OXFORD MODERN LANGUAGES
AND LITERATURE MONOGRAPHS

PRIVILEGED MORTALS

The French Heroic Novel, 1630–1660

by

Mark Bannister

OXFORD UNIVERSITY PRESS
1983

Oxford University Press, Walton Street, Oxford OX2 6DP

London Glasgow New York Toronto
Delhi Bombay Calcutta Madras Karachi
Kuala Lumpur Singapore Hong Kong Tokyo
Nairobi Dar es Salaam Cape Town
Melbourne Auckland

and associates in
Beirut Berlin Ibadan Mexico City Nicosia

Published in the United States
by Oxford University Press, New York

British Library Cataloguing in Publication Data
Bannister, Mark
Privileged mortals. — (Oxford modern languages
and literature monographs)
1. French fiction — 17th century — History and
criticism   2. Heroes in literature
I. Title
843'.4   PQ247
ISBN 0-19-815539-5

Library of Congress Cataloging in Publication Data
Bannister, Mark.
Privileged mortals.
(Oxford modern languages and literature monographs)
Bibliography: p.
Includes index.
1. French fiction — 17th century — History and
criticism.   I. Title.   II. Series.
PQ645.B36 1983   843'.4'09   82-24531
ISBN 0-19-815539-5

Set by Hope Services, Abingdon
Printed in Great Britain by
St Edmundsbury Press, Bury St Edmunds, Suffolk

For K, T, and G

NOTE

I should like to offer my warmest thanks to Dr D. C. Potts of Keble College, Oxford for his encouragement and friendly advice on my work on seventeenth-century France. I am grateful also to Professor P. J. Yarrow, and to the librarians and staff of the numerous libraries in Paris, Oxford, London, and Aix-en-Provence in which I have worked, particularly those of the Taylor Institution Library and the Bibliothèque Mazarine.

It is a source of regret to me that neither my former tutor, Mr Iain Macdonald, who pointed me in the right direction, nor my D. Phil. supervisor, Dr Will Moore, who ensured that I arrived at the right place, are still alive to receive my thanks.

M. B.

CONTENTS

Il peut y avoir une âme privilégiée, une personne extra-ordinaire, un héros ou deux en toute la terre: mais il n'y a pas une multitude de héros.

Guez de Balzac

INTRODUCTION

Those scholars whose work leads them into the area of the seventeenth-century French novel often feel like explorers on a lost continent, dimly aware that there are great resources to be discovered but lacking maps and points of reference by which to guide themselves. Maurice Lever, who has done more than most to set up signposts on the terrain, has written of 'ce paysage de désolation' in which 'se dressait solitaire l'héroïne de Mme de La Fayette, telle une droite vigie scintillant dans la nuit des siècles et défiant le perpétuel reflux des courants et des modes: admirable figure de proue d'une Atlantide engloutie!'[1] Raymond Picard, shaking his head sadly over the vast negative bibliography that could be compiled of works not written about the seventeenth-century novel, was drawn to the same image of the lost Atlantis.[2]

The picture is not entirely one of desolation, however. Valuable works of synthesis have been produced, notably by Coulet and Adam,[3] which have helped to relate the development of the novel to literary achievements in other genres. Lever has compiled an authoritative bibliography, superseding those of Williams and Baldner.[4] In particular, a good deal of work has been published on the novel in the period after 1660. Leaving aside the continuous stream of critical material devoted to Mme de La Fayette, there have been a number of important studies covering the emergence of a recognizably modern form of novel.[5] Understanding of the *nouvelle* has benefited from numerous critical editions and from analyses such as those by Deloffre and Godenne.[6] In the pre-1660 period, two or three writers (Camus, Sorel, Scarron) have attracted the attention of scholars.[7]

Of the areas of the seventeenth-century novel that have remained relatively unexplored, the most obvious is that of the multi-tomed novels, generally categorized as 'heroic', which appeared in the years between *L'Astrée* (1607–19) and

Clelie (1654–60). This neglect is of long standing. In the eighteenth century, the works of Gomberville, La Calprenède, and Scudéry were often dismissed as 'des productions ingrattes, qu'on ne lit plus, & qu'on a peut-être raison de ne plus lire' because of their 'style diffus, lâche, obscur, & souvent emphatique'.[8] Scholars of the nineteenth and early twentieth centuries tended to approach them with curiosity but little sympathy. Körting saw the heroic novel as an unhappy fusion of two elements, the one borrowed from the classical world, the other from Italian and Spanish taste, neither of them suitable for the French genius: inevitably they produced only a poetic monster.[9] Saintsbury's attitude was one of tolerant acceptance.[10] More generously, Morillot was prepared to grant them esteem, though not his full admiration, despite their imperfections.[11]

With the publication of Magendie's *Le Roman français au XVIIe siècle de L'Astrée au Grand Cyrus* in 1932, it looked as though there might be a new departure in the study of the novels of this period, thanks to his success in revealing the richness and diversity of the material available. Unfortunately, his efforts seemed to be almost counter-productive. The sheer weight of his erudition, added to the problems of using his study as a tool (it lacked both an index and a bibliography), made it difficult for others to follow him and there was a consequent tendency to repeat his judgements and sanctify the categories he had adopted without further question. In recent years, work on the heroic novel has been patchy. Gomberville has found a number of enthusiastic champions;[12] Scudéry has aroused a certain amount of interest; on La Calprenède and the lesser writers, such as Chevreau and Guérin de Bouscal, virtually nothing has been produced.

It would be well to make clear at this point that it is not my intention to start making claims on behalf of a batch of 'neglected masterpieces'. From the literary point of view, only a very few of the novels generally labelled 'heroic' have anything to offer in the way of creative imagination and convincing characterization. What makes them supremely worthy of interest, I would contend, is what they can tell us about the ideological and ethical climate of seventeenth-century France, for the novel reflects, possibly better than

other genres, the ideological consciousness of the period.
Like the dramatist, the novelist was dependent on the appro-
bation of a wide public and therefore tended to reflect ideas
generally held. Similarly, the reading public looked to the
novel for an expression of its own aspirations, as a means of
coming to terms with its own experience. Moreover, novelists
had, for the most part, not yet developed any pretensions to
expressing a subjective outlook or including a confessional
element in their works and, as a result, the novels read by a
generation that was modifying its affective concepts so
rapidly have much to tell us about the major ethical preoccupations of the day, particularly, of course, about the
ideal of heroism.

Since the 1940s, when Bénichou, Nadal, and others
published their seminal studies, the importance of the concept
of heroism for an understanding of seventeenth-century
France has become increasingly clear. What was originally
seen as a rather simple distinction between the affirmation of
man's potential for heroic activity, associated with the
aspirations of the *noblesse d'épée*, and the 'demolition' of
heroism by an opposing ideology, headed by the Jansenists,
has since revealed itself to be much more complex.[13] The
ideal of heroism found a response in every section of society,
not merely amongst the aristocracy, and was interpreted in
the light of each possible concept of liberty. The hero could
be envisaged as a military leader, a peasant rebel, a saint, a
statesman, a magistrate — in short, in any form that corresponded to the aspirations of a section of society, and there
were always writers ready to argue the case for any of these.
The various concepts of heroism put forward were in fact
claims for the recognition of alternative views of the moral
potential in man: in one form or another, heroic status was
felt to be a goal available to all.

Equally, it has become clear that the ideal of heroism did
not, indeed could not, remain static. As the social and
political structure of France was transformed during the
years immediately before and after the Fronde, so the new
order was reflected in new interpretations of established concepts, representing an evolution of heroism rather than
straightforward affirmation and demolition. The *noblesse de*

robe, the *intendants*, and even the *financiers* all felt entitled to express their own codes of values in terms traditionally reserved for the class-myth of the *noblesse d'épée*, which, especially after the Fronde, had been rapidly losing credibility. The change in ethical attitudes between, say, 1635, when Richelieu's internal policies were beginning to have a profound effect on the realities of politics, and 1661, when Louis XIV took over the government, was enormous, particularly as regards the respective values of the will and the instincts. The generation that responded to *La Princesse de Clèves* was separated by an affective chasm from the generation that had first acclaimed *Le Cid*: as Antoine Adam has put it, 'il y a moins de distance entre Thomas Corneille et Marmontel qu'entre Chapelain et Quinault'.[14] And it is precisely during this period of rapid change that the output of prose fiction was dominated by the heroic novel, which, having produced some of the greatest successes of the century with the reading public, offers an excellent method of gauging the extent to which the various interpretations of man's moral worth had found acceptance with the literate section of society.

I should emphasize, then, especially to those who may have raised an eyebrow at seeing a work of such relatively slight proportions presuming to offer a study of 'the French heroic novel', that my concern is solely to investigate the nature of the heroic ideal offered to the reading public by writers of heroic novels, particularly as regards the way novelists responded to the ideological changes taking place during the period in question. Analyses along structural, thematic, or stylistic lines should provide work for scholars for many years to come, but are outside the scope of the present work.

What, then, is a heroic novel? The term itself has been used from a very early stage to categorize the novels of the 1630s, 1640s, and 1650s, though the label has been applied variously to individual novels. Sorel uses the term in *La Maison des jeux* and again in *La Bibliotheque françoise* and *De la connoissance des bons livres* to identify a large number of novels, extending from *Ariane* (1632) into the 1660s.[15] Lenglet du

Fresnoy lists *Polexandre, Ibrahim, Cassandre, Cleopatre, Le Grand Cyrus, Scanderberg,* and *Mitridate* as heroic novels, but includes many very similar novels amongst the *romans d'amour.*[16] The *Bibliothèque universelle des romans,* on the other hand, categorizes *Cassandre* and *Mitridate* as heroic novels and *Le Grand Cyrus* and *Axiane* as historical novels, but *Polexandre* and *Ibrahim* as *romans d'amour.* Körting sees the heroic-*galant* novel emerging with *Polexandre,* reaching its peak with *Cassandre* and *Cleopatre* and declining with *Le Grand Cyrus.*[17] Amongst twentieth-century scholars, F. C. Green uses the term 'heroic novel' when referring specifically to La Calprenède and Scudéry;[18] Saintsbury indicates that for him it includes in addition the works of Gomberville.[19]

Since the publication of Magendie's *Le Roman français,* there has been a tendency to define the heroic novel by reference to the historical pretensions of some authors, so that the kind of hero depicted becomes of secondary importance. Magendie himself differentiates between the *roman d'aventures* and the *roman historico-épique.* Of forty-one *romans d'aventures* listed, all but eight were published before 1636; of sixteen *romans historico-épiques,* all but two were published after 1636. The distinction between the two groups, however, is not so much chronological as formal, the latter being constructed according to the 'prose epic' theory with a historical figure as the hero and avoiding the wilder fantasies of the *roman d'aventures,* especially the supernatural intrusions. Three works (*Histoire negrepontique, Ariane,* and *Polexandre*) are listed as transitional, since they reveal a concern for verisimilitude and a limited commitment to history without entirely escaping the excesses of earlier novels.[20] Adam makes the same basic distinction as Magendie, showing the *roman d'aventures* developing between 1620 and 1635 (about thirty novels) and falling from favour after 1642. It is characterized by a free use of the imagination with little regard for history (Gomberville is included in this category). Around 1640, the *roman d'aventures* is superseded by the *roman héroïque,* a prose epic based on history and offering a reflection of *galant* society.[21]

The establishing of categories based on the historico-epic theory of the novel current in the seventeenth century has

produced a somewhat distorted picture of the development
of the heroic novel in that it has created artificial divisions
between writers whose fundamental aims and outlook were
similar, by drawing undue attention to certain principles of
form. For example, *Cassandre*, as I hope to show, is closer to
Polexandre in conception than to *Clelie*, though a division
along formal lines would link it with the latter. Coulet's
definition, which concentrates on the spirit of the novel after
L'Astrée rather than on its form and its historical pretensions,
therefore represents a welcome return to an awareness of the
importance of the subject-matter: 'nous réunissons sous le
nom de *romans héroïques* les romans parus entre 1625 et 1655
environ, qui racontent de grandes actions et décrivent de
grands sentiments'.[22]

It is the subject-matter which is central to an understanding
of the heroic novel, for, regardless of experiments with form
and debates on the moral function of the novel, a concern
to depict an increasingly superhuman type of character is
clearly discernible as a major characteristic of the novel after
L'Astrée, d'Urfé's pastoral which had been the outstanding
success of the early years of the century.[23] D'Urfé was long
credited with having given to the novel all those features that
made it worthy of esteem. Even Sorel, always ready to mock
anything he considered unrealistic, described *L'Astrée* as an
'ouvrage tres-exquis'.[24] However, in view of this enormous
vogue, it is curious that the pastoral novel did not find more
proponents and have a more radical effect on the subsequent
development of the novel. It may be, as Magendie has suggested,[25] that the very success of *L'Astrée* militated against
imitators, though there was no shortage of playwrights
prepared to borrow plots from d'Urfé. It may be that the
pastoral very soon ceased to correspond to the taste of the
reading public and that the generation that was to fight in
the Thirty Years War had little time for the restraint and
delicacy of *bergeries*.[26]

Whatever the reason, within a few years of the appearance
of Part III of *L'Astrée* in 1619, the last part published in
d'Urfé's lifetime, the novel had begun to take a new direction.
The 1620s are characterized by novels that substitute for the
rather static situations found in *L'Astrée* a concern for

incident and adventure, frequently presented in a disordered way, giving full scope to fantasy and very little place to characterization. There are few novels of this period with any literary merit, and the re-editions of the Greek romances of Heliodorus and Tatius and the *Amadis* cycle had no difficulty in maintaining their popularity in the face of this paucity of talent.[27] From the beginning of the 1630s, however, a pre-occupation with the kind of individual who excelled in physical combat but who, at the same time, possessed all the social virtues considered necessary by the society of the day is discernible. In particular, Desmarets de Saint-Sorlin's *Ariane* (2 vols., Paris, 1632), Hotman de Latour's *Histoire celtique* (3 vols., Paris, 1634), and the early versions of *Polexandre* (1629 and 1632) indicate a shift in emphasis from a series of adventures loosely connected by one or more characters to the depiction of a special kind of being whose behaviour is shown to be qualitatively superior to that of ordinary men. The adventures in which he is involved are related in order to demonstrate his superiority rather than because of their intrinsic interest. As early as 1624, in his *Endimion*, a short work noted by contemporaries mainly for its references *à clef*, Gombauld had sought to establish a new method of presentation.[28] He refers in his preface to the 'discours héroïque' which he considers to be a necessary ingredient in a novel and which manifests itself in his text as the expression of idealized aspirations, the striving to reach a level where man is in touch with divinity, for which an elevated tone and diction are required, very different from the straightforward narrative style of the *roman d'aventures*. Other writers reveal a similar desire to rise above the mere narrating of striking incidents. Boisrobert, for instance, declares that the novelist's aim is to show 'en un plus eminent degré les vertus dont l'histoire nous presente les exemples'.[29] Hotman de Latour, acknowledging the inspiration he has received from Heliodorus, indicates his chief preoccupation when he asserts that Theagenes is not heroic enough.[30]

By the 1640s, heroic novels, as they came to be called, had established themselves and were immensely popular with the reading public. They were long, contained a large number of *tiroirs*, and described the martial and amorous adventures of

wholly admirable heroes, usually figures taken from history,
though the authors permitted themselves a considerable
degree of latitude in the depiction of historical incidents.
The adventures of the hero's close companions often made
up a proportion of the work. The most successful examples
were Gomberville's *Polexandre* (1637), La Calprenède's
Cassandre (1642-5) and *Cleopatre* (1647-57), and Scudéry's
Ibrahim (1641) and *Le Grand Cyrus* (1649-53).[31] The end
of the vogue for these long heroic novels came remarkably
abruptly in the 1660s. Scudéry's *Almahide* (1660-3) and La
Calprenède's *Faramond* (1661-3, completed by Vaumorière
in 1670) were the last notable examples before the *nouvelle*
eclipsed them, though some of the major novels went on
being republished even into the eighteenth century. However,
when Huet defined the novel in 1670 in terms which were in
effect an apology for the heroic novel,[32] he was already out
of date.

   The period of the heroic novel thus corresponds broadly
with the period when the concept of heroism was exercising
the minds and talents of writers in many different genres.
It parallels the popularity of heroic tragedy and tragi-comedy
in the theatre, and the publication of innumerable panegyrics
aimed at turning public figures into heroes, treatises on the
heroic potential in man (and woman), epics, and heroic odes.
(Those who wrote heroic novels very often made a contribution to one of these other genres as well.) It embraces,
too, the period during which the French turned the Prince de
Condé into a living legend and then proceeded to deprive
him of much of his heroic status, and it is in the light of such
phenomena that I propose to investigate the nature of the
heroic ideal offered to the seventeenth-century reading public
by the writers of heroic novels. In order to make clear the
extent to which the heroic novel ties in with the movement
of ideas and the general preoccupations of its time, I have set
out firstly to ascertain (in Part I) the norms of heroism in the
novel between 1630 and 1660 and to trace the modifications
made to them in response to changing social and ideological
attitudes. Part II is an analysis of the most important heroic
novels taken individually, particularly as regards the concept
of heroism they embody and the contribution they made

to the pattern of development of the novel as a whole. Part III provides some suggestions as to why the heroic novel should have declined so suddenly and so rapidly.

PART I

The popularity of the heroic novel during the years 1630–60 is not hard to establish, if only by the sheer volume of output and the eagerness of publishers to be associated with the more significant works. To ascertain why it should have been so is, however, a different matter. Novelists responded to what they felt to be a public demand, but the demand was a complex thing, made up of needs differing from one group to another and no doubt from one individual to another.

On one level, there was simple escapism, the need to fill in an hour or two of the ample leisure time enjoyed by the upper classes, a need which the novel had been fulfilling for generations. More positively, there was a desire to be stirred by accounts of the exploits of great men, to feel that one was in some way sharing in the actions and the thought-processes of those who stood out from the ordinary run of mortals. For some, there was perhaps a need to believe in an ideal version of man as a palliative to the evidence, abundant in everyday life, of man's weaknesses and shortcomings. Such an ideal might best be embodied in the figure of a military leader, an epitome of all the virtues of the *noblesse d'épée*'s class-myth, or it might emerge as an expression of the aspirations towards politeness and *galanterie* characteristic of the period.

The novelists who wrote in response to these needs made their own assessment of how they could best please the public, but their response was necessarily conditioned by their own personal attitudes and by the changes taking place in the society for which they wrote, for the period in question was marked by particularly rapid and far-reaching changes in the political, philosophical, and social ethos.

On the one hand, the political situation underwent violent fluctuations. The steady movement towards a centralized system of government pursued by Richelieu at the expense of the old aristocratic and legal establishment was met, after the Cardinal's death, by a resurgence of aristocratic individualism. The upheaval of the Fronde with its shifting alliances seriously weakened the independent rôle of the aristocracy and confirmed the trend towards absolutism. The external politics of the time had an effect on attitudes towards military activities. The early campaigns of the Thirty Years War, and particularly those in which the duc d'Enghien won a series of brilliant victories, were greeted with enormous enthusiasm, and the return of the officers to court for the winter was treated as the triumphant return of demi-gods. By the time the Treaty of Westphalia was signed in 1648, the mood was much less euphoric. The Prince de Condé's reputation stood much lower and, after his behaviour in the Fronde, the former hero lost much of the admiration he had enjoyed. The writer of novels therefore needed to be aware of the changes in the mood of the public for which he was writing and to modify the type of individual he presented as a hero. The kind of morally independent aristocratic warrior who would have corresponded to the general mood in 1640 would not necessarily be so acceptable in 1655.

On the ideological plane, the period 1630-60 saw a progressive decline in the belief accorded to the supremacy of the will and its gradual replacement by an awareness of the irrational factors influencing human behaviour. The average reader of novels was perhaps not particularly concerned with philosophical concepts and arguments as such, but he would certainly have been interested in the way they affected the popular representation of idealized romantic love. The whittling away of man's presumed control over his passions and the assumption of the existence of powerful forces which could be defined no more precisely than as a *je ne sais quoi* had a profound influence on the type of hero presented in the novel. Taken in conjunction with the strong feminist movement which built up towards the middle of the century and which took on an extreme form in the *précieux* salons of the 1650's, it indicates the emergence of a new sensibility, adumbrating the faith in the passions characteristic of the eighteenth century.

In the following six chapters, an attempt is made to define the heroism depicted in the heroic novel, a definition which must necessarily be broad in view of the background of changing circumstances, mentioned above, against which individual novels were produced. Chapters I and II deal respectively with the generally acknowledged characteristics of the hero and those features that were the subject of conflicting interpretations. Chapter III is concerned with the concept of *prudence*, a quality much debated by political writers but one which is also of importance to the heroic novel because of the fundamental question, explicit or implicit in virtually every episode, of how the hero responds to the onslaughts of fortune. Chapters IV and V cover the area of the passions, particularly love, and the influence of feminism on the kind of heroic relationships depicted. Chapter VI deals with the relative importance accorded to imagination and truth, whether conceived of as historical truth or truth to life, by those writers who offered the reader an admirable and imitable model of heroism. These parameters define the aspects of human activity that the writers (and presumably also the readers) of heroic novels considered to be suitable material for an exercise in the exaltation of man's greatness, but they also reveal areas where a belief in that greatness was not so firmly rooted and which consequently became the starting-point for a rejection of the concept of heroism.

CHAPTER I

THE NATURE OF THE HERO

The heroic novel was normally constructed around the exploits of a great warrior, usually a well-known figure taken
from history, endowed with many of the qualities of the
knight errant familiar to readers of medieval romances of
chivalry. Despite the superficial resemblance to the knight
errant, however, the hero of the heroic novel had his own
separate pedigree, derived mainly from three forms of the
novel which had proved their popularity in the late sixteenth
and early seventeenth centuries, namely, the group of Greek
romances written in the second or third centuries AD and
known generally through translations of medieval transcrip-
tions; the pastoral, or more specifically *L'Astrée*; and the
descendants of the medieval romances of chivalry, particularly
the *Amadis de Gaule* cycle. From each of these the heroic
novel took certain features and united them in a glorification
of man.

Of the three major Greek romances known in the seventeenth century,[1] the most influential and admired was the
Histoire ethiopique of Heliodorus. Amyot's translation of
1547 was still accepted as the standard one in the seventeenth
century, having gone through seven reprints by 1626, but
other versions also appeared. D'Audiguier produced a modern-
ized edition of Amyot in 1609 which was reprinted in 1614,
1616, and 1626; Montlyard's new translation of 1622 was
reprinted in 1623 and 1626. Jacques de Rochemaure published a translation of Achilles Tatius' *Clitophon et Leucippe*
in 1556, superseded by Baudoin's version in 1635. Eustathius'
Ismene et Ismenie appeared in translation in 1625.

Each of these tales relates the adventures of a young and
virtuous couple who fall prey to pirates, brigands, and
lubricious merchants and ladies to whom they are sold.
They are separated by shipwrecks, transported across the

Mediterranean to be sold into slavery, subjected to near-disastrous punishments, and reunited by miraculous coincidences. Through all this, their virtue remains intact and they eventually achieve happiness and security in marriage. If there is heroism in these stories, it is a heroism of pathos, for the central couple are unable to do more than raise a feeble opposition to the enemies threatening them. They are overwhelmed and can only lament their misfortune: if they are saved, it is thanks to the gods watching over them. Most of the features of the heroism characteristic of the heroic novel are lacking in these romances. Théagène in *Histoire aethiopique*, for instance, is physically striking, but his exploits are restricted to winning a race, capturing a runaway bull, and defeating an Ethiopian wrestler, which he does by a David-like dexterity against a clumsy Goliath rather than by any superior strength or skill.[2] The battle episodes contain no individual exploits, either by Théagène or even by the generals concerned, but are given over entirely to descriptions of the tactics used and the methods of fighting employed by soldiers from different regions.[3] Amyot himself comments that the work lacks *grandeur* because the author does not give his hero any memorable exploits to perform, and the same lack of heroic action is noted by Sorel and Hotman de Latour.[4]

The heroes of Tatius and Eustathius are similar. They are capable of putting up some resistance to the pirates and others who constantly seek to carry them off, but they never succeed in imposing their will on those around. They are victims, and their authors, like Heliodorus, prefer to play on the pathos of the situations into which fate has pushed them rather than make them capable of a level of activity sufficient to free themselves from the control of others. Both *Clitophon et Leucippe* and *Ismene et Ismenie*, being related by the hero in the first person, have the added disadvantage that the reader is not able to obtain an objective view of the central character.

These Greek authors had their French disciples who faithfully reproduced the same framework, with the hero and heroine pretending to be brother and sister, sailing to and fro across the Mediterranean, being shipwrecked, captured by pirates, threatened by the lusts of masters and mistresses, and in each case displaying the same passivity in the face of fortune's apparent hostility. In *Du vray et parfaict amour*, Théogènes is sufficiently martial to be put in charge of the Scythian army, but none the less finds it impossible to retain his liberty against various brigands, royal favourites, and other enemies.[5] The *Histoire afriquaine* presents a hero who, though he is claimed to be capable of 'des prodiges de valeur pour la deffence des siens', is constantly being captured and, when given the opportunity to reconquer his kingdom from a usurper at the head of an army, prefers to enter the country disguised as a merchant to try to win over the people by stealth: he is again taken prisoner.[6] The *Histoire negrepontique* employs the same stereotypes. The hero, Alexandre Castriot, though a descendant of the great Skanderberg, is essentially passive. He and his beloved, Olimpe, are subjected to a series of adventures inflicted on them by other people and from which they have to escape. When Alexandre is condemned to death by a sea-captain, he does nothing to resist but resigns himself to his fate: 'Il se met à genoux avec un visage Chrestien & resolu tout ensemble, mesprisant la mort, mais *mesprisant aussi la gloire*.'[7] He is thrown overboard and is washed ashore at the very spot where the captain is talking to a magistrate; the question of honour and vengeance is, however, settled not by a duel but by a contest of harangues in court.[8]

In his *Histoire indienne*, Boisrobert made a genuine attempt to offer something new, but the influence of Heliodorus is still paramount. The points at which the hero might have made an impact by his physical prowess are allowed to pass unmarked: he and his companion abandon the defence of the besieged town of Visapore because the enemy are too numerous, and the feats of arms in a tournament are scarcely accorded a mention though the dancing that precedes them is described in detail.[9]

Though radically different from the Greek romances in its inspiration, *L'Astrée* shared with them a reluctance to emphasize the aggressive side of the hero's character. The shepherds who represent the central area of interest are not lacking in courage and are quite capable of defending their own interests or protecting the innocent. Filandre, for instance, sees a stranger molesting Diane and, going to her aid, is run through by the stranger's sword, but he succeeds in ramming the metal end of his crook so far into the other's head that it will not come out.[10] However, the urge to measure one's strength against an opponent is never applauded as an admirable thing in itself. There are knights who follow chivalrous pursuits, but the author never allows them to build up a heroic image. The fight between Damon and Tersandre is recounted in two lines.[11] Égide, Ligdamon's squire, describing a battle in which his master performed 'tant de merveilles que l'une me fait oublier l'autre', gives no general account of the fighting and cuts himself short with 'je ne veux icy vous ennuyer par une particuliere description de ceste journée, aussi bien n'en sçaurois-je venir à bout'.[12]

When war comes to the Forez region and the town of Marcilly is besieged, the shepherds and townsfolk cope impressively with the assaults of Polémas and his troops, but they always act as a group: there are no individuals who stand out above the general body of defenders.[13] Céladon, who had been captured by Polémas while still disguised as the shepherdess Alexis, finds himself having to fight outside Marcilly with five companions, covering the escape of Astrée and Silvie into the city. D'Urfé's intention seems to have been to show that Céladon could fight valiantly, yet his description of the scene is curiously negative, emphasizing what is done to Céladon more than his exploits, implying that what is remarkable is the fact that he is fighting at all:

Son rondache estoit tellement herissé de fleches qui s'y estoient plantées, que les dernieres ne trouvoient plus de place vuide, et falloit que par necessité elles frappassent sur d'autres fleches. Son espée estoit toute teinte de sang, et la poignée mesme en desgoutoit. Il estoit blessé en deux ou trois lieux, et mesme en l'espaule droicte d'un javelot qui avoit esté lancé, et qui luy avoit fait une grande playe; et quoy que la perte du sang l'affoiblist beaucoup, si est-ce que le desir extréme qu'il avoit de se venger de l'outrage qu'on avoit fait à Astrée, le transportoit de telle sorte, que presque il ne la ressentoit pas. Mais, en effect, toute cette deffence eust esté vaine sans le secours de Damon . . .[14]

Such an approach on the part of d'Urfé is in keeping with the ethic of *L'Astrée*, in which the greatest expression of man's striving lies in the renunciation of his claims to self-fulfilment and the absorption of his aspirations by the beloved. If heroism exists in *L'Astrée*, it is a heroism of self-sacrifice, epitomized by Célidée who disfigures herself to resolve an impossible situation. It is an ethic almost completely opposed to that of the heroic novel, in which the hero's projection of himself is of paramount importance.[15]

The pastoral disappeared fairly rapidly after *L'Astrée*, though there was a good deal of borrowing of episodes by other novelists for a number of years. When attempts at fully-fledged pastorals appear during the period of the heroic novel or when episodes of *bergerie* are introduced into heroic novels,[16] the contrast is so striking as to illustrate clearly the difference between the objectives of the two types of novel.

The romances of chivalry had survived since the Middle Ages in various forms, but they entered the seventeenth century in a degenerate state. Those which were still being printed were relatively few in number, the main ones being *Huon de Bordeaux*, *Les Quatre Fils Aymon*, *Ogier le Danois*, and *Maugis d'Aigremont* in a combined version with *Mabrian*, but they seem to have maintained their popularity at least with the less sophisticated section of the reading public, since the *Bibliothèque bleue* of Troyes continued to turn out editions for many years.[17] They moved progressively further away from the mainstream of literature, however. The edition of *Mabrian*[18] published in 1625, for instance, presents a primitive kind of prose chronicle, offering a long series of events without order, psychological interest, or style. The publisher evidently assumed that the reader would be sufficiently held by the superhuman blows of the hero, since almost no attention is paid to love: women, when they appear, are often unwanted distractions, trying, like Delilah, to reduce strong men to weakness. From the point of view of production, the work is of a very low order, badly printed, lacking pagination, and in places impossible to decipher.

What had in some measure ensured the survival of the romances of chivalry and subsequently superseded them was the publication of the *Amadis de Gaule* cycle. The translation by Herberay des Essarts of eight volumes of the Spanish original between 1540 and 1548 created a tremendous vogue, and other translators hurried to produce their own sequels, so that by 1580 twenty-one volumes had been published, taken from Spanish and Italian sources. According to Pasquier,[19] the vogue was over by the end of the sixteenth century, but the decline cannot have lasted long; for in 1615 a further three volumes were produced, ostensibly translated from the Spanish, and French authors began to create their own sequences of adventures.[20] Du Verdier intended his *Romant des romans* to be a conclusion to the cycle, but he seems to have been persuaded to extend the work from six volumes to seven: the fact that a number of respectable publishers were associated with it and that the production is of a high standard suggests that this kind of story was still popular or at least was expected to be.[21] A similar type of adventure continued to be written by Logeas, who evidently felt that the public had an insatiable appetite for stories of questing knights. He refers to the author of *Amadis*, 'de qui je suis contraint de louër les agreables inventions, suivant en cela le goust de la pluspart des beaux esprits de ce temps',[22] but in fact he does not attempt to add to the *Amadis* cycle itself in his three volumes.[23]

The heroes of *Amadis de Gaule* and its imitators are concerned primarily with feats of valour. They are capable of tremendous blows and the authors feel it to be part of their function to regale the reader with detailed descriptions of the carnage inflicted in battle or the types of wound suffered in hand-to-hand conflict. The battle in *Amadis* between the armies of Britain and Ireland is typical: the description is long and gory, arms are cut off, eyes put out, heads split in two, combatants hack and heave and roll on the ground. Quarter is neither requested nor offered, and the survivors are driven into the sea and drowned.[24] When Amadis catches up with Arcalaus who has abducted Oriane, the blow from his sword cuts right down Arcalaus' back and into the saddle-bow.[25]

On the whole, *Amadis* remains within the limits of possibility, but some of the imitators allow their imagination to carry them over into unreality. Du Verdier has two knights killing 472 others in one session, and elsewhere another two knights kill forty to sixty tigers in four hours.[26] Superhuman blows are so common as to be reduced to the level of cliché

— an enemy 'croyoit estre sous les ruines d'une tour que la
foudre abat' or 'fut contraint de donner du menton contre
l'estomac' or 'voyoit les estoilles, quoy que le soleil ne fust
qu'au milieu de sa course'[27] — and there is the same emphasis
on combat made up entirely of shattering blows, e.g.

le chevalier incogneu . . . poussa une estocade dans le ventre d'un avec
tant de fureur qu'il le perça de part en part l'envoyant roide mort sur
l'herbe; . . . prenant son espée à deux mains Fulgoran la feit tomber
sur un avec une force si grande que le poil n'ayant peu retenir le tren-
chant luy meit la teste en deux pieces.[28]

It is this physical prowess which is central to heroism in the
romances of chivalry. The other chivalric qualities established
since the Arthurian romances were usually found in the hero
as well, but they were all subject to some degree of modification according to circumstances. In *Amadis*, loyalty, the
defence of the weak, religious scruples, and chastity are all
interpreted flexibly at some stage. Only the hero's martial
pre-eminence stands out as an absolute.

The hero in the heroic novel shares certain features with each
of the three types described above. He has the strength and
skill of Amadis, the sensibility of Théagène, and the fidelity
of Céladon; but he surpasses them all. His creators set out to
depict a man who was felt to be qualitatively different from
the ordinary run of human beings and whose every action, or
indeed whose very existence, was surrounded by an aura of
superiority such that the reader had to respond to the individual rather than to the deeds.

The difference between the heroic novel and the Greek
romances is measurable in *Peristandre*, in which De Moreaux
took *Du vray et parfaict amour* and rewrote it as a heroic
novel. The result is not very convincing because the original
work was by its nature committed to a basic passivity on the
part of the hero and heroine, but a good deal of restructuring
has taken place: the complaints against the gods have been
cut out, the long descriptions of scenes and ceremonies
which were such a feature of the Greek romances have been
considerably reduced, and the whole text has been liberally
sprinkled with the epithets of heroism (*glorieux*, *généreux*,
etc.). Whenever there is a scene containing action, it has been

rewritten. In *Du vray et parfaict amour*, for instance, there is a scene in which Théogènes, Adraste, and a group of sailors have left their vessel to look for food, leaving Charide on the shore near the ship:

en peu d'heure elle apperçeut ses gens refuir vers eux au grand pas, lesquels estoient suivis d'une multitude d'hommes portans arcs, flesches & dards, lesquels ils lançoient contre les fuyans, dont Theogenes fut atteint d'une flesche dedans un bras. On conseilloit à Charide de se sauver promptement dedans le vaisseau: mais elle feit responce qu'elle n'en feroit rien que premierement elle ne veist Theogenes à sauveté, aymant mieux mourir sur la place que retourner sans luy. La blesseure de Theogenes le contraignoit de retenir ses pas: parce que la flesche ayant le fer dressé en barbillons estoit demeurée en la plaie, & s'esbranlant par le moyen de la course, luy causoit une grande douleur. Il prie Adraste de courir vers Charide pour la faire monter dedans le vaisseau. Mais ces Scythes pour estre legiers à la course furent aussi tost qu' Adraste parmy ceux qui estoient restez sur le bord du fleuve, & se saisissans de tous emmenerent avec eux les uns & les autres.[29]

In *Peristandre*, Féliciane (Charide), Péristandre (Théogènes), Adraste, and Atalante have all gone off and are pursued by a group of Scythians twice as large as their own, but the encounter this time is very different:

Peristandre au souvenir de sa maistresse tourna visage, & fit tant de beaux explois contre ces barbares par son courage & par sa valeur qu'il fut aisé à juger par celle qui l'animoit que les Scites n'auroient pas si bon marché de luy qu'en avoient eu les Bisantins. Que ne fait point cét Amant, il seme la terre de corps: mais comme s'il eust eu un Hydre à combatre, pour un homme qu'il tuoit, il en renaissoit cent autres. Le nombre ne l'étonne point, Adraste le seconde vaillamment, & chaque autre personne de leur suitte se defend assez bien pendant quelque temps: Mais comme il faut de necessité que l'addresse cede à la force, les matelos recreus & de leur faim & de la peine qu'ils avoient eu au combat, lâchent le pied, s'enfuyent & gaignans le vaisseau veulent se mettre dedans & se sauver. Feliciane s'y oppose si genereusement, & en leur faisant honte, elle les oblige à retourner au combat & y va elle-méme avec Atalante.
   Quand Peristandre vid à ses côtez son Amazone, armée d'un javelot, faire trop de merveilles pour une fille, Ha! Madame, retirez-vous, luy dit-il en combattant, enviez-vous la gloire à Peristandre, & voulez-vous la luy ravir? Sans repartir Feliciane ne laisse pas de combatre: mais pour la couvrir des coups des ennemis, luy & son brave compagnon se mettent au devant d'elle pour empêcher qu'elle n'en fust atteinte.
   Enfin ce valeureux Amant & ce courageux ami font leurs derniers efforts pour vaincre ou pour mourir. Il ne s'est jamais rien veu de semblable aux puissans fais d'armes que ces deux Grecs firent contre les

Scittes. Pensant avoir à faire au Dieu meme de la Trace, ces barbares, qui croissoient à veuë d'oeil d'hommes vivans aussi bien que de mors, augmenterent leurs forces pour venir à bout de ceux qu'ils avoient ataquez, & dans ce temps-là, Peristandre fut blessé d'un coup de fléche qui le mit hors de combat. Sa blessure fut la victoire de ses ennemis. Adraste fit bien tout ce qu'il pût pour retirer son ami d'entre leurs mains: mais luy-méme fut fait captif, & Feliciane n'eut pas une meilleure avanture, voyant prisonnier son Amant, elle fit gloire d'étre aussi captive.[30]

These lengthy quotations indicate the way in which a simple encounter could be turned into a heroic exploit. The outcome is the same in either case, but in the former the reader's attention is drawn to the pathos of the situation as he watches the hero suffer defeat and capture; in the latter, the hero's actions inspire admiration as he resists his enemies. His final capture is of little significance compared with the moral victory he has gained. Admiration is in fact the key to the new heroic tone: the relationships between the major characters depend on it. A simple statement in *Du vray et parfaict amour* — 'Puis Scyeles remerciant Theogenes du bon devoir qu'il avoit fait en ceste guerre pour feu son pere, pour luy, & pour son Royaume, le pria de vouloir demeurer avec luy',[31] — becomes an acclamation in *Peristandre*:

Peristandre, dit Scieles, qui parloit bon Grec, je sçay trop bien quels sont vôtre courage, vôtre valleur, & vôtre experience, & quels sont les prodigieux explois de guerre que vous avez fais contre Eurus, & les Nomades, ses sujets & nos ennemis, pour douter d'une chose que j'ay veuë & que la Renommée publiera par tout l'Univers, etc.[32]

Comments on the nature of man have been reformulated to express a heroic view of human aspirations. For instance, Charide's comment that the Romans had perverted the Greeks' sense of public duty by offering triumphs to victorious generals[33] is converted to approval of the Roman attitude and scorn for the *naïveté* of the Greeks.[34]

The same process of conversion to a heroic register by the emphasizing of an individual's capacity for spectacular physical action and by the refining of relationships between admirable characters through the use of a certain kind of impressive diction can be seen applied to the romance of chivalry in *Le Polemire*,[35] the only novel by an otherwise unknown writer. It is a poor work and seems to have been written over a lengthy period, since Book I is very different from Books II and III. In Book I, the hero is used to link up a series of disparate incidents, very much in the tradition of the romance of chivalry, full of magic and spells: he finds himself, for instance, entering a cavern, past *la porte venimeuse* guarded by a monstrous creature with a pike, in which he finds, surrounded by severed heads, a magician inside a circle of vipers, casting spells over the captive Charisbée. In Books II and III, the difference is remarkable. Polémire has become a morally admirable individual, searching for his Amaranthe in a world of heroic endeavour, and the plot consists of situations chosen not for their strange or terrifying nature but because they demonstrate his exceptional character. Each duel or battle is a chance to build up his heroic stature, e.g.

le grand courage de ce jeune Prince qui se joignit à son pere fit reprendre cœur aux soldats & les fit retourner au combat, . . . Et Polemire demeura dans le champ de bataille où il fit des merveilles de sa personne, tuant tout ce qui se presentoit devant luy, & faisant toutes sortes d'efforts de peur qu'ils ne se r'alliassent pour revenir à la charge en leur desespoir. Jarmeric fut fait son prisonnier de guerre, & (chose estrange) ces deux jeunes Capitaines s'embrasserent aussi-tost que l'un fut au pouvoir de l'autre & se jurerent une eternelle amitié.[36]

The type of hero presented in the heroic novel is very much an idealized character. His creators came as near as it was possible in a Christian society to assimilating him to the classical definition of the hero as a demigod, a being who shared the attributes of both mortals and immortals. He can always be seen to be an exceptional being. His face, bearing, and presence make an immediate impression, which causes those around to respond positively: 'parmy les hommes il y en a dont les ames sont plus vigoureuses les unes que les autres, & si puissantes qu'elles forcent secretement la resolution d'autruy à condescendre à leurs volontez.'[37] Lesser mortals immediately feel the effect of the charisma and take up an appropriately subordinate position. Other extraordinary individuals offer respect and esteem on a basis of equality, because of 'la difference qu'il y a des ames élevées, en qui les belles actions ne forment qu'une impression d'estime & de respect aux ames basses, en qui elles produisent l'envie &

l'inimitié'.[38] His natural authority is easier to experience than to define: it sometimes appears like flames round his face[39] or more simply as 'je ne sçay quoy de majestueux & de Martial'.[40] It enables him to take his place as a natural leader and inspire those around to give of their utmost for his sake. In war, this is usually achieved by the force of example, but it is frequently reinforced by an ability to harangue which has a galvanizing effect on his troops.

He is possessed of superhuman courage which allows him, like Orodes, to pick up burning coals to demonstrate his devotion to a cause.[41] In combat, he displays a physical strength and skill which are frequently carried to the very limits of credibility but rarely exceed them, as they had done in the medieval romances. In the heroic novel, it is not uncommon for a hero to kill a dozen opponents in single combat or to account for a few hundred dead in a full-scale battle, but the fabulous numbers slaughtered by the heroes of romance were felt to be so exaggerated as to be unacceptable. 'Je ne donne pas plus de force & de courage à mes Heros qu'un homme genereux en peut avoir,' wrote the anonymous author of *Axiane*, '& je ne remplis pas leurs veines de plus de sang qu'elles ne sont capables d'en tenir ... Je descris mes Heros comme des hommes dont les ames & les vertus participoient veritablement de la Divinité: mais qui avoient un corps dont les forces n'excedoient pas le pouvoir d'un mortel, & qui estoient proportionnez à sa condition,'[42] and most authors agreed with him.

These outstanding physical characteristics are paralleled by an immense intellectual prowess. Nature has endowed the hero with the propensity to learn which allows him to attain full maturity while still a boy, and in some cases it is evident that he was actually born with innate knowledge. While still a youth, Polexandre already knew what even the cleverest men could only learn after years of study and experience.[43] At the age of twelve, Pyrrhus had mastered the most difficult elements of philosophy;[44] at ten, Pacore was capable of the same mental operations as a man of thirty;[45] more modestly, Polémire managed to learn all the natural sciences and four languages within the space of three years during his adolescence.[46]

Above all, the hero is a man of action. He is always ready to react to any situation with the appropriate means: he usually moves swiftly to avert danger or attack injustice, and often appears impulsive in the spontaneity of his actions. Action is in fact an indispensable ingredient in heroism, which is why the martyr cannot strictly be considered heroic.[47] On occasion, circumstances may dictate the need for deliberate restraint from direct action, but such cases merely underline the hero's grasp of all the factors involved in action: he delays in order to obtain better results from action at a later stage.

The hero always remains true to his own honour. He will repay debts of honour, even, or perhaps especially, towards his enemies. He will never lie (though he may occasionally deceive in a good cause), because lying implies that he cannot win by legitimate means. He will fulfil his obligations to his king and country, his family and friends, provided they do not conflict with other aspects of his honour, and he will unhesitatingly prefer death to the remotest possibility of his not being able to hold true to these ideals.

His sense of honour is indissolubly linked to his sense of liberty. Freedom is essential, not necessarily on the physical level, but certainly in the moral sphere. Even though he has been taken prisoner, he will maintain an attitude of moral independence (which usually has an immediate effect on his captors). Similarly, his subjection to an acknowledged sovereign is seen to be a moral contract with responsibilities on both sides.

It is ultimately by this moral independence alone that his right to be considered a hero must be judged, for all his other qualities are meaningless if he does not possess it. It is not a question of status or power or prestige. The heroic aura stems from an inner conviction that he is destined for greatness, combined with the capacity to carry out the actions necessary to achieve that greatness. Any situation can be turned into a demonstration of heroism by allowing the urge to sublimity and a superhuman ability to operate freely, as Ibrahim does when he establishes himself as Sultan Soliman's superior by making a personal decision to fight actively, in the moral sense, that is, to take the course of events into his own hands, which he does with spectacular results, rather than remain under orders in the ranks with the other slaves.[48]

All these features of the hero were found equally in other branches of heroic literature, such as plays, odes, and panegyrics, and they were freely attributed by eulogists to the real-life heroes of the time. According to his biographer, Montmorency could break in wild horses at an age when most boys can hardly stay in the saddle, and, later on in his career, he revealed an innate capacity for commanding a naval battle, even though he had never been in one before, since 'les personnes que Dieu destine aux actions extraordinaires viennent au monde avec les vertus qu'il faut pour les achever, & n'ont pas besoin de l'estude ny de l'exercice'.[49] The Comte de Harcourt 'sçait commander avant que de commander . . . l'usage ne luy a rien appris; sans experience il est sçavant; l'exercice l'a confirmé, il ne l'a pas instruit.'[50] The duc de Guise had such a charisma that 'on a veû des Assemblées, qui n'estoient pas petites, se rendre en un instant à sa bonne mine. Il n'y avoit point de coeur qui pust tenir contre ce visage: il persuadoit avant que d'ouvrir la bouche: il estoit impossible de luy vouloir mal en sa presence.'[51] The Great Condé's admirers found him beyond comparison: 'son Esprit enfin est le Miracle de tous les esprits, parce que n'ignorant rien de tout ce que l'esprit humain peut sçavoir, il est luy seul effectivement comme un Illustre Abregé de tous les hommes'.[52] Clearly, those who wrote heroic novels were simply building on foundations already established in the mind of the reading public.

The hero was invariably noble, though the precise interpretation of the term was the subject of debate in some novels. Since he was usually represented as a king, prince, or highly-placed aristocrat, he was assimilated to the seventeenth-century aristocratic class-myth, according to which nobility was the prerogative of a particular class, the *noblesse d'épée*, who existed as the defence and bulwark of the state. The only justification they needed was that their lives were ready to be sacrificed in the service of the king. By virtue of being descended from generations of noble ancestors, they had inherited a kind of distillation of *vertu*, each generation passing on to the next the essence of its own highest qualities.

'La matiere & la premiere semence de la vertu des hommes se fait de la bonne naissance':[53] every true-born aristocrat had a predisposition to *vertu* which could only come from high birth. Though it was possible for a commoner to display *vertu*, there was felt to be an essential difference in the quality: 'Quoy que la vertu naisse au village, elle retient tousjours son merite; la bure ne luy oste pas sa valeur, mais elle estouffe sa majesté. Au contraire, une bonne naissance luy donne de nouveaux rayons, elle augmente sa splendeur.'[54] While birth was the beginning of *vertu*, education had to work upon the seeds implanted in the soul and bring them to fruition — education understood not as a means of developing the intellectual faculties and stimulating the curiosity, but a process which ensured that the young nobleman had absorbed all the beliefs and prejudices, the manners and airs of his class. The word most frequently used to describe the imperceptible process whereby the young man was moulded into the required form was *nourriture*, a gradual influencing towards the right reactions by exposure to the world of which he was to form a part.

The discrepancy between this myth and the reality of the *noblesse d'épée* was no doubt made frequently evident in the everyday life of the time, and the moralists were quite prepared to point out that things were not always what they ought to be, with aristocrats frequently behaving in a most ignoble manner.[55] They therefore separated the issue of birth from that of *vertu*, insisting that high birth was of no intrinsic significance unless it accompanied personal merit. Dubosc was particularly outspoken, declaring that the actions a man performs outweigh any considerations of birth: 'il n'importe pas beaucoup de qui nous ayons receu la vie, pourveu qu'elle soit bonne'.[56] He removes nobility from its framework of hereditary privilege and offers it as an objective standard of virtue accessible to all.[57] La Mothe le Vayer compares noble birth to a zero which has no value of its own but serves to increase the value of other figures when united with them, and again to 'une lumiere qui éclaire & fait paroistre davantage le bien & le mal de ceux qui la possedent'.[58] Vulson de la Colombière looks back approvingly to the days when nobility was indistinguishable from virtue and questions of lineage were of no relevance.[59] In *Le Vray Theatre d'honneur et de chevalerie*, a work in which he particularly censures the aristocracy of his day for having degenerated from its glorious origins, he warns the nobles not to pride themselves on the actions of their ancestors, for nobility is not a legacy to be transmitted automatically: 'la Noblesse demeurera toute entiere à celuy seul, qui l'auroit peû esperer de son propre merite'.[60]

This insistence on the pre-eminence of *vertu* was taken up by one particular section of society, the *noblesse de robe*, and exploited in the interests of their own class-myth. The theme of the *homo novus* can be traced back to the later Middle Ages, but in the sixteenth century it was widely debated, and, after 1604, when the institution of the *paulette* made it possible for the *robins* to pass on their offices and titles by hereditary succession to their descendants, it developed a new dimension. The *noblesse de robe* saw themselves no longer distinguished qualitatively from the *noblesse d'épée*, but only by the nature of their commitment to the state. They could claim that they represented the true backbone of society by virtue of the services they rendered, interpreting *vertu* as the carrying out of public duties for the maintenance of civil society, with ennoblement as its just reward. Some apologists went so far as to claim that the bearing of arms and the exercise of military skills were subordinate to the arts of peace.[61]

The heroic novel purveyed an idealized world in which disputes between various branches of the aristocracy had no place. The only hierarchy that existed in it was moral rather than social, though it reflected closely enough the class-myth of the *noblesse d'épée*. However, discussions on the relationship between nobility and *vertu* found their way into several novels, because the hero, belonging as he did to the highest level of the social order, might have been considered to owe as much of his *vertu* to his ancestors as to himself. Novelists wanted to make it clear that the glory of their heroes was in no way dependent on the deeds of their ancestors, but at the same time they did not want to deprive them of those ancestors. One of the simplest devices for resolving this dilemma was to make the hero leave his homeland, assume another name, and impress the world without the benefit of borrowed glory. Thus, Oroondate makes a reputation for himself under the name of Oronte; Cyrus first presents himself to the reader under the cryptonym, Artamène; Pacore, Prince of the Parthians, leaves his home and gains glory as Alcide in Bactria; Armetzar, son of Tamerlane the Great, spends most of his career as Phocate in a neighbouring kingdom.[62]

As an extension of this device, the hero could be shown believing himself to be of low birth. The full value of his *vertu* can then be weighed, and when, as invariably happens, it is revealed that he is in fact of noble birth, the impression already formed by the world is simply confirmed. In *Cleopatre*, for instance, a character called Artaban appears in volume III, 'jeune capitaine, qui selon le bruit commun d'une naissance obscure estoit parvenu par sa vertu aux plus hautes dignitez en peu d'années'.[63] His awareness of his own abilities makes him capable of changing sides in war if these abilities are not taken as the sole criterion for judging him. He is in love with the Princess Elise, who is taught by her *confidente* to distinguish between the real man and his social background. Elise agrees to accept Artaban subject to her father's approval. When her father refuses, Artaban's reply is uncompromising: 'Si la recompense que j'ay demandée est au dessus de mes services, mes services sont au dessus de toutes les autres recompenses que vous me pouvez donner.'[64]

In volume V, a character called Britomare, who had already appeared in volume I, recounts his life-story. He is of low birth, but has always felt himself drawn to the highest honours. When he falls in love with the King of Ethiopia's daughter, he is not dismayed but perseveres: 'si je n'ay pas la naissance, j'ay le courage digne d'elle & si par le courage je ne puis suppléer au deffaut de la naissance, il faut perir noblement plustost que d'abaisser nos pensées'.[65] In volume VII, it emerges that Britomare is in fact the same man as Artaban. He continues his career, acquiring glory and fame until, in volume XII, at the height of his renown, it is revealed that he is actually the son of Pompée and he is made king of the Parthians. Elise is pleased for his sake, but is not unduly impressed: 'je crois avoir tesmoigné que sans le

secours de la naissance, Artaban m'estoit plus considerable
que tous les plus grands Monarques'.[66] None the less, the
world-order has been reaffirmed; nobility has been shown, as
always in the novel, to be a conjunction of birth and virtue.

The theme of birth and virtue is treated very seriously by
Juvenel, who made it the major element in one of his works,
pursuing it beyond the point to which most novelists were
prepared to go, and in so doing touched upon important
social implications. The hero of *Dom Pelage* is the son of the
Spanish king who is deposed by the wicked Vitiza and
thrown into prison. The boy's mother gives him to an aged
servant to bring up before going to share her husband's
imprisonment. The servant, however, hands the baby on,
without revealing the circumstances of his birth, to a peasant
woman whose own child has just died. As a result, Pélage's
adoptive parents are unaware of his true identity and treat
him exactly like their other children, giving him the name
Hidaspe. His innate *vertu* begins to work in spite of his environment and he runs away to the wars at the age of thirteen,
convinced that he must have been born 'pour quelque exercice
plus noble & moins ravallé que l'agriculture'.[67] He is fired by
the ideal of the great men who have risen from nothing and
refuses to see himself held back by his birth. Inevitably, he
makes a great impression in the ranks of Charles Martel's
army and increases his reputation after returning to Spain
and fighting against the Moors.

Throughout his career, Pélage succeeds by refusing to
contemplate failure. He is convinced that, at the sight of
vertu, everyone will be filled with admiration and put aside
all considerations of birth. He and his 'brother', Cratile,
decide to give such great proofs of valour in war that, when
their base origins are revealed, their *vertu* will be all the more
admired.[68] Similarly, far from despairing when he realizes
he has fallen in love with the king's daughter, he tells himself
to persevere and to raise himself to the level of the greatest
kings: 'force le Ciel d'accorder à ta vertu les avantages qu'il a
refusez à ta naissance'.[69] And, with one notable exception,[70]
the *généreux* characters in the book respond in exactly the
way he has predicted. He is elected King of the Asturias by
the Christians. Sacar, a Spanish nobleman, loves 'Hidaspe' for

his *vertu* no less when he hears of his apparently base origins. It is Sacar who spells out the underlying philosophy of the book to his daughter, whom he hopes to marry to the hero he so much admires:

Deux choses, ma fille, elevent ordinairement quelques hommes si fort au dessus des autres: . . . C'est la grandeur de la naissance ou l'excellence de la vertu. Quiconque a l'un & l'autre n'a rien à souhaiter au de-là, mais qui possede seulement la derniere en un degré bien eminent, quoy que sa naissance ne soit point illustre, ny sa fortune éclatante, va tousjours plus haut que l'ordinaire des hommes & s'acquiert à la fin, en bien faisant, les avantages que la nature avoit refusez à sa condition, avec plus de gloire que s'ils avoient precedé sa vertu.[71]

This argument is, of course, to a large extent invalidated by the fact that Dom Pélage is really of royal blood, but it is re-established by the parallel figure of Cratile, his supposed brother. As a boy, he had felt none of the stirrings in the soul that had so troubled 'Hidaspe', but he was so impressed by the latter's magnanimity that he determined to follow him to the wars. He is to be found throughout the novel ably seconding Pélage in battle, establishing a sound reputation for valour in his own right, and falling in love with and eventually marrying a noble lady.[72]

The implication in *Dom Pelage* is that *vertu* is latent in everyone and can either be stifled by a base environment or liberated by contact with the higher things of life.[73] The possession of *vertu* is what gives entitlement to nobility and, given the necessary will-power, anyone can achieve it. It is a view which would have been approved of by the moralists of the day, but it was too radical for the heroic novel in general. It was certainly the inherent qualities which mattered most in the hero and the world of heroism was open theoretically to anyone with the requisite merit, whatever his origins, but the novel avoided the awkward social implications of such a view by simply identifying moral nobility with social nobility. Anyone who demonstrates that he has true heroic virtue must automatically belong to the highest aristocracy. Even when a man has been washed up by the sea and is lying unconscious, 'des que la genereuse Oriane eust jetté les yeux dessus, elle ne douta plus qu'il ne fust de sang illustre'. When he recovers and sees his benefactress, he is similarly impressed:

'cette auguste majesté qui eclatte si visiblement sur vostre
front & cette haute generosité dont vous me donnez aujourd'
huy de si sensibles tesmoignages m'ont d'abord appris la
grandeur de vostre rang & l'excellence de vos vertus'.[74] In an
ideal world, all virtuous people could belong to the highest
rank without any of the anomalies to be found in real life.

Many of the features mentioned above were retained as
constants in heroic literature throughout the seventeenth
century and, to a certain extent, are common to heroes in
other, very different, periods of literature as well.[75] However,
there are essential differences between the kind of hero
offered by the heroic novel and the kind depicted in the
other major forms of seventeenth-century novel. What sets
the heroic novel apart from the Greek romances and their
derivatives is that its hero always sets out to impose himself
on the world rather than suffer a series of *coups de fortune*.
His will drives him on and it always brings him through
victorious at the end. When fortune seems to turn against
him, he responds energetically and determinedly, and forces
circumstances to second his design.

The principal difference between the heroic novel and the
romance of chivalry of the *Amadis* type lies in the quality of
the hero's response to those around. In *Amadis* and its
successors, the hero is only one energetic element in a world
which contains other positive figures, such as giants, sorcerers,
and dwarfs. *Généreux* knights do not fight against each other,
except in tournaments, because there are enough ignoble
opponents for them to deal with.[76] The code of *courtoisie*
only applies between knights who live by the chivalric oath,
not between such knights and anyone else they may encounter, and enemies are disposed of in any way that suggests
itself at the time, if necessary by the aid of a magician or
fairy. There is, too, a certain moral ambiguity apparent in
these romances. The giant Gandalac, 'un Geant si horrible,
qu'il n'y avoit homme qui à le voir ne fust surpris de tres
grand'paour',[77] who steals Galaor, the brother of Amadis,
none the less appears later on fighting alongside Amadis in
the army of King Lisvart. Amadis fights the giant Balan who
has killed a knight for no good reason, admitting 'je crains la

condition des Geans, lesquelz peu communément sont gouvernez par raison, ains de furie & dure cruauté',[78] but subsequently befriends him. Astramond, a pagan giant twelve feet tall, behaves in a thoroughly arrogant and unheroic way, killing enemies who have begged for mercy, carrying off a ten-year-old princess, and cursing heaven and the gods.[79] He appears in Constantinople and challenges Amadis de Gaule (well advanced in years by this stage), but has to admit himself beaten.[80] He is thereupon given a royal reception and, after becoming Christian, is eventually made Emperor of Ethiopia.[81] The implication here is that it is not the man himself who matters so much as the nature of the feats he has accomplished and that anyone who is not behaving in an obviously wicked way is entitled to be considered heroic by virtue of his valour.

In the heroic novel, the hero's physical feats are secondary to his moral status. As Scudéry put it, 'ce n'est point par les choses de dehors; ce n'est point par les caprices du destin, que je veux juger de luy; c'est par les mouvemens de son ame & par les choses qu'il dit.'[82] As a result, his opponents are no longer wicked. Heroic novels contain a series of combats between characters who share the highest ideals of justice and courtesy, whose conceptions of virtue and *générosité* are identical, but whose interests have, perhaps temporarily, overlapped. They are enemies only in the sense that each is trying to assert his superiority over the other, but they by no means desire the annihilation of the other. When the fighting is over, the combat is one of magnanimity: who can treat the other with the greater chivalry? They can offer each other respect and friendship, because they both belong to the universal commonwealth of courtesy and *générosité* which unites all those, in whatever country or continent they may be and in whatever age in history, who aspire to the highest calling of man, the heroic bearing of arms. The same norms of honour and politeness are found in ancient Persia and Greece, classical Rome, medieval Denmark, and modern Turkey. Fighting therefore becomes not so much a matter of good against evil, innocence against injustice (though it sometimes is), but a morally neutral expression of personal prowess, and thence a contributory factor towards *gloire*.

The hero in the romances of chivalry was heroic because he had fought and won. He was a conqueror who had earned his laurels; his heroic status was a consequence of action. For the new hero, the situation is reversed. Fighting is a consequence of being a hero. For him, heroism is a state, not a goal. He fights because he *is* a hero and has to demonstrate that he possesses the necessary qualities, and the only valid way of establishing moral superiority is against an opponent on the same moral level, who by definition cannot be evil. The point is illustrated by an episode in *Mitridate*. A stranger (who turns out to be Mitridate) has killed six out of eight of Pyrrhus' men who had tried to rob him. Pyrrhus gives him the remaining two to punish as he sees fit, but the stranger lets them go and asks Pyrrhus to pardon them. It is this gesture of magnanimity that validates the stranger's bravery and marks him out as a true hero: 'Pyrrhus n'avoit jusques alors reconnu sa vertu que par des marques exterieures & qui pouvoient tromper; mais il ne balança plus sur l'estime qu'il en devoit faire, quand il vit cet excez de generosité.'[83]

The features of the hero outlined above give an idea of the area of consensus amongst the writers of heroic novels. However, it should not be assumed that all such writers shared a common view of the relationship between the heroic individual and the rest of mankind. There were considerable differences of opinion as to the obligations and rights that heroic status carried with it, differences which can usually be traced back to conflicting assumptions about the source of human motivations and about the relative proportions of self-interest and altruism within morality. The differences manifest themselves mainly in the type of episode created and in the use made of the terminology of heroism, though sometimes more obviously polemical passages are introduced. It is these debated aspects of heroism which will be considered in the next chapter.

CHAPTER II

THE AREA OF DEBATE

The trauma of the Religious Wars was still affecting the French mind long after the cessation of hostilities, and it is not surprising to find that many writers in the first decades of the seventeenth century expressed a profound pessimism about the state of the world. The traditional doctrine of man's fall from grace and his condemnation to a life of toil and sorrow was reinforced by the experiences of civil war to create a climate of teleological gloom, the belief that any progress man made must be downwards. The process of degeneration was often felt to have gone so far that not even the theory of the cyclical decline and revival of empires provided any real hope of ultimate resurgence. Balzac maintained that permanent decline was now inevitable: 'le Monde a perdu son innocence il y a long-temps. Nous sommes dans la corruption des Siecles, & dans la caducité de la Nature. Tout est foible, tout est malade, dans les Assemblées des Hommes.'[1] Political commentators frequently adopted the position that man's baser side had infected the system under which he lived and ensured that imperfections in the political structure were perpetuated. Richelieu saw no point in trying to reform the state machinery, since its defects had become a matter of habit;[2] Silhon maintained that the days when men worked zealously for good were gone for ever;[3] Naudé considered the great European empires to be at just the age at which they were ripe for collapse.[4] War was held to be a constant corrective, necessary to maintain some sort of equilibrium in society, likened to a public bloodletting which restores a certain health to a sick kingdom poisoned by ambition.

Moralists frequently pointed to ambition and avarice as the besetting sins of the age, sins which made it impossible for man to achieve harmony and which were blamed as the major cause of the upheavals which marked the regencies of Marie de Médicis and Anne d'Autriche. Chevreau's view reflected the outlook of many:

> Jamais on ne se servit plus avantageusement de la liberté pour mal faire: La coustume authorise tous les crimes que les loix defendent; & pour treuver de l'innocence & de la pureté parmi les hommes, il faudroit remonter jusques au premier âge du monde. Le vice est tellement respecté, qu'il a par tout des amis & des partisans: . . . Les plus saints d'aujourd'hui ont l'ame noire, & les mains soüillées . . . [L'avarice] est la cause & l'appui de la corruption du siecle.[5]

This was not some reforming cleric writing, but a soldier and man of letters who moved amongst the polite circles of Parisian society and wrote novels for their entertainment.

Not everyone was so pessimistic. There were those who took a more charitable view of the positive features of human nature and who believed that, though man had fallen from his original state, he still had in him the seeds of universal love which made him want to live in society with his fellow men. The interdependence imposed on man by his social nature provided an opportunity for him to transcend to a certain extent his natural egotism by contributing to the good of the community. Some found it possible to claim that the contemporary world represented a new Golden Age.[6] Others, without going so far, saw enough positive factors in the way in which the world was developing to justify faith in man's capacity to improve himself and his environment, an attitude which was to come into its own in the *Querelle des anciens et des modernes* and the optimism of the Enlightenment.

Both these concepts of man, which may be loosely termed pessimistic and optimistic respectively, allowed a belief in the existence of heroes and supermen. In terms of the pessimistic view, the hero represents the exception to the general rule, the man who is not subject to the normal degeneration which afflicts the rest of humanity. He consequently tends to be seen as something of a moral island, cut off from other men and having no real contact with them, so that all they can do is admire from a distance: 'Qu'il y a de plaisir à voir les saillies d'un esprit genereux: C'est un Aigle volant, qui mesprisant la terre qu'il regarde par dedain, n'a des yeux que pour envisager le Ciel, & se mirer dans l'esclat des Astres & du

Soleil.'[7] This kind of hero has certain affinities with the Stoic sage in that his heroism exists more or less for its own sake, an end in itself, though that is not to say that he does no more than contemplate his own virtue: the hero is always a man of action and needs to have an audience to whom he can display his virtue and so increase his *gloire*.

For the partisans of the more optimistic view, the hero was not isolated from the rest of mankind, but was one of 'ces hommes qui semblent n'exceller au dessus des autres que pour leur bien & n'estre bien partagez dans les avantages du Ciel que pour en faire part avantageusement à ceux du commun',[8] an idealized projection of man who never loses the links which bind him to his fellows. His heroism is seen as a combination of all those elements that give grounds for hope about human nature, extended to the highest level compatible with human limitations. He is not a separate species but an exceptional specimen who puts his exceptional qualities at the service of the community, like Guérin de Bouscal's Hercules who '[caressoit] les affligez avec la mesme main qui domptoit les monstres' and who 'voulut partir de la Capadoce, disant qu'il ne pouvoit sans honte estre si long-temps sans faire quelque chose pour le bien commun des hommes'.[9]

The pessimistic view puts a premium on self-assertion, the hero being primarily concerned with establishing his own *gloire* and maintaining it at all costs. It derives from a some-what Hobbesian view of society. The natural tendency to want to impose oneself on others, chiefly from a vain esteem of oneself; the right to use all the means and carry out all the actions without which one cannot preserve oneself; a state of nature in which profit is the measure of right and each man is constantly at war with all other men: all these, expounded by Hobbes, are merely an unflattering statement of the same will to power, self-preservation and self-perpetu-ation which, in the egocentric heroic ethic, are expressed in a terminology borrowed partly from Christian altruistic morality — *vertu*, *devoir*, *générosité*, etc.[10]

Such a philosophy was entirely incompatible with the more optimistic view of man, according to which heroism only had any validity in so far as it made a contribution to the good of the world. *Générosité* only existed in terms of other people, since it could not be said to have come into being until some recipient had experienced it. Guérin de Bouscal demonstrated the unacceptable nature of the type of heroism that existed for nothing but its own advantage in the person of Sinis, a brigand who lives in the forests of ancient Greece. Like Hobbes' natural man, Sinis judges everything in terms of profit and power. He glories in being the enemy of the whole human race and claims to live in accordance with the law of nature. He has evolved a quasi-Nietzschean theory according to which it is moral weakness that has led the mass of mankind to agree not to harm the interests of others; he who is free from fear has no need of traditional morality: 'nous ne nous retenons jamais d'outrager autruy que de peur qu'on nous outrage nous mesme: & si nous n'avons pas cette crainte, nous n'avons pas cette retenuë.'[11] The domination exercised by men over women, by kings over their subjects, by fathers over their children — these are merely institutionalized forms of the will to power enjoyed by the strong, and, if men were honest, they would heed no law except that of their own will.

The value of these theories is indicated by the way of life they oblige Sinis to lead. He lives alone (except for his daughter, who does not share his beliefs) in a cave in the forest, living by hunting and robbing travellers. He knows no one other than another brigand some miles away, and he has to be constantly on the alert against enemies. The moral independence he prizes so much has produced a life that is nasty and brutish. He is not even left with the possibility of joining a society of like-minded superior beings, since the same anti-social law of power would apply, though he does feel a certain affinity with other valiant men:

Je vous fais ce discours . . . pour vous desabuser en particulier d'une creance generale, & pour justifier l'eternelle guerre que je fais aux hommes. Ce n'est pas qu'il me fâche d'estre accusé par des lâches; mais il me seroit fâcheux que les vaillans, au nombre desquels je vous conte, eussent des pensées desavantageuses de ma vie.[12]

However, a sufficient comment on this is provided by the fact that, shortly after this speech, he pushes his interlocutor over a precipice. It is evident that Guérin wished his readers to accept that no way of life could be considered admirable if it ignored obligations and merely asserted its privileges.

The principles on which a worthwhile society and a proper appreciation of heroism must be founded are set out later in the same novel by Theseus, who explains that the natural love of man for his fellows can be used to destroy the tyranny of self-interest: the precepts of altruism reinforce the sentiments instilled by nature, so that the properly educated would consider themselves to have committed a crime if they missed an opportunity to do good.[13] These principles produce a society in which the highest manifestations of heroism can appear but where the hero never loses sight of what he owes to his fellow men. He corresponds closely to the ideal set out by Couraud for his Christian hero, 'dans lequel l'humanité & la religion; bien faire aux hommes & bien servir Dieu; se rendre aimable à eux & à luy; en un mot dans lequel perpetuer sa memoire en obligeant les creatures & en obeïssant au Createur, feront les deux parties de sa vie heroïque'.[14]

Though few writers were as explicit as Guérin de Bouscal, there were others who evidently felt that an entirely self-centred ideal of heroism was not acceptable and who wanted to prevent the hero from turning himself into a moral island. It is possible to talk of a debate as to the nature of heroism between those who held to an egocentric ideal and those who postulated an altruistic ethic, the standpoint of the author being indicated by the kind of action he considered praiseworthy and the interpretation he gave to the terminology of heroism, for the frequent use of certain terms, such as *gloire*, *générosité*, and *vertu*, is a marked characteristic of the heroic novel as it is of the heroic theatre. Earlier novels had used these terms more sparingly or without the aim of building up a heroic atmosphere: Boisrobert, for instance, uses *gloire* very little in his *Histoire indienne* and *généreux* mainly as a courtesy epithet.

Those scholars who have studied the manifestations of the heroic ideal in the seventeenth century stress the importance of a correct interpretation of such terminology for an understanding of heroism and point out that it had already changed its meaning by the end of the century. Definitions have been put forward of its various meanings in Corneille's plays[15] and modifications offered with reference to other forms of literature.[16] An analysis of the use of the terms made in the novel reveals that on the whole they are applied in a similar way to their use in the theatre but that there are distinct attempts by some writers to impose an alternative definition of heroism. It would be useful at this point to consider each of the main terms in turn and to determine the different values attributed to them.

Générosité

Of all the qualities associated with heroism, *générosité* is the most essential. It is the one which enables the hero to maintain the position consonant with his own and the world's view of him and thus to remain true to himself. The inborn propensity to greatness which drives him on relies on a 'grandeur de courage' without which no one can be considered heroic, and which is in fact often used synonymously with *générosité*. It is the external manifestation of moral striving. Differences of interpretation arise when it is a question of deciding what the aim of such striving should be.[17]

On the one hand, if the hero is seen as morally responsible to no one except himself, then *générosité* need be no more than straightforward courage, since this is all that is ultimately necessary to enable him to defend his prerogatives; 'les hommes genereux . . . n'apprehendent jamais rien, ils sont preparez à tout, & s'ils craignent, c'est plutôt pour leur reputation que pour leur personne'.[18] Thus it is possible for men to be described as *généreux* even though they are cruel, tyrannical, discourteous, or devious, simply because they show courage in defending their cause, whether it can be approved of morally or not:

encor qu'il ait quelque cruauté, il est pourtant genereux.

la response d'un genereux courage estoit toute preste [from the tyrannical and unjust Admiral].

la surprise l'estonna plus que le danger du combat, & comme il [the unchivalrous slanderer Zadarem] estoit veritablement genereux, apres quelques paroles nous en vinsmes aux mains.

parmy les Turcs il y en a presque tousjours eu de resolus & de genereux, ils se sont servis de la ruze, de la force & de la vaillance pour se maintenir.

[Serefbeg has] une generosité brutale, qui le portoit dans les perils sans les connoistre.[19]

This sort of *générosité* can even arise out of hatred:

une mesme affection jetta dans leur ame ces profondes racines d'une hayne qui leur fist entreprendre plusieurs genereux desseins sur leur vie.

si vous avez quelque haine secrette pour moy, vangez-vous genereuse-ment.[20]

There are some writers who never go beyond this point in their use of the term, notably the authors of *Alcide*, *La Prazimene*, and *Le Polemire*: they are concerned only to depict the courage displayed in the immediate interests of self.

Exponents of the more altruistic view of heroism, on the other hand, see *générosité* as necessarily attached to ethical and social values. They set relationships with others higher than the demands of self-aggrandizement, and lay particular stress on sympathy and help for those in trouble:

une ame genereuse est hors de son element, lors qu'elle est contrainte, ou de se ressentir des injures qu'on luy a faites, ou de refuser de la compassion à ceux qui sont tombez, quoy que justement, en quelque infortune.

un esprit genereux ne peut se resoudre à opresser les foibles.[21]

Only those actions which benefit others can be qualified as *généreuses*. 'Le Prince n'est pas genereux qui travaille plus . . . pour son interest que pour celuy des autres,' declares Du Bail.[22] Gomberville's hero displays 'cette genereuse humanité par laquelle vous entrez dans les sentimens de vos ennemis & prenez part à leurs disgraces'.[23] Thésée reminds himself that 'la generosité n'est pas entiere, si elle est melée de quelqu'autre interest que de celuy de la personne qui l'a fait [i.e. has caused it to be exercised]'. His altruism is acknowledged by others: 'comme vous estes parfaitement genereux, il vous suffit de sçavoir que j'ay besoin de vostre secours, pour croire que j'en suis digne,' declares Egée.[24] Cyrus is told that 'c'est estre bien genereux de vouloir plustost vous interesser dans les malheurs d'autruy que dans les vostres'.[25] In short, it is the concern for others that turns courage into *générosité*.[26]

Though it is not his primary aim, the hero who has a genuine concern for others, especially his enemies, reaps considerable rewards in terms of esteem. Pure self-interest usually has to give way before altruistic *générosité*. Pyrrhus, concerned with his own *gloire*, refuses to allow his enemy Ptolomée to arrange to have his wounds tended. Straton argues with him: 'Est-ce que vous ne voulez pas devoir quelque chose à ceux que vous avez haïs? Considerez, Seigneur, qu'en ne l'acceptant pas, vous n'estes pas moins obligé à leur generosité, que si vous en aviez ressenty les effects, & que vous ne pouvez à present mourir que leur redevable,' but to no avail. Ptolomée, however, asks him to recover as a favour and at this, Pyrrhus is won over: 'la generosité du Roy d'Egipte l'avoit tellement touché, qu'il n'avoit peu luy refuser ces marques de sa recognoissance'.[27]

Gloire

Gloire is the hero's reward for action. He achieves it by being successful or by imposing himself morally on to any situation in which he may find himself. Those for whom heroism was largely a question of moral independence depicted their heroes devoting all their energies to the pursuit of *gloire* and subordinating all other aims to it: 'd'obliger nos ennemis à publier nostre gloire sans contrainte, ce doit estre la plus belle de nos esperances, & la plus noble récompense de la vertu'.[28] Every action is referred to the ideal vision that the hero maintains within himself; every action must help him to keep the position that he sees himself already occupying. *Gloire* is thus elevated to the level of an absolute; the hero acknowledges only one essential element in the order of things — himself — and the rest of the world has to be made to fit in with this simple plan.

Since the heroic novel was concerned almost exclusively with military leaders, the area in which *gloire* manifested itself in the novel tended to be dominated by the battlefield or tournament, though acts of unselfishness and altruism also attracted *gloire*. Novelists must have been aware, however, of the questions raised by moralists as to whether *gloire* was a legitimate end in itself or whether its only value was as a spur to virtue. There were those who were prepared to accord it an important place in the scale of moral values. Chevreau, despite his Stoic leanings, rejects the idea that virtue must necessarily be its own end and reward. Virtue in fact needs *gloire* to illumine it: 'si l'on nous ostoit la gloire, nous ne pourrions pas distinguer la vertu d'avec le vice, ni ce qui nous est permis d'avec ce qui nous est défendu'.[29] A similar argument is used by Montausier in Chapelain's *Dialogue de la gloire*.[30] Those who assume that man will be virtuous without this stimulus are being hopelessly unrealistic, it is suggested. One hero at least concurs, basing his desire for *gloire* on a profound disillusionment with the rest of the human race: Polexandre assures the *généreux* Zelmatide, who has advised him not to bother justifying himself since his conscience is clear, that he would do as he says if all men were like him, 'mais quand je considere que le plus grand nombre des hommes est composé de sots & de meschans; & d'ailleurs, que nostre reputation est servilement attachée aux sentimens de cette multitude; je croy que nous sommes obligez de tesmoigner ce que nous sommes, & tiens que quand on vit parmy des gens qui sont incapables de la souveraine Sagesse, il est plus vicieux d'aller contre la coustume que contre la vertu'.[31]

The limiting factor as far as the moralists were concerned was that *gloire* required a balance to be maintained between the internal ideal that the hero strove to achieve and the external view of him in relation to the accepted moral norms: 'se voir également accompli en soy-mesme, & en l'opinion d'autruy'.[32] Such a balance can only be ensured if the hero has the necessary self-knowledge, and this in its turn is dependent on his resisting the temptation to pass from *amour de soi* to *amour-propre*.

Amour de soi is perfectly legitimate and indeed is a necessary quality in anyone who is to stand out amongst men. It enables him to confront the world and fulfil the demands made by his position. It is an acknowledgement of his true worth: 'S'il y a du merite en nous, & que nous ne le voyons point, c'est estre aveugle; si nous le voyons sans le vouloir confesser, c'est estre ingrat.[33] The approach to self-knowledge must be calm and detached if it is to produce the right results: when a just appraisal of the self has been achieved, it will lead to a mode of life in which consideration for others plays a central part. Camus goes so far as to claim that *amour de soi* is an element in charity and is expressly commanded by God's law.[34]

Amour-propre, on the other hand, arises when the individual develops a false perspective of himself and loses his awareness of the demands of the world around. He gives in to pride (*orgueil*) which makes him feel that only he is of importance and that his own worth is greater than it actually is: 'que l'amour propre est un grand Imposteur! il nous depeint nos merites plus grands & nos defauts plus petits qu'ils ne sont.'[35] *Amour-propre* is obsessed with personal advancement and loses sight of the true relationship of the individual to the creation of which he is a part:

Tout amour propre est bien amour nostre, mais tout amour nostre, c'est à dire, de nous mesme n'est pas amour propre . . . par l'amour propre j'entends le vicieux amour de nous mesme, ce foyer du peché, . . . cet amour par lequel nous nous arrestons volontairement & deliberement à nous mesmes . . .

l'amour nostre . . . est tousjours . . . de sa nature rapportable à la fin derniere, au lieu que l'amour propre n'y est jamais ny rapporté, ny rapportable, & ainsi tousjours injuste.[36]

This distinction between *amour de soi* and *amour-propre* leads on to a further important distinction between *gloire* and ambition. The latter was one of the major passions to which the hero was expected to be susceptible, but it was at the same time dangerous because it could take over his moral sense and force him into unheroic postures. In particular, it could lead him into thinking that the end was more important than the means. So, just as *amour de soi* requires the individual to have a proper appreciation of the qualities he possesses, *gloire* is found only where the aim is commensurate with the abilities deployed to achieve it and where only morally acceptable means are used. If the aim is beyond the scope of the individual and is not in some way in the general interest of man, then *gloire* has given way to ambition:

Ce desir de gloire vient donc d'un courage relevé qui par le chemin de la vertu se fait un passage aux grandes charges; il ne tente que ce qui répond à ses desseins, il ne s'attache qu'au bien public, & dans ses honneurs il fait confesser, quelque chose qu'on luy donne, qu'il en merite encore davantage. Mais l'ambition se jette dans les dignitez par toutes sortes de moyens, elle ne consulte point s'ils sont permis ou defendus.[37]

... l'ambitieux ne mesure point son dessein à ses forces, & n'employe pour reüssir que des moyens deffendus ... l'on voit qu'il n'est pas permis à toutes sortes de personnes de butter aux grands honneurs; il faut bien sçavoir ses forces, ou autrement, c'est ambition.[38]

Gloire must be the unsolicited reward for action undertaken in some virtuous cause: if the action is carried out for the sake of acquiring *gloire*, it is the product of ambition, 'le defaut d'un courage bas, puisque l'on se declare inferieur à tout ce que l'on desire au dessus de soy. Une ame n'est eminente que lors qu'elle voit tout sous elle; à mesme qu'elle pretend s'eslever, elle publie sa bassesse.'[39] Amasis proves himself to be such a base man when he sets out to usurp the throne he does not merit: 'il n'escouta ny la generosité, ny la raison, ny mesme la veritable gloire, qui ne se trouve pas à regner par une injuste voye: & se laissa emporter aveuglément à l'ambition toute seule'.[40] Desmarets carefully defines *gloire* in terms which exclude all ambition but retain the element of moral superiority. If victorious, the hero gains *gloire* by his treatment of his opponents, particularly by showing clemency; if defeated, his *gloire* derives from his constancy in the face of adversity and his refusal to submit morally.[41]

A number of writers of heroic novels chose to ignore the fact that the gap between *gloire* and ambition was dangerously narrow, and extolled the greatness of heroes interested only in their own reputation, but on the whole there was an awareness that the elevation of personal *gloire* to the level of an absolute was undesirable and that the hero lost none of his superhuman quality if he showed he had a concern for the claims of the world around. Some were explicit, as in the case of Araxez, who makes a point of letting his enemy, whom he is freeing, know that he is 'ne se proposant pas mesme la gloire pour la fin de son action, mais l'action elle-mesme'.[42] Coriolan, too, feels as much compassion for the misfortunes of others as love of his own *gloire* and disregards his own interests to help the afflicted.[43]

Particular attention was often paid in the heroic novel to the hero's abilities as a military tactician, since the traditional

heroic practice (still seen in *Alcide, L'Illustre Amalazonthe,*
and *Mitridate*) of spending an entire battle heaping up
honours and *gloire* for personal prowess with never a thought
for the overall conduct of the battle was felt to be out of
keeping with the self-control and the commitment to the
common good required in a hero. Scudéry takes care to
stress that Ibrahim, though capable of individual heroic
actions, also kept a firm hold on the development of the
battle as a whole. On the one hand, he saves Sinan from
death with a magnificent stroke of his scimitar: 'mais faisant
le soldat en cette rencontre il ne laissoit pas d'agir en General
d'Armée & d'avoir l'œil à toutes choses', sending reinforce-
ments where they are needed or leading an attack himself
where necessary.[44] In *Berenger*, when the Christians come off
worst in a tournament against the Saracens, they draw the
appropriate moral, recognizing that they had been motivated
by vanity, 'au lieu que les hommes de cœur doivent reserver
leur valeur pour la gloire & l'avantage du public.'[45] In *Cassandre*, Memnon and Oxiarte carry their personal rivalry onto
the battlefield, with the result that the common cause begins
to suffer.[46] Golème, one of Scanderberg's generals, rides
alone into a squadron of Turks to capture a flag and is nearly
killed in the process: such an action would be laudable in an
ordinary soldier, but needs to be censured in a general:

Il faut donc dire que Goleme fut heureux, mais non pas vaillant, puis
qu'il y fut plus poussé par un sentiment d'honneur que par un sentiment
de vertu, que le bien public le toucha moins que le sien propre, & que
le profit qui devoit revenir de cette action n'estoit pas si grand que le
dommage qui pouvoit revenir de la perte de sa vie.[47]

Thus, though the acquisition of *gloire* was universally
considered to be a legitimate aspiration in the heroic novel,
there were those for whom it could not be simply a matter
of self-fulfilment, the attainment of whatever goal the
individual had set himself: it had to be achieved within the
area prescribed by the interests of the community as a whole,
an attitude in line with the altruistic version of the heroic
ideal.

Vaillance
Vaillance is widely taken as the manifestation of courage

required in the pursuit of *gloire*. It therefore has a close affinity with *générosité*, and again, like *gloire* and *générosité*, was subject to interpretations stressing its more moral elements. This is particularly noticeable in the political writers, who want to prove that heroic qualities are not necessarily limited to the sphere of physical action. Richelieu dissociates courage from *vaillance* so that he can claim the latter as an attribute of the statesman as well as of the general.[48] Balzac reinforces *vaillance* with intellectual capacity so that he who regulates the civil sphere can be put on the same level as the military leader.[49] Chevreau, too, stresses the part played by reason in his portrait of *le Vaillant*.[50]

A certain amount of this modified meaning found its way into the heroic novel. Desmarets elevates *vaillance* to the point where it becomes an end in itself, very close to *gloire*:

la vaillance n'a point de satisfaction qu'en soy-mesme; & c'est ce que nous appellons honneur, qui n'est autre chose que la gloire qui est en nous de ne manquer jamais à ce que la vaillance nous ordonne, quelque disgrace qui puisse arriver; . . . la victoire & les honneurs ne peuvent estre ses objects principaux, pource que ce ne sont pas des choses que l'on soit asseuré d'acquerir.[51]

The episode of Golème in *Scanderberg* illustrates the fact that true *vaillance* involves far more than mere courage: 'son ardeur fit bien voir que les plus courageux ne sont pas quelquefois les plus vaillans, que c'est peu d'avoir un bien si on n'en sçait pas user'.[52]

Vertu

Though *vertu* was acknowledged by seventeenth-century writers to be one of the primary qualities in heroism, there was a certain constraint on their part in deciding what exactly it involved, because of the strong Christian overtones inherent in the term which frequently militated against the other aspects of heroism (e.g. François de Sales asserts that *vertu* practised for the sake of *gloire* alone is not genuine).[53] Those who undertook to define *vertu héroïque* often revealed uncertainty as to what it consisted of, other than that it was somehow specially elevated. For Dubosc, the difference between heroic and ordinary virtue is that the former has 'une certaine grandeur, ou une eminence qu'elle adjoute aux autres'.[54] Le Moyne sees its object as 'l'Honneste consideré dans la plus haute élevation qu'il puisse avoir'.[55] Cériziers suggests that 'la Vertu s'appelle Heroïque quand elle est arrivée jusques à nous eslever au dessus du commun, & qu'elle fait un estat môyen entre Dieu & les hommes ordinaires'.[56]

The one aspect that is generally agreed upon is that *vertu* presupposes action. The moralists all stress the point and writers of heroic novels agree: 'la vertu de l'homme consiste toute en l'action'.[57] Some interpret *vertu* as no more than a source of strength which enables the hero to pursue his aims, whatever they may be. It is synonymous with energy, like the *virtù* of Machiavelli: it is constantly poised ready to work for self-fulfilment. Any action it initiates must be spontaneous, and a failure to respond with action leads to the unheroic situation of being morally subject to fortune, like Mélinte who 'languissoit abbatu d'ennuy, sans aucune apparence de vertu' instead of trying to 'se relever par les sentimens de la vertu, qui enseigne à mespriser les accidens humains'.[58]

It is possible, therefore, for *vertu* to imply no more than great strength and courage: 'leur seule vertu extermina les ennemis'.[59] It could be a source of fortitude, moderating despair in affliction.[60] However, the term usually contained within itself an element that gave it an added moral dimension. Without being assimilated to any specific ethic, it presupposed in the hero an ability to concentrate all his force on the attainment of a particular objective which is seen by him as a duty. This duty might be simply an obligation to maintain an image of himself or of his social group. From those who demanded a greater awareness in the hero of the claims of humanity as a whole, on the other hand, there came the suggestion that the better part of *vertu* was not courage — 'cette aveugle ardeur, qui procede du temperament & non pas de la vertu'[61] — but the rectitude of the intention, judged in terms of its contribution to the good of mankind. *Vertu* acted as the bridge between the hero and the rest of the community from which he was inevitably in some measure set apart: 'les personnes qui portent ses marques se discernent & se separent du commun par ce puissant caractere qu'elle a imprimé en elles'.[62] It is the quality which prevents him from developing too great an opinion of himself.[63] Its commitment to a sense of duty may lead it to overrule other heroic inclinations, even the desire for *gloire*.[64] One particular feature which is referred to frequently as being indispensable to it is an ability to show gratitude, since this indicates immediately that the hero does not consider himself to be outside the normal world of human relationships, obligations and interdependence: he shows his solidarity with his fellows by 'une juste recognoissance, qui est le premier mouvement d'une vraye vertu'.[65]

The area of debate amongst those novelists who affirmed the existence of heroism as an idealized expression of man's potential covered its application rather than its essence. Both sides would have agreed with Herminius, that 'pour faire qu'une action soit toute heroïque, il faut non seulement que le motif en soit juste, mais encore que les moyens en soient nobles & innocens'.[66] The divergence was between those who wanted to raise personal aspirations and the individual's moral independence to the level of an absolute, and those who saw the need to relate the individual to some sort of ethical order. This is not to say that the second type had a social conscience in the modern sense or was necessarily imbued with any more Christian charity. It is rather that the exponents of the former view, amongst whom may be counted Lemaire, d'Astorgues, and Deschaussée, set out to depict an exceptional being who exists on a different plane from the rest of mankind, whereas those who expounded the latter view, including Chevreau, Guérin de Bouscal, and Segrais, presented a model to be not only admired but imitated.

The fact that so many writers were careful to present their own definitions of the terminology considered above suggests that the heroic novel needs to be studied in the context of the search for man's moral identity, a search which we know to have been of great importance in the seventeenth century, thanks to the work of many scholars in recent years. Those who so avidly read heroic novels no doubt needed to believe in a world in which Oroondate and Cyrus could exist, and the freedom embodied by the literary hero might well have seemed attractive to people with everyday lives to lead, but, as some novelists pointed out, it brought with it its own responsibilities and obligations — self-restraint, the suppression of false grandeur, allegiance to a code of social ethics. To those who proposed an ideal of aristocratic self-fulfilment based solely on fidelity to the individual's image of himself, these other novelists opposed a kind of heroism based on duty towards the society that had made that heroism possible.

The concept of heroism in the novel appears, therefore, to have been affected by the conflict in France between those who still maintained the supremacy of the values associated with the aristocratic class-myth and those who affirmed the need for a new order. Direct political comment is not found, and it would be wrong to identify the latter view with the theory of state expounded by Richelieu and his spokesmen. It is rather a concern that the individual should moderate his personal aspirations and submit them to a generally applicable code of *honnêteté*. He could certainly allow *générosité*, *gloire*, and *vertu* to carry him on to greatness, but it must never be at the expense of his fellow beings.

In one respect at least, the question of the morality involved in the relating of means to ends, the heroic novel was fundamentally opposed to the principles on which Richelieu's state was founded. It is this question of *prudence* which will be considered in the next chapter.

CHAPTER III

PRUDENCE AND PROVIDENCE

The Greek romances were suffused with an awareness of the power of fate, an inscrutable force which relentlessly pursues certain individuals, inflicting on them disasters and tribulations far beyond the burden that most human beings are called on to carry. Other people can sympathize: they themselves can do nothing, for as soon as they have escaped one misfortune, another catastrophe strikes. They may survive a shipwreck only to be captured by pirates, or be bought out of slavery only to find that their new master or mistress has designs on them. In all this, they are victims. Seeing no pattern or justice in the apparently arbitrary persecution, all they can do is suffer and lament, sometimes inveighing angrily against the gods:

Ha! Dieux & Demons, . . . en quelque lieu du monde que vous soyez, si mes complaintes vous touchent, respondez-moy je vous prie, si Leucippe & moi avons commis un tel forfait qu'il faille qu'en si peu de temps nous soyons accablez de tant d'infortunes & de miseres?[1]

. . . je suis le trophée de la fortune, le spectacle des miseres du monde, le joüet du Ciel & de la mer, & le theatre du toutes les Furies de l'Enfer.[2]

Behind the sequence of events, however, there is a providence protecting the hero and heroine and ensuring that none of the disasters that befall them is fatal. The reader is made aware that some kind of pattern exists and that the conclusion is likely to be a happy one. Sometimes the characters themselves give a hint of insight, but, more frequently, it is dreams which indicate how the future is to unfold, though the dreamer remains a victim and has no way of avoiding the danger of which he has been forewarned, using his knowledge merely to strengthen his fortitude.[3] Oracles often establish the path of the hero's destiny. Heliodorus in particular builds up the reader's awareness of the providential framework as the *Histoire ethiopique* progresses, to the point where the suspense of the conclusion is weakened because of the constant references to the divine plan for Chariclea.

The French disciples of the Greek romance-writers clung very much to the same passivity in the face of fate. Their heroes and heroines undergo a long series of misfortunes against which their only consolation is their lamentations.[4] They list the catastrophes they have survived and desperately beg the gods to release them from the persecutions of fate, but their authors constantly present them with some new peril and extract the maximum of pathos from their situation. The episode in the *Histoire ethiopique* in which Théagène is to be sacrificed exercised a particular appeal because of the element of suspense broken by the intervention of providence. Théogènes in *Du vray et parfaict amour* and Alexandre in *Histoire negrepontique* are both condemned to death and miraculously saved; Anaxandre in the *Histoire indienne* has to be twice rescued by providence from public execution.

In the *Amadis* cycle and its successors, the framework of providence is there, represented by the fairies and magicians who protect the interests of the heroes. They can foretell the course of the lives of their heroes and quite frequently intervene supernaturally in events to ensure that that course is being followed. They cannot impose or prevent the working out of an ultimate destiny, however. Thus, in the *Götterdämmerung* scene which closes the *Romant des romans*, when the massive battle begins against the pagans, in which Amadis de Gaule, Don Bélianis de Grèce, le Chevalier du Soleil, and many more are to be killed, Urgande, Alcandre, and the other magicians have already created a Temple of Glory for the dead heroes and themselves and burnt their books, but they could have done nothing to influence the outcome of the battle.

As far as the ordinary encounters and trials of strength in the romances of chivalry are concerned, each knight behaves as though the outcome were dependent solely on his own efforts. He relies completely on his own courage and skill, and would consider it unworthy to call for supernatural aid. When Rosidor hears about le Château des Esprits, for instance, his response is immediate and direct: he sets off to find this daunting place, concerned lest anyone should think that he had even considered avoiding it.[5] Each adventure is related with little reference to the problems of fate because, as far as the hero is concerned, fate has nothing to do with the situation confronting him: it can be resolved by the application of his own forces.

In general, the concept of fate and fortune presented in the fiction of the period reflected the prevailing Christian concept of providence. Given that God loves man despite his faults, it was argued, we must accept that any incident that befalls us has been ordained for some purpose which we may very well not be able to grasp: in our ignorance, all we can do is submit in the faith that God's providence is working towards a necessary end:

Quand il t'arrive quelque fascheux accident, il est determiné de Dieu, il ne vient point à toy par inconstance fortuite des evenemens, qui ne sçavent où se placer. Il y a une telle coherence & une concatenation si necessaire d'une cause à l'autre, qu'elles s'entrepoussent toutes comme les flots, sans que nous puissions découvrir quel est le principe de leur impulsion.[6]

While the ultimate outcome is in the providential hands of God, individual incidents may appear to be ordered by a capricious fortune, but this is only because man sees a sequence of events rather than the overall pattern.

It is that view of the forces acting on man which is embodied in the heroic novel. There is universal agreement with Bonnet, 'qu'il y a une providence qui preside sur les actions des hommes, pour donner le chastiement aux crimes & la recompense à la vertu',[7] and the inevitable happy ending is itself an indication of the need to believe in providence. Characters in the novels sometimes reflect on the way in which their lives seem to suggest a plan. Lépante, for instance, having thrown himself off a cliff in despair and been saved by becoming caught in a fisherman's net, is impressed by this manifestation of divine intervention:

qui peut douter ... du soin continuel que les Dieux ont de nous? car il est impossible d'attribuer à la fortune, qui est aveugle & imprudente, quelques assistances que nous recevons aux plus grands hazards de nostre vie, qui ne peuvent estre données que par une meilleure & plus sage main.[8]

The existence of providence in the heroic novel is made

more evident by a comparison with the contemporary tales of horror, from which it is noticeably absent. Those of Camus are full of atrocities brought about by the corrupt nature of man: the innocent suffer and injustice and cruelty seem to flourish, though we are assured that divine retribution will follow after death. *L'Amphitheatre sanglant* contains thirty-five stories offering a good deal of gratuitous violence. For example, a group of soldiers billeted on a village mistreat the villagers. A captain rapes the daughter of the house in which he is staying, is stabbed by her and she in her turn is torn to pieces by the other soldiers. Thereupon the villagers set upon the whole body of soldiers and kill them with carefully described refinements of cruelty.[9] *Les Spectacles d'horreur* present a further fifty such incidents, stressing the horrifying cruelty of which human beings are capable, with no suggestion of a benevolent force protecting the innocent.

The heroic novel, with its more optimistic view of the human condition, assumes a benevolent circle of providential protection, but within which events are, for all practical purposes, ordered by fortune and require the individual to work out his own response to them and carry it through. To the hero, each situation demands a specific endeavour on his part. He must exert himself as though there were no such thing as a divine plan. The relationship between providence and fortune is therefore not usually referred to. As far as the reader is concerned, the hero's adventures involve his overcoming obstacles manufactured by fortune: it is only at the end of the work that the pattern of providence becomes apparent, and the triumph of virtue appears to be due to a combination of human enterprise and divine goodwill.

The key factor is action. The hero must treat any set of circumstances with which fortune has confronted him as an opportunity to demonstrate his heroic stature. He relies exclusively on his own courage and fortitude, and scorns to consider the outcome of his encounters: 'ceux qui se fient à leur courage . . . n'invoquent point la puissance de la fortune.'[10] Action is an end in itself, not a means to some other end, and it is here that the heroic ethic finds itself involved in one of the major areas of debate in the first half of the seventeenth century, the area of *prudence*.

Those who lived in the real world rather than in the idealized atmosphere of heroic novels found that, without the guarantee of a happy ending, the problem of reconciling ends and means was not so easily resolved. The perennial conflict between man's professed freedom and the inscrutable workings of the fate which seems to order his life led them (as it has men in every age) to attempt to anticipate the future and take steps to influence the course of events. On the political scene, there was a particular concern to define the extent to which those in power ought to attempt to mould the future and ensure the success of the kind of structure they took to be the best.

At one end of the spectrum were the partisans of absolute monarchy, particularly the propagandists of Richelieu and Mazarin, whose aim was to put before the people an approach to politics which took account of the realities of power in the kind of state then being constructed. They attacked the pretensions of an aristocracy which took it for granted that it had been entrusted with the well-being of the state, but which took advantage of its privileges to exploit the system in its own interests: the nobles' claims, they argued, were really a cloak for pride and self-aggrandizement. In place of the ideal of *générosité* which the former ruling class held up, the new men preached political realism. According to Sirmond, Silhon, Hay du Chastelet, Balzac, and Richelieu himself, political decisions must be taken, not in the light of lofty aspirations but of a careful consideration of all the factors involved in the situation, and the results desired must be weighed against the means necessary to achieve them. If the end dictates it, it is legitimate to have recourse to dissimulation and double standards, though these would not exist in an ideal world. Balzac argues that justice, which works very slowly and can only take account of actions committed, has to be complemented by *prudence*, which is entitled to look into men's innermost thoughts. It concerns itself not with what has been done but with what might affect the general interest in the future, and it can therefore legitimately employ means justified by necessity though not strictly legal in themselves.[11] Richelieu defends the *prudence* which ensures not only that an individual does not harm the state but also

that he is not in any position to do so,[12] and Silhon justifies
dissimulation as a necessary defence against the danger of
being deceived.[13] All these writers argue that, when all power
emanates from the central authority of the state, the state
must be allowed to decide what means are required to safe-
guard that power. It is *prudence* which prescribes the spheres
of efficacity of justice, conscience, and political necessity.
It emerges as the art of anticipating problems and adopting
flexible and, if necessary, immoral methods to deal with
them.[14]

Such a philosophy was inevitably attacked by those who
spoke for the aristocratic opponents of the absolutist state.
Setting themselves up as the guardians of the old and trusted
values, they denounced such *prudence* as simply another
means of strengthening the power of a megalomaniac cardinal
and rejected it as unworthy of anyone with noble ideals.
Mathieu de Morgues, the chief spokesman for the exiled
Queen mother, dismissed it as 'fourbe' or 'finesse', totally
distinct from true *prudence*: it destroyed the basis of trust on
which the nobles depended for their relationships with their
allies, servants, subjects, and even their enemies.[15] The manifesto of the Soissons rebellion of 1641 condemned Richelieu's
prudence as *imprudence* for the same reason.[16]

While the rival political forces argued, there were those
who preferred to analyse the factors affecting the most
popular road to success, a career at court. For much of the
century, a series of aulic treatises offered advice to the young
man wishing to reach the heights of prestige and influence
within the orbit of the sovereign. Taking their tone more or
less from Castiglione's *Cortegiano*, they warned that the
court was a breeding-ground for self-interest and corruption,
and that the courtier who wished to make a name for himself,
though not necessarily contributing to the total of wickedness,
would need to adopt a flexible standard of integrity and
unashamedly make use of others to further his own advancement. He should be prepared to turn himself into whatever
the situation required.

Du Refuge acknowledged that it was sometimes necessary
for the courtier, *homme de bien* though he might be, to
'laisser faire les meschans & vivre à leur accoustumée': he

should be ready to swallow his pride and cultivate the prince's servants, provided they could bring him to the notice of the sovereign.[17] Faret encouraged his courtier to forget his ideals of disinterested heroism and to ensure that any spectacular action he undertook was carried out in the sight of the prince.[18] Gerzan du Soucy considered the essential quality in the ambitious young man to be 'l'esprit souple & complaisant',[19] and Jacques de Caillière, writing in 1658, carried realism to new lengths when, having established that the men of wealth and influence in the post-Fronde world were the financiers, he urged the fortune-seeker to suppress his natural pride in his birth and to attach himself servilely to one of these rich *parvenus*: 'qu'il fasse taire cette sotte gloire qui luy rend les reins trop fermes pour ployer sous un homme que la Fortune a fait, qu'il pense plutost qu'il y a de l'avantage à s'en aprocher.'[20] The realities of making a living in the world could not be presented more starkly.

The devotee of the heroic novel would no doubt have argued that these treatises were aimed at second-rate men, those who had to rise by devious means because they did not have the necessary qualities to raise them naturally above the crowd, and that such cynical opportunism had nothing to do with heroism. There were, however, some who were prepared to claim that the road to heroism was only an extension of the process whereby a gentleman could establish himself at court. They introduced the idea of flexible moral standards into the domain from which idealized heroism took its values, suggesting that destiny can be created and that the hero does not necessarily have to be born as such but can build himself up into one if he approaches the task in the right way. Gracian's *El Heroe*, for instance, which found its way into French in 1645, provided the ordinary man of good family with a textbook on the method of raising himself to the level of the greatest heroes. Though certain qualities are indispensable, such as courage, there are many faults which can be hidden or even turned to advantage, provided the aspiring hero is careful not to reveal his whole self: 'O homme dont la passion ne travaille que pour la renommée, toy qui aspires à la grandeur, que tout le monde te connoisse, mais que personne ne te comprenne! avec cette adresse, le mediocre paroistra beaucoup, le beaucoup infiny, & l'infiny davantage.'[21] He will cover his weaknesses by using his will-power, since uncontrolled passions are the surest means of betraying the real man.[22] Hence, the faculty that he should cultivate most is judgement. To establish his pre-eminence, he will look for a field of activity that has not been tackled before, and when faced with several possibilities, he will select the one 'qui s'execute à la veuë de tout le monde, & avec la satisfaction d'un chacun, tousjours avec fondement de la reputation.'[23] Nor does this reputation automatically accompany 'l'eminence des belles qualitez': it has to be worked for, the goodwill of the people has to be cultivated by 'artifice'. Throughout, heroism is shown not as something that derives from an inner necessity but as the result of ambition, careful manipulation of circumstances, and, on occasion, dissimulation.

Cériziers, wishing to establish a specifically French road to heroism, suggests in the preface to Le Heros françois that 'Gratian croit faire le Heros, à peine fait-il son phantosme', but he nevertheless follows him at many points in his book, advocating the same careful nursing of reputation and even justifying hypocrisy if it leads to some positive advantage in terms of gloire. Going further still, the detachment required for the exercise of 'political' prudence is brought fully into the heroic activity par excellence, direct military action, in an anonymous work, Le Guerrier prudent et politique, dedicated by the publishers, Sommaville and Courbé, to the comte de Harcourt whom they praise as the living portrait of the prudent and politic warrior. The book provides advice on every aspect of warfare — raising troops, maps, sieges, spies, etc. — but the philosophy on which this advice is based is very different from that found in heroic literature. War is shown to be a hard-headed business which should not be mixed up with vague aspirations. Gloire and vertu are motivating factors which should be recognized and used in other people, but which the prudent general should not take as his own guiding principles. Loyalty and bravery, which can ultimately be reduced to self-interest, are also qualities that can be harnessed to achieve success. The real aim in war is 'de prevoir & de prevenir ce qui pourroit causer une issuë

contraire à nostre dessein'.[24] To do this, the general should
ensure, as far as it is possible, that his venture will succeed
by anticipating difficulties and by not estimating his own
capabilities too highly. The author, though he is dealing with
the field of activity that heroism claimed as its own, unashamedly preaches the political maxims of Naudé or Silhon
— whatever benefits the ruler's interests is legitimate; breaking
promises is permissible to him who stands to gain by so
doing; if the world observed the laws of justice, it would be
reprehensible to be other than totally honest, 'mais aujourd'
huy, que qui fait mesme les loix les corrompt, qui enseigne
trompe, & qui conseille ruine, le meilleur est de se deffier,
de dissimuler & de ne croire pas trop tost, de peur de s'en
repentir trop tard.'[25]

Though La Rochefoucauld had not yet begun to suggest the
extent to which heroic virtues derived from self-interest, it is
clear that not everyone was prepared to abandon their critical
faculties when considering the class of exceptional beings
acknowledged as heroes. Many were ready to argue that,
though the feats accomplished might be sublime, the motivation was basically no different from the range of desires
and aspirations experienced by the mass of humanity. Heroes
were different from the rest of us, certainly, but only because
their enterprises had succeeded, and, as Saint-Évremond was
to explain, their heroism was likely to be the product of a
particular set of circumstances as much as of an indomitable
spirit. Julius Caesar's temperament would not have allowed
him to embark on some of the daring exploits that brought
success to Alexander, but, conversely, Alexander would
probably have perished in all the political manœuvrings of
the Roman Republic.[26]
   In the midst of all these relative values, however, the
heroic novel stands out as a bastion of moral absolutism,
totally separate from any concept of flexible integrity and
diametrically opposed to any position which implied that it
is possible to turn oneself into a hero. According to the
novelists, the hero *is*: if he is not born a hero, there is nothing
he can do to become one. His destiny is to respond in a heroic
way to anything that fortune may confront him with. There

is no question of his having to weigh ends and means, because for him there is only one end, not to *become* a hero but to *continue to be* one. Whether or not he is successful in his enterprises is irrelevant: what matters is the way he goes about them, constantly resisting the onslaughts of fortune by direct action.

Prudence has no place in the hero's world, because it involves anticipating fortune with the aim of avoiding its worst effects and, hence, anyone who relies on *prudence* is automatically not heroic. Those who need to do so are trying to avoid action by rendering it unnecessary, a response which would never occur to the hero, who prefers to lose a fight rather than refuse a challenge. When Chrisante counsels caution — 'se retirer devant un ennemy trop fort n'est pas une fuite honteuse, mais une prudente retraite: & il ne faut pas confondre la temerité & la valeur' — Cyrus gives the instinctive reply of the true hero: 'Je ne sçay pas encore trop bien . . . faire toutes ces distinctions: c'est pourquoy de peur de me tromper en une chose où il va de mon honneur, je veux prendre le chemin le plus asseuré, qui est celuy de combattre.'[27] It is this determination to surmount every danger by demonstrating their scorn for it that characterizes Cyrus, Polexandre, Coriolan, and all the host of their fellow heroes. They refuse to worship Fortune, seeing in her inconstancy a sufficient reason for discounting her. To acknowledge her power would have been to surrender their most treasured possession, their moral autonomy. Whereas the heroes of the Greek romances had found the terms of their lives dictated by her caprices, these new heroes concentrate on maintaining their own *vertu* in any circumstances in which they find themselves, thereby rendering her morally powerless.

The need to defy fortune and preserve one's moral independence at all times is stressed repeatedly in the heroic novels, illustrated in numerous episodes and often expressed in maxim form:

. . . la vertu sçait agir avec la fortune, comme avec un ennemy qu'elle mesprise & dont elle sçait tourner tous les efforts & les stratagemes à sa propre confusion.

La Fortune cede à quiconque la violante, & veut que le respect qu'on luy porte soit meslé d'audace.

... dans les combats, plus on est valeureux, moins on court de for-tune.[28]

Prudence stems from fear and weakness. It counsels flight from dangers which ought to be faced, and is often a charac-teristic of the old, who, having lost their physical force, are likely also to lose their moral courage. (They may well also succumb to avarice, another manifestation of the same 'fausse prévoyance.') Ménalippe, being young and heroic, is shocked to hear her mother argue that 'la prudence veut que nous conservions ou changions nos inclinations selon qu'elles nous sont avantageuses ou qu'elles nous sont nuisibles': such a view is contrary to all her natural impulses.[29] But, young or old, those who claim to be prudent usually lack openness and honesty: they have a 'vaine curiosité de connoistre l'advenir'[30] whereas 'le sage remedie aux choses presentes & laisse l'avenir à la conduite de la Providence.'[31] Worrying about the future indicates a false scale of values, since instead of relying on oneself and on providence, one assumes that providence has to be forestalled or influenced, which, besides being presump-tuous, is ultimately impossible: 'Le Ciel nous fait naistre pour suivre l'arrest de nos destinées, & la prudence dont nous pensons appuyer nos desseins flechit malgré nos intentions aux volontez de celuy qui peut à son gré disposer de toutes choses.'[32]

The only sense in which the heroic novel accepts *prudence* is in its mildest interpretation, as the opposite of impulsive-ness. It may well be a good thing on occasion for a hero to learn to control his wilder impulses, but it must never lead him to compromise on the means he employs to reach his aims. He never stoops to dissimulation. If fortune presents two possible courses of action, it is legitimate to choose the one which may appear the more prudent, but there must be no attempt to force the hand of providence.[33] Such *prudence* does not enable the hero to win through, since that can only be achieved by action, but it helps him not to lose. In heroic terms, it could perhaps claim to be a half-virtue.

The distance between the attitude towards *prudence* adopted by the writers of heroic novels and the political view is well illustrated by a comparison of the version of the Fiesco conspiracy included as an episode in *Ibrahim* with that given by Retz. In *Ibrahim*, Fiesco himself (the comte de Lavagne) is depicted as a man totally devoted to the heroic life: 'l'ambition & le desir de la gloire estoient ses passions dominantes, & les seules choses pour lesquelles il faisoit toutes les autres'.[34] His view of heroism is firmly committed to the public good. It is his mother whose scheming results in his being converted to the idea of the conspiracy. She sends three pernicious counsellors to him with strict instructions on how to approach the subject:

souvenez-vous sur toutes choses, dit-elle à Raphael Sacco, de ne luy rien conseiller de violent, que vous ne puissiez pretexter du bien public, de l'equité & de la gloire: car, poursuivoit-elle, je connois le Comte; si vous ne luy proposez que sa conservation, son utilité, l'advancement de sa fortune & la perte de ses ennemis, vous ne le vaincrez jamais. Il faut picquer son esprit du desir de l'honneur & le tromper adroitement pour l'empescher de tromper nos esperances.[35]

Because the plot is presented to him in terms of virtue and heroic altruism, he accepts the leadership but steadfastly refuses to countenance anything that might be construed as deceit.

In Retz's version of the same conspiracy, though Fiesco is justified against the suggestion that he was naturally of 'un esprit couvert & dissimulé', the author none the less approves of his use of political *prudence*:

je ne pense pas que l'on puisse blâmer avec justice la dissimulation du Comte, parce que dans les affaires où il s'agit de nostre vie & de l'interest general de l'Estat, la franchise n'est pas une vertu de saison; la nature nous faisant voir dans l'instinct des moindres animaux qu'en ces extremitez l'usage des finesses est permis pour se defendre de la violence qui nous veut opprimer.[36]

Calcagno is shown trying to dissuade an eager Fiesco from joining the plot. To Retz, *gloire* is an end in the pursuit of which it is legitimate to employ means that could not strictly be considered *généreux*. In the heroic novel, the means must be *généreux*, otherwise the enterprise, whatever its conclusion, is damned from the start and cannot lead to the acquisition of *gloire*. *Gloire* is gained as much from the striving as from the achievement.[37]

Though there is no evidence that writers of heroic novels

were consciously taking up a position against the philosophy of Richelieu's state — indeed, some of them were admirers and supporters of his — the concept of man embodied in the heroic novel, with its commitment to individual liberty, none the less represented a definite response to the question of the morality of power being widely debated at the time. The novel associated itself firmly with an ethic which allowed no place to flexible moral standards and insisted on the primacy of the individual's responsibility to his ideal vision of himself; no political advantage, no collective benefit could justify the betrayal of that vision. The virtues proclaimed by the novelists as necessary to the maintenance of the heroic ethic were, broadly speaking, the ones which the *noblesse d'épée* had always claimed as their own, and, in that respect, since Richelieu's propagandists were busily pointing out that the aristocratic ideals were a well-worn myth with little relevance to the contemporary world, the novel can arguably be seen to be representing an anti-absolutist position. We must assume, too, that there was an element in the educated public which was prepared to be allured by the heroic myth, if only in novels. No doubt for many it was simply a question of escapism, a longing for a simpler world in which perfect beings could exist; for others, a response to the need to believe that the destiny of the world was ordered by a special category of human beings who worked in conjunction with the forces of providence, rather than by competing factions who varied the norms of morality for their own ends. In any case, the literary hero seems to have been appreciated by a large number of readers as an inspiring or a consoling model in the endless struggle against the unpredictable force of fate.

CHAPTER IV

THE PASSIONS

The neo-stoicism which exercised a considerable influence on French thought at the beginning of the seventeenth century taught that man's reason was supreme. The greatest aim of the wise man must be self-knowledge and, since the passions distorted his perception of the world and of himself, they were opposed to the reason and could only impede his search for enlightenment. It was therefore the function of the will to extirpate the passions, those maladies of the soul, and raise the wise man to a plane of *ataraxia* from which he could contemplate with detachment the world and its weaknesses. The will was the key to a correct ordering of the human faculties and the attainment of the self-mastery which was the aim of virtue. The hero in stoic terms was thus the man whose will rigidly excluded all passions such as ambition, *gloire*, love, or jealousy, and who practised virtue without necessarily having any sense of involvement with his fellow men.

A number of writers of heroic novels were known for their stoic leanings. Gomberville produced in 1646 *La Doctrine des mœurs*, in which he expounded a strict stoic philosophy and showed a sage who achieves a 'divine immobilité, s'attache tout entier à la consideration de soy-mesme, pese serieuse-ment les mouvemens de son ame'.[1] Desmarets de Saint-Sorlin published his *Morales d'Epictete* in 1653. Chevreau's *L'Escole du sage* has strong stoic elements, despite the author's careful inclusion of disparaging references to the impracticability of the stoic ideal and his advocacy of Christian precepts. The same dual attitude is evident in his *Tableau de la fortune*.[2]

It is natural that some measure of these sympathies should find its way into the novels they produced, but it tends to be in the form of moral maxims offered by tutors and hermits, and does not affect the action of the novel to any great extent.

The hero of *Cytherée* is constantly being plied with philosophical advice by wise old men. *Rosane* contains an important
figure called Uranie, who has succeeded in rising above the
tyranny of the passions. The supposed authoress of *Orasie*
is lauded because, when she is obliged to describe a passion,
'elle ne la flatte point, elle n'en farde jamais la deformité
avec de belles paroles: mais elle en parle comme d'une
maladie de l'ame',[3] and the moral tone of the work frequently
betrays a leaning towards stoicism.

It is certainly possible to interpret some of the heroic
concepts in terms of the stoic ideal. The view of the hero
as a kind of moral island, separate from the rest of mankind
and untouched by the weaknesses that assail them, parallels
that of the stoic sage. For some writers, heroic *vertu*, like its
stoic equivalent, is not exercised for the benefit of others,
but as an end in itself, to be contemplated in solitude. On the
whole, however, the fundamentals of heroism cannot be
reconciled with the tenets of stoicism, because all the stoic
sage's striving is towards withdrawal from the world, inner
contemplation, and passivity in the face of fortune. The
hero's reactions, on the other hand, are towards self-assertion
and, above all, action to resist the challenges offered by fate.
He is dependent on the rest of the world as a theatre in which
to display his superiority. Battles are not to be watched as a
detached observer, as the stoics would urge, but to be used
as an opportunity for moral self-aggrandizement. Suicide,
the supreme stoic affirmation of independence, is the negation
of heroism. Death has to be assimilated into the hero's
outward-looking ethic: 'elle est plus belle quand on la treuve
par le danger, que quand on la treuve par le desespoir, &
ceux qui s'en éloignent avec raison ont tousjours plus de
gloire que ceux qui s'en approchent avec joye'.[4] On the
occasions when heroes turn their swords against themselves,
it is an impulsive reaction to a sudden emotional shock,
almost invariably rejection by a mistress, and not a rational
response to disaster or danger. When they have had time to
consider the situation, their natural urge to survive and resist
reasserts itself.

The heroic ethos had much more in common with the
catholic humanist outlook which largely superseded the

neo-stoic morality. According to this view, the stoic ideal of suppression of the passions was misconceived, because it did nothing to help struggling man come to terms with his divided nature. It ignored the fact that the will, provided it was exercising its proper sovereignty, could draw on the potential of the passions and employ them in the cause of virtue. The passions were rehabilitated. They are, it was argued, morally neutral and can only be classed as good or bad by reference to the end to which they are applied. Thus, circumstances have to be taken into account in assessing the morality of a passion. If the will is functioning properly, it can moderate the passions and allow the energy involved in them to be directed towards the cause of virtue.

Such a theory is propounded by a number of moralists, all of whom reject the stoic attitude to the passions as false. Coeffeteau accuses the stoics of ignoring the complexity of human nature and trying to turn man into either a rock or a god.[5] Senault denounces their beliefs repeatedly in stronger terms, claiming that they are capable of appealing only to those arrogant enough to want to rise above the human condition and become angels.[6] Cériziers sees stoicism not simply as an impracticable philosophy, but as a positively subversive force within the religious life of the community.[7]

Anthony Levi has shown that one of the effects of the reaction against neo-stoic ethics was the rehabilitation of *gloire* as the supreme moral value. From having a pejorative sense in Justus Lipsius and du Vair, the word 'gloire' had evolved by the 1630s to the point where it was considered the highest personal quality and had been assimilated to the ethic of energy and activity which was replacing the passive emphasis of stoicism. As the force of stoicism declined, so too did the distinction made by the stoics between reason and passion, and the passions could even be seen as an ingredient in heroic virtue, transcending the norms of reason.[8]

Some of the proponents of this theory gave added encouragement to the heroic ethic by arguing that special value inhered in those passions associated with action, which were held to reside in the irascible appetite. Coeffeteau claims that the irascible side of man's nature has more *générosité* than the concupiscible, because it was ordained by nature for the latter's defence. Thus,

la Force ou la Valeur qui reside en l'Irascible est une vertu plus digne
& plus loüable que la temperance qui reside en la Concupiscible. Aussi
experimentons-nous que ce nous est chose bien plus honteuse de ne
refrener pas les mouvemens de la Concupiscible que de n'arrester pas
ceux de l'Irascible: d'autant que ceux-cy offensent moins la raison que
ceux-la.[9]

Senault shows how all the passions can be turned towards
positive action by a proper use of the reason, with the
implication that the hero is the product of his own will-
power: fear can be applied to reinforce self-assurance, hope
can drive us to perform *généreux* and difficult actions, daring
can make soldiers invincible.[10]

The idea that any passion could work positively towards
virtue, provided it was controlled by the reason, was taken
over by the novel and used to justify the actions of warrior
lovers in the grip of strong emotions. The heroes depicted by
novelists were by nature spontaneous creatures, liable to
react impulsively when their passions were aroused, and there
could be no suggestion that they were the victims of disordered
faculties. They were not statues cast in the stoic mould; their
hearts were 'ny de pierre, ny de bronze', as La Calprenède is
fond of putting it. Since their aims were dictated by reason,
the purity of their passions was guaranteed, and the experiencing of violent emotions was in fact an indication of the
sensitivity of their souls. Coriolan's reply to his *confident*
who has urged him to apply his philosophy in the face of his
misfortunes is that philosophy and fortitude might help with
ordinary troubles, 'mais ils ne peuvent m'oster le sentiment
pour un mal de la nature du mien sans oster à mon ame cette
faculté sensitive de laquelle elle est composée en partie'.[11]

The Thomist classification of the passions into the irascible
and concupiscible appetites, five in the former and six in the
latter, was unimportant to the novel and was largely ignored.
Only those passions were of interest which aim at good and
which arise from a forceful character. *Fuite* and *désespoir*,
for instance, are disregarded, and some of the secondary or
mixed passions become correspondingly more important
(*miséricorde*, *émulation*, etc.). Desmarets goes so far as to
suggest that there are only certain passions (he mentions

love, hatred, desire, and fear) which reside in us: ambition, pride, avarice, anger, envy, and the other 'mauvaises passions' are not naturally found in man but are produced when the judgement is perverted.[12]

In fact, the novelists' interest centres on two passions which are accorded the dominant position, namely, love and ambition. They are felt to fulfil a special function in that they stimulate the individual to aspire as high as possible, ambition in terms of self-fulfilment and love in service towards his fellow beings (though it almost always manifests itself as service for one particular being of the opposite sex). The hero is expected to be susceptible to both, especially love, for 'la Nature . . . crie qu'il faut aimer, & . . . en inspire la passion en mesme temps qu'elle inspire la vie'.[13]

In concentrating on these two passions, the novel was taking up a point made by a number of moralists who argued that love and ambition interacted and complemented one another to form a vital force which could inspire men to reach out for the higher virtues. 'Il semble que tout ce que l'Amour a de force, il l'emprunte de l'ambition. C'est elle qui luy allume son flambeau; c'est elle qui le rend sensible, c'est elle qui l'anime aux plus grands desseins & aux plus genereuses entreprises.'[14] Temperamentally, the man who is capable of one will also be drawn to the other, and it is that sort of individual that the heroic novel set out to portray — active, enterprising, sensitive to the influence of the opposite sex. His susceptibility to passion is a part of his claim to heroic status. Scudéry identifies love and ambition as the noblest of the passions.[15] Love is 'la plus noble cause de toutes les actions heroïques';[16] it turns mere bravery into heroism.[17] It can make old men perform 'des actions plus heroiques que celles qu'ils ont exercées en la plenitude de leur vigueur'.[18] Ambition and love (represented as 'pleasure') are 'les plus puissans genies du monde'.[19]

In *Polexandre*, the function of ambition and love in the great pattern of providence, bringing the heroic individual the closest of all humans to God's purposes, is explained by a hermit. The perfect harmony of the universe is dependent on the most discordant elements counterbalancing one another. Ambitious men have their part to play in this scheme: 'leurs desseins qui n'ont jamais de fin sont comme autant de machines dont la Providence se sert pour faire mouvoir le pesant corps du monde, & empescher par des secousses & des agitations frequentes, qu'il ne tombe dans une mortelle letargie'.[20] In heaven, all is tranquil, on earth all is movement, and God has made us active, impatient, and ambitious so that we can work towards felicity: 'Que ne produit point cette fiévre de l'ame, insolente, dangereuse & temeraire que nous nommons valeur? A quelles extremitez ne nous engage point, avec plaisir, cette autre qui s'appelle Amour?[21] The interaction of love and energetic striving, whether it be called ambition or *gloire* or valour, is the process required to raise man above his normal limitations and set him on the path towards perfection:

Si vous me demandez qui a poussé les premiers hommes à se rendre les deffenseurs des foibles, & les extirpateurs des monstres & des tyrans, je vous respondray que c'est l'Amour. L'Amour eschauffe l'ame encore plus que le sang, la remplit du desir de la Gloire; & luy arrachant tout ce qu'elle a contracté de bas & de terrestre par la contagion du corps, la purifie & la porte dans cette supréme perfection à laquelle elle est destinée.[22]

It is significant that most writers of heroic novels chose to call this passion *ambition* rather than *gloire* when referring to it as a morally neutral passion to be found in anyone with determination.[23] If it is divorced from the reason and allowed to take control of the faculties, it devours all moral sense and forces the individual to perform ignoble acts. It blinds him and puts him in the unheroic position of caring more about the end than about the means. So it is that Dicéarque, the persecutor of Mélinte and Ariane, confesses on his deathbed that 'l'ambition a esté la passion forcenée qui m'a toûjours agité, à laquelle celle d'amour se meslant encore, ces deux furies ensemble m'ont tourmenté si cruellement que je n'ay point esté maistre de mes actions & me suis laissé conduire à elles sans appeller en aucune façon la raison à mon secours'.[24] If his reason had been sufficiently strong to enable him to direct these two passions, he could have been an honourable man, possibly even heroic. Ambition would then have been transmuted into *gloire*, since its aims would have been virtuous, and the love he felt would have been devoted to service rather than self-interest.

The rehabilitation of the passions as the source of energy necessary for heroic actions was therefore dependent on the supremacy of the will. Many of the earlier heroic novels stress the need for rational control and illustrate the disastrous consequences when the passions become stronger than the will. In *Cytherée*, the reader is informed that 'tant que la raison & la bien-seance sont assez fortes pour s'opposer à l'impetuosité de la passion, ... elle [i.e. love] apporte de grands avantages à la personne qu'elle possede', and the dire effects of an epidemic of irrational love which strikes all the women of Cyprus are described.[25] Guérin de Bouscal distinguishes between the love felt by 'les grandes ames' whose passions are subject to rational principles and that of 'les hommes communs' who allow themselves the licence that leads to infidelity and dissimulation.[26] The hero of *Polexandre* at all times subjects his love to his will.

The supremacy of the will was, however, already being questioned in certain quarters and a more determinist explanation of man's behaviour was beginning to be felt. Already in 1624, the Jesuit Caussin had made out a case for environmental determinism, describing the way of life of a child born in poverty, unable ever to escape from its yoke, regardless of the talents and determination with which he has been endowed by nature.[27] Religious attitudes were changing, with the arbitrary God of Jansenism replacing the benevolent deity of François de Sales. A treatise on heroic education postulated a predetermined propensity to virtue or vice, with temperament and experience dictating the general direction to be followed. The soul is 'un hosti nud [*sic*], qui vient habiter dans un Palais meublé, où il trouve les dispositions et les semences, les habitudes que le temps et l'exercice meurissent par apres. Nous portons dans nos veines le germe de nos bonnes & mauvaises qualitez et la masse du corps, insensible d'elle-mesme, contient neantmoins le principe des sentimens que l'esprit vivifie.'[28]

The traditional explanation of the operation of love had postulated a rational basis along neo-platonic lines. The eye is struck by beauty, but since this is only a symbol of the spiritual beauty beyond, the beholder's reason carries his

mind from the beautiful to the good, that is, the virtue embodied in the beloved. If reason is functioning properly and
not allowing itself to be clouded by the senses, it will dwell
only on the spiritual qualities of the object it loves. There
can therefore be no question of possession or demands to be
made or met, but simply satisfaction to be gained from the
contemplation of goodness, the honouring and adoring of an
ideal which can be cherished equally well in its absence as in
its presence. Jealousy is inadmissible, because it presupposes
some kind of right to possession. Love can therefore only
exist in a context of virtue, subject to the rational control of
the lover: any emotion that leads to behaviour contrary to
the prescriptions of virtue is by definition not love. The will
must remain paramount; as a good lover, Scanderberg rejects
the arguments of those who try to devalue it:

D'une puissance souveraine, qui est la volonté, ils en font une malheureuse esclave, ils ne sçauroient souffrir qu'elle suive le bien qui l'attire,
ils croyent qu'elle est emportée par la violence & veulent qu'une force
étrangere fasse tous ses mouvemens, comme si pour estre aveugle elle
ne pouvoit pas estre libre.[29]

As the power of the will came more into question, such a
view with its simple categories and its rejection of the more
complex aspects of emotion was to be superseded by an
awareness of the involuntary features of love, inexplicable
elements which render the will powerless and force love upon
the unsuspecting individual. The attraction exercised by one
person upon another could not be explained in terms of
absolute truth or goodness, nor was it possible to reject
passions such as jealousy as being outside the confines of
love. This was obviously an area of human behaviour that did
not lend itself to simple analyses: what had been seen as
straightforward moral responses were now revealed as ration-
alizations of wishes.[30]

There had, in fact, never been in the seventeenth-century
novel a complete commitment to a neo-platonic concept of
love, even in *L'Astrée*.[31] Novelists were concerned to offer
their readers situations based on emotions not too far removed
from those they might themselves have experienced, rather
than illustrations of abstract theories. Consequently, even
in those novels in which the only true love is presented as

rational and controlled, there is an indication that love has its unexplored and incomprehensible areas. Ibrahim declares that 'il y a une puissance superieure, qui nous pousse malgré nous & sans l'aide de nostre connoissance, à aymer souvent une personne que la raison commune nous deffendroit de regarder.'[32] An argument about how real love should manifest itself, in which Hipolite claims 'L'amour doit estre plus fort que la raison: il ne la détruit pas, mais il la trouble . . . la colere & la jalousie sont les veritables marques d'amour: . . . la jalousie est la seule marque indubitable de cette passion', is allowed to remain unresolved.[33]

It was not long before such indefinable aspects of love were occupying a much more prominent place in the emotions of the major characters in novels. *L'amour d'inclination*, a dangerous aberration according to the moralists of the time, became a force to be reckoned with and effectively eclipsed *l'amour d'élection* as the motivating factor behind the deeds of heroes. Whereas in *Ariane* and *Polexandre* the characters who fall victim to this sort of irrational passion are shown to be morally corrupt and inspire horror in the right-thinking characters and in the reader,[34] there is an increasing number of novelists who recognize that the human condition cannot be explained simply in terms of how man would like to be and that the contradictions within human emotions are masked rather than resolved by an insistence on the supremacy of the will. Characters are created who are admirable for the most part, but whose actions become questionable when love takes control. An honourable man may lose all moral sense when he falls in love: 'cette violente passion qui le maistrise le transporte tellement qu'il se resout avec facilité aux choses les plus injustes & les plus des-honnestes, si elles luy font esperer la jouyssance de ce qu'il ayme'.[35] Pacore abandons the woman he loves for another, pleading in his justification: 'j'en fus si mortellement attaint, je l'advouë, que je mourus dés le moment en moy pour ne vivre qu'en elle & pour elle. Il se fit donc un tel changement en moy-mesme, que j'avois de la peine à me recognoistre.'[36] Araspe, charged with the care of Panthée, has the best of intentions, but is unable to prevent himself from persecuting her with the 'insolence de sa passion'.[37] Entirely virtuous ladies feel no shame in explaining their feelings in terms of 'ce je ne sçay quoy qui nous fait mépriser les services de tous les autres & qui par des causes qui nous sont inconnuës & qui ne peuvent s'exprimer, nous fait trouver dans luy seul tout ce qu'il y a d'aymable & d'accomply'.[38]

Two of the major heroic novels, *Cleopatre* and *Le Grand Cyrus*, are based on the assumption that love is a product of involuntary inclination rather than recognition of merit and election,[39] and the novels of the 1650s follow their lead entirely. A scene such as the one in *Polexandre*, where Zelmatide surmounts his natural desires '& se destacha si bien de l'homme & de la matiere, que son amour devint tout intellectuel'[40] would have been considered unrealistic if it had been offered to the public in a novel published during the 1650s.

It was perhaps natural that a recognition of the autonomy of the passions should lead to attempts to justify them. Since the will could not control the emotions produced by the heart, no blame could attach to those who found themselves borne helplessly along. Such an attitude appears in *Le Grand Cyrus* in the argument put forward by Stésilée:

je ne voy pas que la vertu consiste à n'avoir point de passions: la Nature les donne à tous les hommes: on ne s'en sçauroit deffaire qu'avecque la vie: & je suis fortement persuadée que pourveû que ces passions ne nous facent rien faire contre la veritable gloire, nous ne sommes point coupables de ne les pouvoir surmonter dans nostre cœur.[41]

It is developed in *Clelie* into a full discussion about the validity of the passions. Though they have been the cause of all the greatest crimes the world has seen, that is not a reason for condemning them, as though one would stop loving roses because they have thorns. The passions are the source of all pleasures and the instigators of all the heroic actions ever performed.[42] If there were no passions, civilization would not exist, since they are the basis of all the aspirations and activities that have ensured man's progress. 'Ne nous pleignons donc point des passions, puis qu'elles font seules toutes les occupations, & tous les plaisirs de tous les hommes.'[43] If it is hard to overcome them, that is a clear indication that opposition is the wrong attitude to adopt: 'abandonnez-vous à elles; & au lieu de vous amuser à les vouloir vaincre, cherchez plustost à les satisfaire, & vous n'en serez pas si tourmenté.'[44] Condemnation of them is misguided: 'elles donnent des plaisirs infinis à ceux qui cherchent à les satisfaire: & elles ne font presques jamais de mal, qu'à ceux qui les veulent détruire.'[45]

The tone of the discussion is light-hearted, and it is the playful Amilcar who expresses the most complete faith in the passions. No one takes up the implication behind Stésilée's proviso: what is the moral position of someone who is obliged by his passions to act against the demands of *gloire* or of society? In fact, much of *Clélie* is taken up with explanations of how the dangers inherent in the passions can be avoided if relationships are established on a correct basis. The ideal of *amitié tendre* expounded in *Le Grand Cyrus*[46] is modified and extended. Love needs to be tempered with *amitié* if the lover is not to be tormented by his passion, explains Herminius. The ideal relationship begins with *amitié*, a response to virtue, modesty, and decorum in a woman; gradually it turns to love, but the element of *amitié* remains: 'l'amour & l'amitié se meslent comme deux Fleuves, dont le plus celebre fait perdre le nom à l'autre. Mais apres tout, les eaux du plus petit y sont effectivement aussi bien que celles du plus grand.'[47] *Amitié* ensures that the power of passion is not allowed to control the relationship completely:

il n'y a rien de si doux que cette espece d'amour. Car toute violente qu'elle est, elle est pourtant toûjours un peu plus reglée que l'amour ordinaire, elle est plus durable, plus tendre, plus respectueuse & mesme plus ardente, quoy qu'elle ne soit pas sujette à tant de caprices tumultueux que l'amour qui naist sans amitié.[48]

Some of the admirable characters in *Clelie* have succeeded in avoiding all the dangers inherent in the passions by holding to an ideal of *repos*. Térame maintains emotional equilibrium: 'regardant l'ambition comme une passion pleine d'inquietude, il luy a deffendu l'entrée de son cœur. Il n'y a mesme jamais laissé entrer l'amour avec tous les suplices qui le suivent dans le cœur des autres Amans.'[49] Théandre, a heroic figure, 'met le souverain bien au repos. Aussi pour ne s'exposer jamais à le perdre, a-t-il ôsté à l'amour tout ce qu'il a de fâcheux & de penible. Il aime les beaux objets en general, sans qu'il y en ait aucun en particulier qui puisse avoir la force de l'attacher jusques à le rendre malheureux; de sorte que l'amour est plustost un simple plaisir dans son cœur qu'une passion.'[50] How they are able to resist the passions if the passions are not subject to the will is not explained. Madeleine de Scudéry acknowledged that the passions were a source of vital energy, ultimately outside the control of the individual, and welcomed what they had to offer in the way of pleasure, but she preferred to believe that the darker side of the passions need not impinge on ordinary people if they followed a sufficiently strict set of emotional rules. The 'Carte de Tendre', with its indications of the correct paths to be followed in love, is an attempt to keep the lover well away from the dangerous sea and the unknown territories of real passion. It solves the problem by ignoring it.[51]

The heroic novel never ventured into the more complicated areas of emotional analysis: that was left to the *nouvelle* and the novels of Madame de Lafayette. None the less, the realization that love and the other passions lay outside the control of the will had a considerable effect on the concept of heroism, since it directly concerned the moral autonomy of the hero. Both forms of the heroic ideal, that which saw the hero as an exceptional individual responsible only to himself and the one which stressed his obligations to the rest of mankind, were originally based on the premise that there were certain moral norms to which the hero had to remain constant. His obligations — either to the maintenance of his image or to the ethic of service to mankind, depending on the outlook of the author — had to be fulfilled at any cost. Falling in love would not diminish such obligations: any emotional relationship had to be subordinated to the values that made the hero what he was. Ibrahim could not break his word to the Sultan, merely to stay with Isabelle; Oroondate could not cease pursuing his *gloire* simply because Statira had required him to do so. If, however, the hero was liable to fall victim to an emotion over which he had no control and which could influence every aspect of his behaviour, he could no longer claim to be in command of his destiny. The one factor above all others which had entitled him to be considered heroic, namely his ability to impose his will on every situation and on himself, was to become meaningless if his actions were to be dependent on an arbitrary movement of the humours, a *je ne sais quoi*. Moral independence was to become a pretence.

The loss of the belief in the supremacy of the will was one of the major factors in the eventual decline of the heroic novel.[52] Writers who depicted their characters at the mercy of passions stronger than their will contributed, perhaps without realizing it, to the decline of the concept of heroism. Once La Rochefoucauld had provided insights into the nature of the passions and Racine had illustrated their destructive potential, the hero-figure in the tradition of Oroondate could no longer exist in literature. The decline was accelerated by the strong movement towards feminism which reached its peak in the 1650s: the values of heroism had been largely male, but the new feminism led to a conflict between male and female values. It is this conflict which will be considered in Chapter V.

CHAPTER V

LOVE AND FEMINISM

Though the *romanesque* hero was always expected to be susceptible to love and usually devoted much of his energy to fighting on behalf of the woman he served, his relationship with her was subsumed by his heroic status. It is not that love was subordinate to *gloire*, but rather, as Rodrigue and Chimène both understood, that love had no real meaning except in a context of heroic affirmation. Love could only be expressed in terms of action: if the hero withdrew from action in order to pursue his love separately, he would do so in opposition to all his natural impulses and would be unable to continue for long. Like Achilles among the daughters of Lycomedes, Oroondate abandons Statira because 'il eut dépit de la vie qu'il menoit tandis que tout le monde estoit en armes'.[1] There is no conflict between love and heroic values, simply a recognized scale of priorities. Justinian considers for a moment the possibility of breaking his word to the Sultan for the sake of remaining with Isabelle, but he very quickly tells himself that such an action would be self-defeating: 'tu crois que cette genereuse Princesse que tu sers te trouveroit digne de son affection apres cette lascheté?' His view is confirmed by Isabelle: 'sçachez que je suis assez genereuse pour ne pouvoir souffrir que vous me tesmoigniez vostre amour par une lascheté: & je suis ravie de voir que vous aymiez la gloire autant que moy.'[2]

This kind of heroic love-relationship derives from the inequality in strength between the sexes. The weaker sex has to accept the dominance of the male, because his strength provides her with protection. Hence, the only way in which a woman can avoid the secondary rôle demanded of her by love for a hero is by literally taking over the primary rôle in heroism; in other words, by taking up the sword and equalling man on his own terms. Sémiramis, Hérone, Meyrem, Polinixe[3]

and many others scornfully reject the passivity that characterizes the traditional function of woman and demonstrate
that they have as much courage and martial spirit as any man.

The Amazon, the woman who has refused from the start
to submit to the physical superiority of man and who relies
on her own strength to establish her position in the world, is
a perennial figure in the heroic novel. It is a poor story which
does not contain at least one heroic female who dons armour
and faces men on equal terms, declaring 'quoy que je sois
femme, mon métier est de combattre les hommes'.[4] Those
set in the ancient world of Greece or Persia were almost
bound to include an episode or two involving the Amazon
tribes of Scythia. Opinions varied as to whether these tribes
contained any males. According to some, the Amazons lived
cut off from men. In *Cassandre*, their queen, Talestris,
eventually persuades them of the error of their ancestors
'qui ayant creu par l'institution de leurs loix s'affranchir de la
tyrannie des hommes, s'y estoient soumises avec infamie &
s'estoient reduites à les aller chercher dans leurs terres & à se
prostituer à eux par des voyes horribles'.[5] In *Rosane*, the
Amazons accept men, only in order that their race shall not
perish.[6] In *Antiope*, however, the men of the race exist in
the subordinate position occupied by women in the rest of
the world, and would feel extremely aggrieved if they were
made to go to war or take on the running of the state.[7]

In all cases involving Amazons, woman has achieved heroic
status by wholeheartedly adopting the criteria accepted in
the world of men. In pursuing *gloire*, she renounces love as a
part of her life (not necessarily definitively), and frequently
acts as an example of how love's debilitating effects can be
counteracted by a suitable devotion to physical action. When
Zénobie, the Amazon queen, marries Odenat, the wedding is
not celebrated in terms of male/female submission, 'en festins
superflus, ny en delices effeminez', but as a union of two
sources of strength, with tourneys and physical combats of
all sorts. The sensual side of love is severely restricted:
'Jamais Zenobie ne coucha que deux fois en sa vie avec
Odenat, dont elle eut deux fils, Herennian & Timolas, &
depuis se contentant de ces deux enfans, elle ne l'a plus receu
dans son lit, & ils n'ont vescu ensemble que comme un frere

& une sœur.'[8]

The woman who lacks the strength or physical *vertu* to establish her own position in the world must rely on the efforts of her champion to maintain her status. Her *vertu* thus consists in protecting her moral independence during the period while the hero is proving his devotion to her, so that she can be sure of her position when the time comes to hand her honour over into his keeping. The 'severity' which is a general feature of the female characters in the main stream of heroic literature is clearly understood by both author and reader to be a temporary measure safeguarding the woman's honour in the transitional period between first acquaintance and marriage. The hero accepts it because the ultimate relationship will be one in which he will be the undisputed master.

In the Greek romances and in *L'Astrée*, the heroine maintains her independence by a strict chastity which requires her to reject her lover's advances. While freely admitting her love for him and her intention to marry him, she firmly resists his physical approaches. This purity sometimes reaches a quasi-mystical level. In the *Histoire ethiopique*, it is a necessary condition of the working out of the divine plan for Chariclée; in *Clytophon et Leucippe*, the heroine is subjected to the test of the Grotte de Syringue, inhabited by Pan, and is hailed as almost superhuman when she emerges triumphant, her virginity proved by the playing of the magic flute.[9]

In *Amadis de Gaule*, no importance is attached to chastity. Indeed, there are a number of episodes in which the delights of physical passion are described at some length, which is no doubt what led Camus to exclaim that the work was 'une eschole d'amour, mais, Dieu, de quelle amour!'[10] On the other hand, great stress is laid on fidelity. The test of the Isle Ferme, which plays an important part in the adventures of the various heroes, is so devised that no one can pass through who has 'faulsé ses premieres amours', and Apolidon and Grimanèse, who established the test, and later Amadis and Oriane pass through gloriously, even though they are not chaste. There is also, however, a certain ambivalence towards women: an element of latent brutality towards them lies not very far below the surface, and the stage had certainly not

yet been reached at which any woman was worthy of respect
and deference simply by virtue of her sex. When a spear is
hurled at Amadis, he pursues his assailant, who shouts that
she is la Géante de l'Isle Triste, his enemy. 'Quand Amadis
entendit que la personne qu'il poursuyvoit estoit femme, ne
la voulut plus avant suyvre: Mais commanda à Gandalin aller
apres, & la tuer s'il povoit.'[11] It is not chivalry that restrains
him, but the fact that there is no honour to be gained from
fighting a woman. In *Le Romant heroïque*, those women
who are not an unattainable ideal seen in visions in mystic
grottoes are debauched temptresses who try to bring knights
to their ruin.[12]

In all these predecessors of the heroic novel, the assumption
is made quite openly that the object of the male's pursuit is
possession of the female. The heroine acknowledges the fact
equally straightforwardly and, within the limits prescribed by
the need to preserve her moral independence, she responds
positively. Astrée assures Céladon that his love for her cannot
surpass the feelings she has for him and that she longs for the
day when they can be united.[13] Oriane submits to Amadis
when his desires become too strong for him and skilfully
combines her own pleasure with 'une delicate & feminine
plainte de l'audace d'Amadis'.[14] At times, the directness of
the approach leads to situations of an impropriety which
would not have been tolerated later on in the seventeenth
century.[15]

In some of the earlier heroic novels, the same acknowledgment of the male attitude is apparent. The need for the
woman to hold him at a distance with her 'severity' is thus
self-evident. Oroondate, for instance, finds that conversation
with Statira is not enough:

goustant des douceurs inconcevables dans les legeres faveurs qui luy
estoient accordées, il trouvoit sa mort dans la deffence de celles qui
estoient reservées à un autre plus heureux que luy: il s'en plaignoit à la
Reyne assez souvent, & còmme enfin il estoit homme, & n'estoit point
entierement destaché des sens, il s'emancipoit quelquefois au delà de ce
qui luy estoit volontairement permis, & tesmoignoit par quelqu'une de
ses actions qu'il n'estoit pas maistre de ses desirs. Mais ceste sage
Princesse quoy qu'elle ne les peut legitimement condamner, les reprimoit
avec une douce majesté.[16]

The hero's submissiveness towards his beloved in this

respect is an essential part of his testing, but when his probationary period is brought to an end by the formalizing of
their relationship in marriage, his subjection ceases and the
relationship takes on its proper form, with the hero acknowledged as the moral centre of the union, the source of *gloire*
and honour. Thus, Alcidiane, who had received absolute
obedience from Polexandre at all times, proclaims at the end
of the novel that he deserves to be the master of herself and
of her people 'par la merveille de ses actions' and hands over
to him in marriage both her power and her glory.[17] *Cassandre*
ends with the central characters married and the men's régime
of respect and obedience discarded:

Ce fut pour lors que les plus grandes beautez de la terre furent mises en
proye aux passions de leurs impitoyables vainqueurs, & qu'ils se ven-
gerent des peines qu'elles leur avoient fait souffrir avec des ressentimens
que tout violens qu'ils estoient, elles ne peurent raisonnablement
desapprouver. Aussi estoient-ils en quelque façon pardonnables, & il
estoit juste que ceux de qui les maux avoient esté si longs & si cruels
en tirassent de grandes reparations.[18]

The influence of women on Parisian polite society during the
first half of the seventeenth century has long been acknowledged as one of the most important factors in the literary
history of the period. The development of the salons and the
civilizing effect they had on society were the subject of a
voluminous scholarly literature during the nineteenth and
early twentieth centuries, the most influential study being
that of Magendie.[19] More recently, scholars have begun to
analyse the wider implications of the rôle of woman, setting
the feminist movement against its sociological and political
background. In particular, Maclean's important study,
Woman Triumphant, has revealed the complexity of the
feminist forces, of which the salons were only one manifestation, and of the corresponding anti-feminist trend, and
Lougee's investigation into the socio-economic and ideological
bases of the salon culture has helped to explain why feelings
on the feminist question ran so high.[20]

Maclean has identified two periods during the first half of
the seventeenth century in which feminist activity in literature
was particularly intense, viz. 1617–29 and 1640–7. During

the first of these, a debate was conducted on the criticisms aimed at women by Trousset in his *Alphabet de l'imperfection et malice des femmes*, a debate which continued the somewhat crude polemics of the traditional *querelle des femmes*. The second period coincides partially with the early years of the regency of Anne of Austria, when feminists were able to adopt a more aggressive attitude, supported by an increase in social and cultural activity by women.[21]

Though it would be unrealistic to look for exact equivalents of these dates in the development of the novel, it is none the less true that, in the 1620s and 1640s, the novel underwent significant modifications in response to the pressures for a greater degree of *honnêteté* in society. During the 1620s, before the heroic novel had emerged as an identifiable genre, writers of novels revealed an awareness that the reader wished to see a more refined relationship between the sexes than had existed in the romances of chivalry and many of the novels of adventure. *Le Romant des romans*, for example, contains some episodes imitated directly from *Amadis de Gaule* with the same licentiousness, and others embodying a much more sophisticated concept of man overcoming his passions in the name of *bienséance*.[22] When Marcassus came to produce his condensed version of *Amadis* in 1629, he considered it necessary to change the tone even of some of the central scenes in order to accommodate the new sensibility. The original version opens with Elizène going at night to the room of Périon who has arrived as a stranger at her father's castle, urged on by her maid Dariolette. Marcassus has reduced Dariolette to a mere supporting rôle, while Elizène becomes a paragon of reserve and modesty. It is Périon who seduces Elizène, and the whole encounter, like all the relationships between the sexes portrayed in the book, is wrapped up in the language of *galanterie*, with a good deal of stress on the external manifestations of emotion — 'ces souspirs, ces propos interrompus, ces paroles imparfaites, ces frequentes allées & venuës, ces devoirs & ces respects qu'il vous rend,' etc.[23]

By the time Anne of Austria began her rule as regent in 1643, the feminist movement had gained in confidence and competence: rather than merely reacting defensively to the traditional attacks of anti-feminist polemicists, it was adopting a more assertive stance and arguing the case for the superiority of women.[24] Eulogies of womankind proliferated, and feminist propaganda appeared on every bookseller's stall. *Le Triomphe des dames*[25] sets out to refute the slanders perpetrated by men about women and to show that woman is superior to man intellectually, morally, and even, on occasion, physically. Dubosc, who had spoken out strongly in favour of education for women in *L'Honneste Femme*, reiterates his support in his new work, *La Femme heroïque*, ridiculing those men who are opposed to their wives becoming educated for fear of being surpassed.[26] Le Moyne demonstrates in his *Gallerie des femmes fortes* that, for every male heroic virtue, there is a female equivalent, worth just as much, if not more. Gilbert pursues the same argument, maintaining that the one way in which men surpass women, namely in physical strength, is rather a proof of their inferiority.[27]

All these works, together with the multitude of panegyrics addressed to the Queen Regent, consciously devalue the qualities traditionally ascribed to heroism and substitute for them the moral virtues to which, they claim, women have a natural propensity. According to Gerzan, men see their honour as dependent on fighting on almost any pretext and losing their chastity as early as possible: such 'virtues' betray brutality and weakness, whereas women choose those virtues that are more agreeable to God, those that resist the senses.[28] Le Moyne echoes him: 'pour faire un Homme vaillant, il faut moins de force & moins de courage que pour faire une Femme chaste'. Chastity is no longer seen merely as a withdrawal from the ordinary pathways of life but as an essential factor in the maintenance of a woman's independence. With her moral liberty guaranteed by her chastity, the new woman can aspire to the heights of heroism which had traditionally been the preserve of men, since physical strength was no longer considered a prerequisite for heroism: 'Ce n'est pas la hauteur de la taille, ny la force du corps qui fait les Heros: c'est la grandeur & l'élevation de l'ame; c'est la vigueur & la fermeté de l'Esprit: . . . De ce costé là donc il n'y a rien qui puisse diminuer les droits des Femmes.'[29]

As the confidence of the feminists increased, some were

drawn to challenge one of the most entrenched of the commonplaces about women, that she was spiritually the weaker
vessel. Traditionally, the fact that the serpent had chosen to
tempt Eve, knowing that she was more likely to succumb
than Adam, was taken as evidence of her inherent inability to
control her passions, from which could be deduced the need
for the female to be subject to the male throughout her life,
her incapacity for intellectually demanding exercises, her
predisposition to infidelity and vanity, and many other moral
prejudices. However, as the age-old belief that the will was
the dominant faculty in the properly ordered mind gave way
before an acknowledgment that the irrational elements in the
passions, especially love, might have their own validity,[30]
some of the feminists were able to argue that, though the
rational faculty of even the most balanced of human beings
could be affected and sometimes swamped by the irresistible
force of passion, the sexes were not uniformly susceptible
to this kind of disorder. Nature had given woman a greater
capacity for resisting her passions and listening to the voice
of reason: 'la Volupté ne la touche pas à l'esgal de l'homme,
ou si elle le fait, son sexe a des retenues qui manquent au
nostre, & qui repriment la violence de leurs Passions'.[31] The
will could still retain some sort of control in woman's mind:
'la raison est plus absolument obeye dans leur esprit que
dans les esprits des hommes'.[32] Man, on the other hand,
disregards his reason with fatal abandon, once love has been
allowed to creep into his mind. All his honourable resolutions
count for nothing when he is confronted with the one he
loves or with physical temptation. Most damning of all, he
has no idea how weak he is.[33] With her moral superiority
clearly recognized, woman could take her rightful place as
the dominant force in the world. Saint-Gabriel goes so far as
to suppose a world in which women are in control: there
would be no war, the golden age would reappear and everyone would live happily in harmony.[34]

Since novels were written predominantly for the female
part of the reading public, the effects of this increase in
feminist assertion were quickly felt. Not only the terms in
which relationships were expressed but also the nature of the
relationships themselves were reinterpreted in the light of the

greater respect due to woman and her superior moral strength. Her greater ability to control her passions entitled her to a different kind of relationship with the hero who loved her. Instead of accepting a subservient position in which her honour was dependent on the male's maintenance of his own *gloire*, she could retain her own moral independence intact and require her lover to pursue honour and glory with the aim of setting them unconditionally at her feet, to acknowledge or reject as she thought fit. During the early 1640s, heroic novels were still presenting an essentially traditional kind of relationship. In *Ibrahim*, the hero's reputation dictates the heroine's submission: Isabelle bids Ibrahim disregard her qualms at his departure and ensure that he does not give in to her weakness.[35] *Cassandre* depicts something of a struggle between male and female interests. Oroondate is shown eager to be off to the wars, while Statira is equally eager to keep him with her. They each declare an undying passion, while in fact working somewhat coldly towards their own ends. Oroondate murmurs that Statira will quickly forget a suitor as unworthy as himself:

Cruel, luy dit-elle en l'interrompant, ma douleur vous devoit contenter sans m'en faire naistre de nouvelles par vos soupçons desobligeans, vous parlez contre vostre pensée, & vous ne laissez pas de m'affliger veritablement. Ah! Oronte, & maintenant Oroondate, que j'ay bien plus de sujet de craindre que l'abscence effaçant ces legeres idées de vostre esprit ne vous fasse repentir de la peine que vous avez prise, pour une personne que vous n'aviez veue que de nuict, & dans le trouble, & en qui du depuis le temps, & la longue frequentation vous auront fait remarquer des deffauts que les tenebres vous avoient cachez. A cela, repondit-il froidement, il y a si peu d'apparence, que je ne vous feray point de nouveaux sermens pour vous oster une creance de laquelle je m'asseure que vous estes tres-esloignée.

In the end, a compromise solution is reached to this emotional blackmail. Oroondate insists on departing, but Statira commands him

de ne hazarder que bien à propos ce qui n'est plus à vous, si vous ne voulez revoquer le don que vous m'en avez fait . . . Je vous ay voué tant d'obeissance, repliqua-t-il, que je ne m'esloigneray jamais de vos commandemens, & me conserveray pour vous revoir d'aussi bon cœur que je me fusse dispensé de ce voyage, si l'honneur & le depart d'Artaxerxe, que je ne puis ny ne dois abandonner, me l'eussent peu permettre.[36]

In novels published only a few years later, it is more likely that the hero will ignore the call of *gloire* if it conflicts with his desire to fulfil his obligations to his lady. Pacore disregards his father's request to him to return home and defend his country, because he is with his beloved, 'attaché par des chaisnes si belles & si plaisantes'.[37] Armetzar, son of Tamerlane the Great, not only rejects his father's command to rejoin the army in the fight against Bajazet, recognizing no other title than that of Ladice's suitor, but at a later stage actually abandons Tamerlane's cause and his own chances of glory to subject himself totally to Ladice:

Non, Tamerlam, ne me retenez plus, & plustost que de m'obliger à vous suivre, sçachez que j'ay fait veu d'aimer, & que cette profession dispense les enfans de l'obeissance des peres, quand ils en exigent contre leur amour. Si vous me reprochez que je fay plus d'estat d'une fille que d'un Empire, & que je cheris peu la gloire, à qui je prefere un honteux servage, avouez vous-mesme qu'il y en a plus à temoigner de la fidelité que du courage, & que la constance est la vertu des grands hommes, où l'autre se rend commun jusqu'aux animaux.[38]

Cyrus has little difficulty in making his desire for glory submit to his love for Mandane: 'le desir de la Gloire est une passion aussi bien que l'amour; & une passion dominante; & une passion imperieuse, qui n'a pas accoutumé de ceder. Mais apres tout, je n'ay point d'interest où celuy de ma Princesse se trouve.'[39] For these heroes, the greatest glory is no longer to be found in action and self-fulfilment, but in subjection to the beloved.[40]

In general, a slackening of emphasis on action and a greater concentration on the hero's concern with his mistress can be noted during the period of the heroic novel's popularity, particularly when a novelist made more than one contribution to the genre, as did La Calprenède. His *Cassandre* is full of battles and single combat, a world dominated by men and male values, whilst *Cleopatre* contains very little heroic action, the attention being focused almost entirely on the love intrigues and *galanterie*. Chevreau's *Scanderberg* devotes a good deal of space to descriptions of military actions, including a naval battle and a highly technical account of the siege of a fortified town.[41] The same author's *Hermiogene* avoids all commitment to physical action. The hero's first reported act is not one of great prowess, but an attempt to

have himself sacrificed for the sake of his beloved, over whom
he falls ill. When it is necessary for the author to show his
hero confronting the Romans, he spends as little time on it as
possible: 'Il ne perdit de temps en cette occasion, & sans
occuper long temps vostre patience, apres un combat qui
dura si peu, vous sçaurez en deux mots qu'il n'eut gueres plus
de peine à les defaire qu'à les rencontrer.'[42]

The service performed by a hero for his lady, which had
always been a feature of chivalric literature, was reinterpreted
in accordance with the new position of woman. In the heroic
tradition, the hero justified himself as a suitor by proving
that he was capable of glorious deeds, regardless of whether
the lady had authorized him to do so or not. Thus, Phélismond
is pursued to Denmark by Polexandre for claiming that he
alone is worthy of Alcidiane. When Phélismond turns out to
be courageous and *généreux*, Polexandre gives him permission
to serve Alcidiane: 'Jusques icy vous n'avez esté mal traitté
que pour ce que vous n'avez pas esté connu. Lors qu'Alcidiane
sçaura quel est Phelismond, . . . asseurez-vous qu'elle changera
de sentiment', almost as though Polexandre were empowered
to admit new suitors in Alcidiane's name.[43] Similarly, in
Scanderberg, it is agreed that a woman must accept the
advances of a man who has demonstrated his love for her:
'comme l'amour est une operation vertueuse, . . . il faut sans
doute que celle qui est aimée reponde par sa vertu aux
sentimens de celuy qui l'aime, puis que l'ingratitude ne peut
estre jointe à la vertu . . . la Dame doit donner son amour à
celuy dont elle connoist estre veritablement aimée.'[44]

The new feminism rejected such a concept as perpetuating
the subservience of women. The deeds a man chose to perform had no value other than that which the lady deigned to
place on them: it was she who decided what she would
accept as service. In *Berenice*, Sabine has been rescued from a
fire by Cécinna who declares his love to her, assuming that
the service he has just rendered will carry weight in his cause,
but the ladies listening to the story are unanimous in rejecting
this extraordinary idea which, if applied, would require them
to accept the advances of any man of courage. They are much
more likely to be moved by services arising from fidelity,
such as 'un respect fort grand & beaucoup d'attachement'.[45]

It is not essential for service to require courage at all, as long as it furnishes proof of utter devotion. When Oriane is stabbed by a rejected suitor, her three remaining suitors react in different ways. Polidarque pursues and kills the would-be assassin, Aristide tends the wounded Oriane, and Euridème faints. In the ensuing debate as to who showed the greatest feeling for Oriane, Euridème has the warmest support.[46]

The type of relationship that resulted was one in which the man gave all in total submission, whilst the woman was not obliged to give anything. The severity which a woman had used to protect her honour during courtship, in order to be able to hand it into the keeping of the hero she loved when they married, was replaced in many novels by a cult of male submission for its own sake. Severity became the woman's way of retaining power over her lover. As long as she does not declare her feelings, 'elle tient alors veritablement en sa puissance le bonheur ou le malheur de son Amant: & c'est proprement en ce temps-là qu'elle est Maistresse & qu'il est Esclave'.[47] As soon as she admits to loving him, he feels he has a right to demand further proofs of her affection and loses his subordinate position. It is necessary that he should abandon all hope and surrender his destiny totally to the lady he serves:

C'est ainsi . . . que j'ayme mon adorable Princesse; je l'ayme seulement parce qu'elle est belle, que son esprit est ravissant, & pour ses vertus toutes heroïques. Il est vray que j'espere, mais ce n'est pas contre les regles que je me suis prescrites, & cét espoir n'apporte point de tache à la pureté de mon amour. J'espere, non d'estre un jour aymé de Ladice, mais bien d'avoir la preference de la servir sur tous ceux qui me la voudront disputer.[48]

She can reject him, but still refuse to allow him to turn his attentions elsewhere; she can, like Axiane, tell her lover, after tremendous services on his part, that she can no longer admit him as a suitor, to which the correct response is continued submission, as Cyrus acknowledges: 'allons partout, vivons heureux ou malheureux, mourons, pour quelque subjet que ce soit, il n'importe, si Axiane le commande'.[49] She will not tolerate jealousy, since it would suggest that she had some obligation towards her suitor: 'il me devoit laisser la liberté

de mes actions, s'il est vray qu'il m'ait donné de l'empire sur
les siennes', cries Cléopâtre, furious that Coriolan should have
written her a letter accusing her of inconstancy.[50]

The ultimate expression in the heroic novel of the feminist
trend is found in the *précieux* attitudes of Madeleine de
Scudéry. Indications of an opposition to marriage are visible
in *Ibrahim*, where Axiane rejects it as 'une captivité qu'on
devoit esviter, autant qu'il estoit possible',[51] but this becomes
open hostility in *Le Grand Cyrus*. Sapho asserts that matri-
mony is 'un long esclavage', a form of subjection which
destroys moral equality. All husbands are potential tyrants.[52]
But as well as subjecting one partner to the other, marriage
inevitably kills the love which may have preceded it. The
advice given is uncompromising:

l'amour peut aller au delà du Tombeau, mais elle ne va guere au delà
du Mariage: c'est pourquoy je suis persuadée que quiconque veut tousjours aimer doit n'espouser jamais la Personne aimée.
    Sapho fit connoistre . . . que pour s'aimer tousjours avec une esgalle
ardeur, il falloit ne s'espouser jamais.[53]

More general feminist principles are enunciated. Fathers
should not oblige their children to marry against their inclinations;[54] men should be prepared to accept women on the
same terms as other men, acknowledging their mental abilities
instead of judging them solely by their beauty.[55] Madeleine
de Scudéry has nothing but scorn for the Arnolphes of her
day, 'qui ne regardent les Femmes que comme les premieres
Esclaves de leurs Maisons, qui deffendoient à leurs Filles de
lire jamais d'autres livres que ceux qui leur servoient à prier
les Dieux', though Damophile, her version of Philaminte, is
equally derided: 'comme il n'y a rien de plus aimable, ny de
plus charmant qu'une Femme qui s'est donné la peine d'orner
son esprit de mille agreables connoissances, quand elle en
sçait bien user; il n'y a rien aussi de si ridicule, ny de si
ennuyeux, qu'une Femme sottement sçavante'.[56] Throughout the novel, the portraits of female characters emphasize
their wit, intelligence, and learning.

The kind of relationship proposed as an ideal in *Cyrus* and
Clelie, the *amitié tendre* so derided by satirists of *préciosité*,
was in a sense an attempt to re-establish moral equality
between the sexes. The passions were seen to be potentially

uncontrollable. Though they were the source of pleasure, they could all too easily become the cause of emotional disaster. Love was almost certain to bring with it jealousy and pain:[57] *amitié tendre*, on the other hand, stopped short of overwhelming passion. It was a relationship which cultivated the pleasure to be gained from the interplay of two minds and took away the need for either party to feel subject to the other, but it went deeper than mere esteem arising from the recognition of merit and obligation based on services rendered.[58] It was not, however, a relationship which could have found a place in the world of Polexandre or Oroondate.

It was the strength of the feminist movement which produced the most striking changes in the ideal of heroism as depicted in the novel, and ultimately those changes were to help destroy the very premises of *romanesque* heroism. In the 1630s, the hero had been a man with an urge to self-assertion, ready to oppose anyone who seemed to want to subject him morally, including, if necessary, the woman he loved, since love was only one feature of a life devoted to heroic endeavour. He had become, within a very short time, a man whose sole object in life was to serve the lady he loved, submitting all other aspirations to that one alone. Love had become an end in itself.

To a certain extent, such a progression was a return to the ideals of courtly love, of neoplatonism, of d'Urfé's *honnête amitié*, but the resemblance could never be more than partial, because of the acknowledgment during the seventeenth century that love was an involuntary passion which, however it might be idealized, posed a threat to the carefully elaborated code of emotional restrictions on which heroic love was based.[59] With the power of the passions in mind, certain writers concluded that the only safe relationship was one from which passionate feeling was excluded — the *amitié* of the *précieuses* — but such a relationship had little to do with the sublimity and affirmation of liberty on which the heroic novel had been founded.

CHAPTER VI

HISTORY AND FICTION

The past was a perennial source of interest to the educated during the seventeenth century. The demand for historical works must have been healthy, judging by the number produced, and Martin's analysis of the contents of some of the private libraries of Louis XIII's reign confirms that there was a considerable interest in history, particularly amongst the *noblesse de robe*. Pontchartrain, Anne Mangot, and Eustache de Refuge were amongst the notable *robins* whose libraries contained large collections of volumes on history, and the *noblesse d'épée*, not generally noted for bibliophily, sometimes also betrayed a preference for historical works: the duc de Luynes' few books included a small number of classics and 'un peu plus d'ouvrages historiques peut-être'; Charles Thiersault, a *gentilhomme ordinaire du Roi*, had quite a large collection, including 'surtout, beaucoup de livres d'histoire'.[1] Overall, as an element in private libraries, history occupied second place only to theology and works of piety.

When assessing the significance of the place accorded to history, however, we need to remember that, in matters of historiography, the first half of the seventeenth century represented the end of a distinct tradition. Although it was to be only a few years before Pierre Bayle, Richard Simon and the rest were to start asking the questions and establishing the principles that laid the foundations of modern historical analysis, the generation for which heroic novels were written still viewed history in much the same way as the men of the Renaissance had done, as a cyclical process of rise and fall, with the same human strengths and weaknesses being endlessly rehearsed in different surroundings. It is rare, therefore, to find them calling for a dispassionate presentation of facts, combining good and evil actions without comment.[2] Certainly, the respect accorded to history was due to the fact that it depicted truth, but it was moral rather than factual truth which was applauded, and the historian was expected to select his material so as to make the maximum moral impact. History was seen as a series of memorable incidents to be studied in isolation rather than as a continuum, and consequently tended to be anecdotal in its presentation: the historian aimed to build up a picture, using a variety of factual, or at least generally accredited, data, to produce the desired edifying effect. Mézeray, the most respected historian of his generation, maintained that history was written for one of three reasons, none of which could nowadays be described as objective: 'ou pour la gloire de ceux qui ont fait les belles actions et pour la honte de ceux qui ont commis des laschetés; ou pour la curiosité et le plaisir, ou enfin pour l'utilité et l'instruction de ceux qui les lisent'. He considered it perfectly legitimate suddenly to recount a number of remarkable incidents which had only the most tenuous of connections with the matter in hand, with an airy 'le lecteur n'aura pas desagreable que je luy rapporte trois choses fort rares'.[3]

The major interest of the historian was in depicting the exploits of great individuals who served as examples to the rest of mankind. He saw himself as the guardian of the reputations of the great men of the past,[4] with the moral duty of impressing on the reader an edifying or monitory spectacle which might influence him in his own life. He was the equivalent in literary terms of the painter who depicted the age-old stories from classical history within the visual and cultural conventions of his own day, for each new generation expected the received tradition to be maintained morally but embellished according to the taste of the day.[5] In pedagogy, this kind of selective presentation of well-known stories was considered valuable, particularly when accompanied by homilies on the moral rectitude necessary to make great deeds possible.[6]

Since history, defined in such a way, could claim to be the art 'qui miscuit utile dulci', it is not surprising that, from an early stage, the novel was condemned by historians and moralists, particularly clerics, because it was based on imagination and fantasy rather than truth and was thus not only devoid of moral value, but could do positive harm by distracting the mind from the reality of the human situation. Camus dismissed all novels, including those which had a basis of truth, such as the romances of Charlemagne and Godefroi de Bouillon, as 'fatras' and 'fadaises'.[7] Dubosc considered that history provided all that the novel had to offer, plus the essential factor of moral utility, and therefore rendered the novel redundant.[8] The danger in novels lay in the attractive picture of worldly love that was presented, seducing young people from the path of virtue and injecting poison into their souls.[9]

The partisans of the novel during the 1620s and 1630s tended to base their response to these criticisms on a justification of the role of the imagination. Why should writers not be granted the same freedom as painters to exercise their powers of invention? Why should novelists be condemned when poets are not? Gerzan could argue confidently that the novel's attraction lay in its inventiveness and that it should contain a large number of intrigues, so that the reader is kept constantly in suspense.[10] In order to strengthen the novel's claim to be the literature of delight, some questioned whether history's much vaunted foundation of truth was in fact genuine: was not much of what was accepted as history suspected of being fabulous?[11] History was seen as a rival, encroaching on a territory which belonged by right to the imagination, and when one considers the bulk of the novels of this period, with their complicated intrigues and their undifferentiated characterization, it is difficult to see what other position could have been adopted.

During the 1630s, however, when the heroic novel was beginning to emerge, the rôle of the imagination was superseded as the main justification for the novel by a new argument, which aimed to establish a less defensive position *vis-à-vis* history. It was claimed that the novel was a kind of prose epic with rules of its own. The novelist had the same commitment to verisimilitude as the historian: he would spend time describing the geography, ethnography, ceremonies, etc. of the countries in which his story was set, in the same way as the historian would, and the intervention of supernatural forces was proscribed. He also had the same moral aim as the historian, to depict the discomfiture of vice and the honouring

of virtue.[12] There was one essential difference between the
novelist and the historian, however, which in the eyes of the
novelists established their superiority. The historian was
bound by the facts of the situation he was describing and was
obliged to reflect the baser and less uplifting aspects of life
as they occurred in his story: the novelist could concentrate
solely on the heroic and inspiring aspects of life and thereby
induce a more effective moral response in the reader. Boisrobert spoke out in favour of novelists on the grounds that
they could prick the conscience of the guilty as well as the
historian could and, much better than he, could inspire men
of courage to maintain justice and reason.[13] Desmarets's
argument, reminiscent of the one expounded by Chapelain
in the *Sentiments sur le Cid*, was that the novel's superiority
derived from its ability to combine history and fiction in an
aesthetic unity, 'pource que la feinte vray-semblable est
fondée sur la bien-seance & sur la raison; & la verité toute
simple n'embrasse qu'un recit d'accidens humains, qui le
plus souvent ne sont pleins que d'extravagance'. Straightforward history could not approach the beauty of a work
in which history and fiction combined to guarantee the
triumph of virtue.[14] The author of *Clorinde* agreed, explaining
that the novelist could illuminate history by making his
readers enter into the sentiments of great figures from the
past, whom they felt they had come to know personally.[15]
Le Vayer de Boutigny proclaimed the absolute superiority
of the novel on moral grounds: 'dans la verité qu'il [i.e. the
historian] nous descrit, l'innocence est souvent opprimée par
le crime; Au lieu que dans les Romans la vertu triomphe
tousjours & que le vice ne manque jamais d'estre puni.'[16]

Truth to life became the novelists' rallying-cry. Total
freedom of invention was henceforth dismissed as the province
of 'ces esprits grotesques, qui entassent une infinité d'avantures mal digerées & sans fondement sur l'Histoire'.[17] Most
novelists established their credentials by constructing their
plot around some historical figure and by building in as much
local colour and accredited detail as possible. Guérin de
Bouscal assures his readers that he has consulted books and
maps to gain an authentic picture of the world of Theseus;[18]
Lemaire claims to have adhered scrupulously to what is

accepted as truth about the age of Sémiramis;[19] Chevreau tells us he has taken the legends surrounding Skanderberg and removed those elements obviously not based on fact.[20] The author of *Axiane* puts forward a rigorous view of truth, arguing that the novelist should produce 'une copie de la verité', neither adding to it nor taking away from it, but himself admits to certain inventions, adding 'pourveu qu'elles soient toutes possibles, je m'assure qu'elles ne seront pas hors de propos'.[21]

In the cause of historical accuracy and verisimilitude, the preface to *Ibrahim* stands out as something of a manifesto. Scudéry declares that without *vraisemblance*, the reading of novels is merely distasteful: 'je tiens que plus les avantures sont naturelles, plus elles donnent de satisfaction'. If necessary, the expression of heroism must be subordinated to the need for realism:

Il est hors de doute que pour representer la veritable ardeur heroïque, il faut luy faire executer quelque chose d'extraordinaire, comme par un transport de Heros: mais il ne faut pas continuer de cette sorte, parce qu'autrement ces actions dégenerent en contes ridicules, & ne touchent point l'esprit.[22]

It would be misleading, however, to conclude that the heroic novel was committed primarily to a realistic portrayal of a historical figure and his world, and to apply modern criteria in assessing the degree of accuracy achieved by the authors.[23] If novelists felt it necessary to declare their interest in history and verisimilitude, it was because they wished to dissociate themselves from the disordered adventure novels written by Du Verdier, Du Bail, and others, with their sequences of disconnected events and incongruous characters.[24] Thanks to these authors, imagination had come to be identified with the most fantastic imbroglios and had to be disowned. But imagination in the sense of an ability to create stirring situations and maintain a level of suspense was still very much a prerequisite for the novelist. Leaving aside the theories put forward in prefaces, the aims of most of the writers of heroic novels, as far as they can be deduced from the novels themselves, were threefold: to stir the reader's imagination, to provide moral edification, and to produce a historical picture (or more accurately a certain amount of atmosphere) of the period and the hero-figure in question.

Those writers who offered imaginative scope and suspense were likely to be successful with the public, who looked for such qualities rather than historical truth. Of Condé, who read *Cassandre* while on campaign, we are told that he read for pleasure rather than for instruction: he was not concerned with the details of the works he read but 'il est touché des beaux endroits, et les choses extraordinaires luy sont tout à fait sensibles'.[25] Segrais, who defined the aim of the novel as 'divertir pas des imaginations vray-semblables & naturelles', mentioned most of the principal heroic novels approvingly, in each case commending them for their imaginative qualities:

Où en peut-on voir de plus extraordinaires [i.e. imaginations], & de mieux escrites que dans le Polexandre? Que peut-on lire de plus ingenieux que l'Ariane? Où peut-on trouver des Inventions plus heroïques que dans la Cassandre? des Caracteres mieux variez & des avantures plus surprenantes que dans la Cleopatre? La seule Histoire du Peintre & du Musicien qui se lit dans l'illustre Bassa, ne ravit-elle pas, & ne vaut-elle pas seule les plus riches inventions des autres? Qu'est-ce qu'une personne qui sçait le monde ne doit pas dire de l'admirable varieté du Grand Cyrus . . . ?[26]

Sorel has much the same attitude, praising *Polexandre*, *Cassandre*, *Cleopatre*, and *Cyrus* for their 'inventions'.[27]

All this debate about the relationship between historical truth and the imagination, which inevitably calls to mind the broadly similar debate being conducted at the same time in the theatre, can ultimately be seen as an attempt to persuade the public of the novel's validity as a vehicle for the expression of truths about man's moral nature. The aim was to present an idealized picture of man's aspirations, a hero capable of reaching a super-human level both in the field of sheer physical action and in the extremely restrained world of social intercourse, as embodied in the concept of *honnêteté*.[28] The reader would be inspired to emulate the deeds of the hero and model his social attitudes on those of the world in which the hero moved, and it was therefore important that the novelist should not be restricted absolutely by the limits of recorded history with its mixture of noble and ignoble deeds and motives. The novel was to be seen to have achieved a new departure, fundamentally different from the romances of chivalry and the novels of adventure, in which an individual had been chosen or invented in order to allow a sequence of events to be recounted with some sort of consistency. In the heroic novel, the events are recounted in order to set off the figure chosen as subject. The hero is not so much put into his historical setting as taken out of his period and elevated to a level where he could be an embodiment of ideals considered to be valid for all ages. It is not surprising in such circumstances that so many heroes seem to be interchangeable, regardless of the period in which they are supposed to have lived, since their creators were all striving in their different ways to express an ideal of heroism. It is for the same reason that the heroic novel so often betrays a marked medieval flavour, even though the plot is ostensibly set in the ancient world. The long tradition of medieval romances still exercised a strong influence, but equally important is the fact that the Middle Ages could offer, more than any other period, an ideal of the heroic individual who, though subject ultimately to the political and social order, carried the ideals of society in himself. The knight errant was justice, honour, and courtesy incarnate and brought them out into the world rather than representing them on behalf of some distant authority.[29]

The medieval elements which seem so incongruous to the modern reader in novels dealing with the ancient world are in fact limited to certain specific and conventionalized areas, viz. those where the highest expression of individual prowess is required. The tournament provides this *par excellence* because it allows a straightforward trial of strength and skill in a properly regulated context of courtesy and honour. Nothing the ancient world had to offer in the way of games or spectacles could do this, and consequently tournaments are made to take place in every age and civilization. Arms and armour are another feature that varies according to the requirements of the plot. If a hero of the ancient world is demonstrating his prowess in a battle, he will probably wear tunic, greaves, and breast-plate. If, however, he presents himself as an unknown challenger in a tournament, destined to win the admiration of all by his courage and skill, with his rank playing no part in his *gloire*, he will wear complete medieval armour covering him from head to foot so that he is not recognizable. The helmet is particularly important, especially in the numerous instances when a woman dons armour and goes to war. Sorel no doubt thought that he had hit upon one of the great weaknesses of the novel when he derided the use of such anachronistic forms of armour,[30] but truth in the novel was not necessarily fidelity to history. Fidelity to the ideal of heroism and the moral function of the novel came first, and seems to have been what their readers looked for. It is often assumed that the public was prepared to suffer the historical anachronisms of the heroic novel for the sake of the *romanesque* entertainment offered:[31] it was surely rather that they found in the heroic novel a statement of the moral reality they acknowledged, expressed in its highest form, and that the historical inaccuracies were consequently considered to be of little importance.

When a reaction against the heroic novel set in after 1660, it was usually justified in the name of truth and *vraisemblance*. The writers of *nouvelles* and the theorists mocked the enormous novels of the preceding generation and what they saw as the unrealistic psychology depicted in them. Du Plaisir is typical when he includes amongst the causes of the heroic novels' loss of popularity 'leur peu de vray-semblance', clarifying his meaning with 'la vraysemblance consiste à ne dire que ce qui est moralement croyable'.[32] He evidently believed that this criterion disqualified the heroic novel from serious consideration, yet Gomberville, La Calprenède, and Scudéry would have agreed wholeheartedly with his definition. Indeed, their claims to superiority over earlier novelists were based precisely on their ability to create situations and characters that were morally credible. They felt that they had created a new genre with something positive to say about man, in the same way that *L'Astrée* had made a contribution to knowledge of the human emotions. They were offering realism in the sense of a depiction of truths about man's capacity for action and glory, as it was understood at the time. They therefore wished to be dissociated from the unreality of the romances of chivalry and the *romans d'aventures*, and made claims to historical verisimilitude as part of their attempt to establish their credentials as serious writers. History gave their works dignity and status.

There was, however, no theory of *éloignement*, no attempt
to set a distance between the reader and the subject. On the
contrary, the ancient and the modern worlds were felt to be
closely linked because they shared common ideals. The
characters chosen to be heroes of novels tended to be those
who were presented to children as models to be imitated,
the great men of republican or early imperial Rome, of the
semi-mythological age of Greece, of the age of Alexander:
they were all assimilated to the seventeenth century and
made part of an entirely contemporaneous expression of
greatness.[33] If Condé could be compared successively to
Germanicus, Alexander the Great, and Julius Caesar for his
military prowess,[34] these heroes of antiquity, when they
appeared in novels, could equally be expected to share the
sensibility he displayed. There was nothing incongruous in
suggesting that Julius Caesar should weep and even faint
when he parted from his beloved, since Condé, his modern
incarnation, could do so.[35]

It is natural, therefore, that, as the type of hero depicted
in the heroic novel was modified to keep pace with the
change from an ideal of aristocratic individualism to one of
social gentility, so the conception of the historical characters
representing those ideals should change accordingly. The
picture of ancient (and modern) virtue given in *Clelie* is
different from that given in *l'Histoire celtique* or *Alcide* and,
to the modern reader, perhaps more ridiculous, but the
object of the authors was the same, to express an ideal which
their contemporaries could recognize as their own in a
framework borrowed from past ages felt to have shared some
of the same aspirations.

PART II

It has been shown in Part I how the heroic novel, outwardly committed to relating the exploits of a particular kind of individual, reflected the evolving aspirations of a generation living through a period of rapid social, political, and ideological change. Once the form was established, authors found it convenient to continue using the same framework — a main plot begun *in medias res*, supporting a large number of *tiroirs*, including the earlier life of the hero and heroine — while modifying profoundly the concept of heroism embodied in the hero and the kind of subject-matter included in the episodes. The novels of 1660 may look similar to those of 1640, but the type of hero depicted had undergone a number of radical changes in order to accommodate the new world-view current after the Fronde. Features which were essential in the earlier novels, such as moral autonomy, have been largely discarded in the later ones.

A number of novels stand out from the majority by their length and by their greater popularity. They were the ones which set the pattern for the rest and were instrumental in imposing the successive modifications to the definition of heroism. Other novelists followed where Gomberville, Scudéry, and La Calprenède, the authors of these major works, led. For instance, novels published before 1641 quite often contained supernatural elements. *La Prazimene* has an airborne chariot pulled by dragons, belonging to the magician Zoroastre;[1] *Polexandre* includes a magic ring left over from the earlier versions;[2] *La Cytherée* contains a monstrous man-devouring snake.[3] After the publication of *Ibrahim* with its insistence on verisimilitude, such elements virtually disappear from the novel. Those that remain are acknowledged rather shamefacedly. Guérin de Bouscal not only tries to justify his inclusion in *Antiope* of supernatural elements such as Médée's airborne chariot — he has not, he claims, brought in any incident 'dont la possibilité n'ait eu des partisans en quelques endroits du monde'[4] — but he also attempts to give quasi-scientific explanations for magic phenomena: the enchanted ring that she had given to Jason to make him invisible, Médée carefully explains to Egée, was simply an extension of the principle by which lenses can make objects appear smaller.[5] Again, the kind of hero portrayed in *Cassandre* provides a direct inspiration for a number of novels, including *Scanderberg*, *Alcide*, and *Axiane*.

The following six chapters analyse these major novels individually (including two proto-heroic works, *Ariane* and *l'Histoire celtique*), showing how their authors used the standard forms of the novel to project their personal interpretation of the ideal of heroism. It is noticeable, however, that in some cases an author would modify his own definition of the hero in order to take account of innovations introduced by other writers. Scudéry's *Cyrus* has absorbed a number of features from La Calprenède's *Cassandre*, but conversely the latter's *Cleopatre* has been influenced by *Cyrus*. The implication here is that the individual author's concept of heroism was, in part at least, conditioned by his response to the mood of the public as he recognized it in the works of rival authors and depended on his assessment of what his readers would like to see. These major works thus provide a valuable indication of the way in which the aspirations of the literate classes evolved from the ideological confidence of Richelieu's day to the moral ambiguities of the post-Fronde period.

CHAPTER VII

THE PROTO-HEROIC NOVEL:
ARIANE AND *l'HISTOIRE CELTIQUE*

Tallemant des Réaux described Desmarets de Saint-Sorlin as having 'un esprit universel et plein d'inventions' and suggested that Boisrobert feared him because of it.[1] Whether Desmarets made a conscious attempt to outshine Boisrobert in every sphere is not clear, but within a year or two of his entering Richelieu's service, he had published a novel which surpassed not only Boisrobert's *Histoire indienne* but all the other derivatives of the Greek romances in its scope and in the manner of its execution. Both *Ariane*[2] and the *Histoire indienne* reveal their authors' indebtedness to Heliodorus but with an essential difference. Boisrobert, while exercising his imagination on the nature of the adventures that befall his heroes and the countries through which they pass, remained within the framework of the French version of Greek romance, as developed by Fumée and Gerzan: Desmarets added to that framework elements which, elaborated by other novelists, were to be taken up in the depiction of idealized heroism.

Certain episodes and features of *Ariane* are clearly inspired by the *Histoire ethiopique*. In each work, importance is attached to the presenting of prizes by the heroine to the hero after his victory in public games; the sacrifice of one of the chief protagonists is narrowly averted; the final assumption of royal rank is found to be in keeping with a divine prophecy. Other features point to the influence of *L'Astrée*, such as the fact that the hero and heroine come from families at feud. Palamède, inseparable companion of the hero Mélinte, is a reincarnation of Hylas, with the same attractive gaiety and incorrigible inclination to inconstancy: he and Mélinte conduct a discussion on the nature of love which closely parallels the arguments of Hylas and Silvandre.[3] Verse is used by Desmarets in the same way as by d'Urfé to underline points of deep emotion.

It would perhaps be unfair to include amongst the list of Desmarets' borrowings from d'Urfé the former's fondness for playing on the reader's prurience, though Guéret imagined Ariane complaining that every book of her novel contains at least one 'lieu infâme' and that she is made to appear naked because Astrée had done so before Céladon.[4] *Ariane* has far more licentious episodes than *L'Astrée*, more than can be accounted for simply by the fact that standards of decorum had not risen very much by 1632. At times, the effect of introducing farcical or indecorous scenes into the narrative is to destroy temporarily the heroic tone built up elsewhere.[5]

Though he owes a good deal to these predecessors, Desmarets is by no means a slavish imitator. He reveals a genuine talent, particularly in the creation of characters who, by the standards of the later heroic novels, are endowed with individual features. The most interesting of these is Epicharis, Ariane's *suivante*, who acts with initiative to deflate the pompous, locking the importunate Marcelin in a pavilion for two days when he thinks he is waiting for Ariane[6] or adding on days of service to the list kept by a boorish suitor who thinks he is working towards the end of his servitude.[7] *Caractères* are introduced into the narrative, such as Garamante, the conceited anti-feminist whose presumption has to be exposed by Ariane,[8] or the melancholic Misandre,[9] or the haughty Zélinde who develops a strange mocking relationship with Palamède.[10]

The introduction of these characters is in keeping with the general 'bourgeois' tone of the work. Almost all the *tiroirs* are concerned with characters from the middle ranks of society, citizens of various Mediterranean cities, and the emotional intrigues in which they become involved. Even those stories that deal with princes and princesses lack a heroic dimension, presenting the same sort of love intrigue and implying that there is no difference between the emotions of a person of royal blood and those of ordinary people. The ideal of ultra-refined feeling, qualitatively surpassing that of ordinary mortals, had not yet become a vital ingredient of the novel.

Mélinte himself is, by the standards of subsequent novels,

a hero of very modest stature. He does not succeed in imposing himself on the world like an Alexander or a Cyrus (nor
does he aspire to), but has to submit to the laws and sometimes the whims of those in power — the Emperor Nero, his
favourite Marcelin, the Roman Governor of Thessaly. He is of
respectable origin, being the son of Hermocrates, the deposed
Sicilian leader, but cannot claim to rival the great Roman
patricians: when Princess Araxie falls in love with him, he
tells her he does not think 'que ce fust une alliance sortable
que celle d'un Gentil-homme Sicilien avec une Princesse du
sang des Parthes'.[11] He and Palamède arrive in Rome, motivated not by a desire to conquer the world but only by 'un
honneste desir de voir le siege de l'Empire'.[12] Though both
of them make an impression on the Romans with their
admirable qualities, Mélinte does not emerge as anything
more than a promising young man.[13] He is more 'retenu',
Palamède more 'prompt & entreprenant'.

The relationship between the hero and the heroine likewise
has more in common with the Greek romances than with the
heroic novel proper. Mélinte and Ariane are drawn mutually
towards one another. Except for a natural sense of modesty
which she shares with all virtuous women, Ariane does not
indulge in the kind of severity that Polexandre was to endure.
She never suggests that Mélinte is being outrageously presump-
tous in daring to love her. On the contrary, having decided
that she loves him, she finds no difficulty in declaring her
feelings unequivocally:

Je promets que je ne seray jamais qu'à Melinte: j'y suis obligée par son
merite, encore plus par son affection; & luy estant redevable de l'honneur & de la vie, je remets l'un & l'autre en ses mains, comme choses
qu'il a acquises, & dont il peut mieux disposer que moy-mesme.[14]

Melinte, je suis à vous, & sans vous je ne puis vivre: Voyez en quel
endroit du monde vous voulez me retirer, je m'estimeray bienheureuse
d'y mourir avec vous.[15]

Nor does she reproach Mélinte for his ardour, but gently
keeps him in the path of virtue.[16] Mélinte responds with
confident respect, having no need for abject deference. The
trust between them is so great that she is prepared to allow
Mélinte to pretend love for Émilie if it enables him to escape
more easily from her influence.[17]

The plot does not therefore derive its impetus from the tensions between the hero and heroine, as was to become normal in later heroic novels. A united couple, Mélinte and Ariane are pushed from one perilous situation to another by the persecutions of the Emperor Nero and of Ariane's uncle and guardian, Dicéarque. Most of the novel is spent in flight: direct retaliation is excluded either by deference and *honnêteté* or by the emperor's authority.

Though all this suggests a parallel with the Greek romances, there are strong indications that Desmarets wanted to create a much more positive and admirable kind of hero than Heliodorus and Tatius had done. For one thing, Mélinte is a man of considerable valour. Desmarets operates on the same principle as the authors of the romances of chivalry, that a hero should be capable of astonishing feats of butchery based on sheer strength:

il donna un tel coup à l'un, que sans qu'il estoit armé, il luy eust separé l'espaule du corps [p. 135].

Melinte se destourna legerement, & en passant luy fendit le bras gauche d'une blessure si grande, qu'il emplissoit de sang toute la place par où il couroit [p. 136].

poursuivant le premier qu'il rencontra il luy fendit le front, & le sang qui luy coula en abondance sur les yeux l'aveugla, & le mit hors de combat [p. 143].

In the first battle against the Scythiars, he fights with the enemy chief, smashes his helmet to pieces and splits his head in two.[18] In the second battle, 'il fendoit les testes, il abbatoit les espaules, & ses ennemis croyoient que ce fust Mars luy-mesme qui fust venu pour les destruire'.[19] The duel against Pisistrate, the man whose hostility had almost led to Mélinte's being sacrificed, ends with Mélinte cutting off his opponent's head with one stroke.[20]

Most of this prodigious energy is expended against ignoble opponents. Only once does Mélinte find himself matched against someone on his own moral level. Amongst the group of pirates who have attacked his ship, he crosses swords with Eurymédon who 'faisoit parestre tant de force & d'adresse, que Melinte jugea que c'estoit là un ennemy digne de luy'.[21] Having beaten him, Mélinte is content to disarm him, and it is from this point that the contest of *générosité* begins.

Eurymédon declares his intention of serving Mélinte with his sword and his life, 'car il faut que vous soyez le plus vaillant de tous les hommes, pour m'avoir mis en cét estat'. Mélinte responds in the only way a true hero could:

Melinte touché de ces paroles, qui partoient d'un cœur bien genereux, & sentant quelque emotion en luy qui le convioit à l'aimer, soit pour la grace qui accompagnoit son visage & son parler, soit *pour une secrette affection que tous les vaillans hommes ont les uns pour les autres*, luy tendit la main, & l'ayant embrassé l'asseura de son amitié.[22]

Desmarets evidently intended his hero to be more than simply one man amongst many. He belonged to a brotherhood of *généreux*, an immediately recognizable higher caste who were to provide the sole centre of interest in many of the later heroic novels.

The encounter with Eurymédon is the exception in a series of fights necessary to prevent oppression. The afflicted look to Mélinte for help and assume correctly that he delights in using his valour to combat what he takes to be the injustices of fortune: his 'grandeur de courage . . . , qui ne voit rien au dessus d'elle, & qui merite que tout le monde luy cede, se plaist à relever la noblesse & la vertu quand elle les trouve abatuës par la fortune'.[23] Before setting out at the head of the Thessalians to do battle with the marauding Scythians, he takes on all the charismatic qualities of the heroic leader, though these attributes had not been particularly noticeable in the earlier books set in Rome. His stature increases (literally, it seems) as he

sembloit ce jour-là plus haut que de coustume, & avoit je ne sçay quoy d'estincelant dans les yeux, & de resplendissant sur le visage, qui le faisoit parestre quelque Dieu descendu en terre pour le secours de la Grece & de l'Empire Romain . . . sa seule mine sembloit inspirer une partie de son grand courage à ceux qui alloient combattre sous sa conduitte.[24]

This valour is founded on a conviction on the part of Mélinte that all difficulties can be overcome by intelligent action. He believes that the gods do not intentionally bring about the ruin of those with a will to survive, but always leave open the possibility of escape if only the individual has the initiative and the courage to pursue it. He is just such an individual, 'd'un courage qui ne s'estonnoit point pour le danger, & d'un esprit qui trouvoit incontinent des expediens'.[25] When Ariane inveighs against heaven in the manner of Leucippe or Ismène — 'Helas! disoit Ariane, il semble que la furie de nostre mal-heur assemble des forces de tous les costez de la terre, pour nous oster tout espoir de salut. Quel crime, bons Dieux, avons-nous commis, pour permettre que les hommes nous poursuivent avec tant de rage?' — Mélinte comforts her and assures her that the gods will provide a way out.[26] When the house in which they are staying is set alight by their enemy Marcelin who is waiting outside to ambush them, he is concerned but immediately sets about finding a solution: 'Esperons encore, Madame, & moderez vos pleurs & vos plaintes, cependant que je vay voir par quel moyen nous pourrions nous sauver, & si quelque Dieu ne m'inspirera point ce que nous devons faire en cette extremité.'[27] When Ariane weeps at the prospect of his being killed in battle, lamenting that it is always the most courageous who run the risks while the cowardly shelter behind them, he explains that facing up to danger is the surest way of nullifying the arbitrary workings of fortune:

quelle distinction feroit-on entre les courageux & les lasches, si jamais il n'y avoit de peril? mais au moins on se doit consoler de ce que dans les combats plus on est valeureux, moins on court de fortune; car il est bien plus avantageux d'aller au devant des dangers en attaquant & en donnant la peur & la mort à son ennemy, que de combattre foiblement ou de fuir avec lascheté en recevant l'une & l'autre.[28]

His belief in the value of self-reliance and individual effort shows Mélinte to be made of heroic stuff. It is a belief which is expressed more firmly as the novel progresses and the extent of his heroic stature is revealed just before he is to be sacrificed. In comforting Ariane, he declares that death is an acceptable alternative to a life of contented inactivity if it comes when *gloire* is at its highest:

Hé bien, Ariane, disoit-il, qu'avions-nous plus à desirer des Dieux, sinon de nous laisser joüir en repos de nostre amitié? S'ils me refusent une vie oisive, & s'ils m'ordonnent la mort lors qu'il ne me reste plus d'honneur à acquerir, dois-je me plaindre d'eux de ce qu'ils me retirent au periode le plus illustre de ma vie?[29]

This feeling in Mélinte that happiness is to be found not simply by avoiding troubles and settling into a peaceful married life but by earning the satisfaction of a great reputation points away from the tradition of the Greek romances and towards the heroic novel proper. Desmarets drew his inspiration mainly from Heliodorus and was therefore led to create a plot in which malevolent opponents were the chief obstacle to success. If he had been created in the mould of Théagènes, Mélinte might never have emerged from the mass of Sicilian citizens to make his mark upon the world, if it had not been for the movements of fate and the passions of others. However, he has been endowed with a force of character which, particularly towards the end of the novel, makes it inevitable that he will be acknowledged as a leader and attain great glory. He has become the sort of man to impose himself upon the situations confronting him, to dictate how life is to treat him, to retain his moral independence by means of action, rather than the kind of figure found in the *romans d'aventures* of Du Verdier and Du Bail, forced by fortune into unlikely situations and saved from ultimate disaster only by luck.

Though Mélinte's commitment to *gloire* is not as developed as Oroondate's or Britomare's was to be, it none the less gives him an honourable place at the head of a line of greater heroes, and marks *Ariane* out as something new emerging from the tradition of passivity in the novel.

Hotman de Latour, the author of the *Histoire celtique*, did not have Desmarets' talent for telling a story or his ability to create convincing characters. His novel, however, represents an important step towards the delineation of a complete hero. The intention, we are told in the *Advertissement*, is to present 'un Heros parfait', such that neither Cyrus, Aeneas, Achilles, nor Odysseus can be compared to him. The setting for his appearance is Gaul in the pre-Roman period, centred on Marseilles at a time when the Carthaginians had established themselves there, and the hero in question is Palingène, recognized eventually as the grandson and heir of Timarque, Roi des Gaules. The whole work is concerned with his success in ridding his country of the Carthaginians and with his love for the fair Célanire. Only five books were published, the author promising a further five if the public's reaction was favourable, so the hero's ultimate triumph at the climax of his monarchical and emotional careers can only be assumed.

From the start, the reader is left in no doubt that Palingène is a being of such exceptional qualities that he exists on a different plane from the rest of humanity. Within the first few pages, his extraordinarily forceful character is established. A prisoner of the Carthaginians, he is driven together with other slaves into a mine, but his expression and bearing are such that his captivity is turned into a triumph:

> Il s'y remarquoit une telle majesté, qu'il ne sembloit pas tant demander de la commiseration, de l'assistance & de l'amitié, que promettre la liberté aux compagnons de sa mauvaise fortune, la clemence à ceux qui soumettroient leurs volontez aux siennes, & aux Barbares, qui le tenoient captif, ou la servitude ou la perte de la vie.[30]

All his fellow-slaves look to him as their leader, even another aristocrat who becomes his contant companion: '[Cleomedon] l'avoit à son arrivée remarqué par dessus tous les esclaves, & reconnu en son visage je ne sçay quoy d'illustre & de grand, qui luy estoit un signe infaillible d'une parfaite noblesse.'[31] Wherever he goes, the effect of his charisma is immediate: 'Les Dieux avoient imprimé sur le front de PALINGENE un si royal caractere que tous ceux qui le consideroient & qui le sçavoient bien cognoistre devenoient incontinent esclaves de ses volontez'[32] From an early age, he had been noted for his wisdom, his skill at all forms of exercise, and his natural grace.[33]

Palingène's valour is affirmed at many points, though without a great deal of space being devoted to descriptions of him in action. The desired impression is mostly achieved by suggestion: in battle, he 'tailloit en pieces autant d'ennemis qu'il en rencontroit: . . . son courage valoit beaucoup plus que cent hommes'.[34] The author is careful too to avoid straining credibility too much. To kill twenty men within half an hour is considered impressive enough.[35] Nor is he invincible, for at a crucial moment in the plot, while defending Célanire, he is beaten down by superior numbers and left for dead.[36] Like his other qualities, however, Palingène's valour is in a different category from that of other mortals: he is clearly differentiated from his companion Cléomédon, 'qui par des effects prodigieux de son courage eust rendu sa valeur egale à celle de PALINGENE, *si elle n'eust esté incomparable'*.[37]

This superhuman status is part of a divine plan, for providence watches over Palingène. His escape from captivity, for instance, is made possible by the intervention of the gods, 'qui avoient aresté de tout temps de le rendre le plus glorieux homme de la terre'.[38] They send a violent storm which scatters the Carthaginians; lightning strikes one of the prisoners dead and burns through the fetters of Palingène who is standing alongside, without harming him. An earthquake completes the destruction necessary for his escape and he succeeds in rallying a small group of survivors, ultimately forming an army and defeating the enemy.

The author constantly impresses upon the reader the idea that heroes operate according to special imperatives, a code of behaviour related to *gloire* and *vertu*. The text is reinforced with maxims stating the general principle behind the action that has just taken place, e.g.

Aussi est-ce l'ordinaire des grands courages de n'aimer point à estre violentez, n'y ayant rien qui les fasche davantage que de se voir forcez aux choses qu'ils ne desirent pas, principalement par des personnes qui leur sont inferieures (I, 165).

les maux servent aux courages nobles d'un fort aiguillon à la vertu (II, 641).

Il n'y a rien qui oblige d'avantage les Grands que la modestie, & qui avance plus à la gloire & à l'honneur que l'humilité (II, 477).

Qu'il est indigne d'un grand courage d'apprehender la mort jusques au point de s'humilier pour une telle crainte envers une personne qui nous est inferieure (I, 73-74).

Similarly, passages of verse are interpolated in the text, not as in *L'Astrée* or *Ariane* to provide lyrical intermissions, but to emphasize noble sentiments and draw attention to particularly important tenets of heroism, such as the duties of kingship or the hero's attitude towards fate:

> C'est le propre d'un grand courage
> De se roidir contre le sort,
> Et de s'opposer à l'effort
> De la tempeste & de l'orage,
> Surtout quand il void en danger
> Son amy pour le desgager (I, 98).

Hotman de Latour was concerned that his readers should be quite clear as to the qualities necessary in a hero and evidently believed that such heroes could exist in an imperfect world.

Though it is created as the abode of supermen, the world in which the story takes place is realistic in comparison with that depicted in the contemporary derivatives of the romances of chivalry, such as those by de Logeas. There are detailed descriptions of Carthage, its buildings, harbour, public places, exports, etc., references to political divisions in Sicily, evocations of ceremonies in Marseilles,[39] and so on. However, by a technique which was to become standard practice in the heroic novel, Hotman de Latour raised this ostensibly normal world to a level of splendour and magnificence which put it outside the range of experience of the ordinary reader: the trappings of life, the clothes, furnishings, and decorations within which the characters display their heroic qualities are superb, too richly made for any but the highest level of society. Each detail is described in turn. Mérissanthe's tent is of velvet and cloth of gold, covered in precious stones with windows of crystal.[40] She invites Palingène into her chariot: 'l'etoffe en estoit d'yvoire & d'ebene enchassée d'or & d'argent: le daiz de velours noir rehaussé d'une riche broderie faite à fleurs naturelles, d'où se formoient des couronnes & des festons accompagnez de trophées d'amour & de guerre'.[41] A substantial part of the story takes place on the Isle de Titan, an earthly paradise with everything to delight the eye and the palate. There are vines and fruit-trees of every sort, flowers and groves, beautiful gardens where the nobles can linger: 'les allées y sont longues & à perte de veuë, accompagnées de berceaux, de cabinets, de solitudes & de labyrinthes, avec des canaux, des fontaines & des cascades d'eaux fort agreables à la veuë & à l'oreille,' etc.[42]

It is implied at certain points in the *Histoire celtique*, however, that this rarefied heroic world shared certain features with Parisian polite society to which the majority of its readers would belong and, by extension, that even the more ordinary person belonging to that society could participate to some extent in the ideals of heroism by observing the code of *honnêteté*. There is, for example, a certain amount of time devoted to involved compliments made up of intricate formulas[43] and the kind of schedule of leisure that no doubt prevailed in salon circles.[44] In places, the concessions made to the salon audience result in a distinctly unheroic tone, as when the conversation turns to the differences between the women of various nations[45] or when Célanire invents a whispering game,[46] but this was no doubt precisely the sort of interlude that appealed to the reader.

Palingène himself certainly has the correct degree of sensibility towards his beloved required by such a readership: he can fix his mind on Célanire, sigh, and faint without further ado.[47] But there is no equivocation over the essentially male basis of heroism. Love is not allowed to take precedence over honour. Both Palingène and Célanire accept that his *gloire* must be preserved at all costs if their relationship is to continue to exist. When one of the stands at a public spectacle collapses and wild beasts escape into the crowd, Palingène's first reaction is to save Célanire from the tiger that is threatening her. Having achieved this, it is honour which dictates the need to continue the rescue work: 'L'amour le vouloit bien attacher pres de CELANIRE, mais l'honneur l'en divertit, ayant porté son courage à servir d'exemple à tous les autres Chevaliers, qui furent tesmoins d'une aventure si noble & dont l'evenement en devoit estre si formidable.'[48]

The main feature of *l'Histoire celtique* which establishes it firmly in the line of the heroic novel and differentiates it from the earlier type of novel is the strong commitment to heroism based on energy. Palingène is a man who is determined to overcome all obstacles. There is nothing in him of the recourse to lamentation favoured by the Greek heroes: disasters encourage him to persevere and calamities produce redoubled effort: 'Ce fut en quoy PALINGENE tesmoigna d'avoir atteint au plus haut point de la perfection, car il se fortifia dans une si longue suite de desastres au lieu d'en estre affoibli.'[49] He draws strength from within himself; his will injects moral courage into every part of his being and will not allow him to succumb to adversity. Even when his greatest hope has been dashed by the abduction of Célanire, he refuses to acknowledge that this is anything more than a temporary victory for fortune; his misery transforms itself into a new resolution and his *vertu* creates the basis of a new hope:

il sceut faire paroistre à ses amis par une force d'esprit & par un courage
invincible, tout le contraire de ce qu'ils avoient pensé: Ce ne fut pas la
nécessité qui le fit roidir contre ce malheur, mais plustost une habitude
qu'il avoit prise à souffrir de grandes infortunes, & une vertu qui se
rencontre en peu de personnes: Que si quelquesfois la foiblesse, qui est
naturelle aux hommes, vouloit s'opposer à sa resolution & à la grandeur
de son courage, il se faisoit alors des leçons secretes, & se disoit à soy-
mesme: Où estes-vous, ma constance, m'avez-vous abandonné? Et vous,
ma valeur, estes-vous endormie? Prenez courage PALINGENE, & portez
le faix de ce nouveau desastre. Voilà comme il faisoit renaistre ses
esperances, & qu'il treuvoit sa propre conservation dans l'adversité.[50]

The actual number of heroic deeds accomplished by
Palingène is not in fact very large. He is always supported
by his companions when required to fight, and in battle is
not particularly notable for his individual prowess. There
are occasions when the chance to indulge in some lengthy
description of valour is ignored by the author;[51] nor has
he taken the opportunity to develop the image of his hero's
virtue by showing him fighting against opponents who share
his ideals, as later writers made a special point of doing.
Palingène only ever pits his strength against wicked enemies
and there are not even any tournaments in which he might
meet his moral equals.

None the less, the *Histoire celtique* stands out as a prototype of the heroic novel by its commitment to energy, the
underlying belief that man's will-power enables him to rise
above the arbitrary workings of fortune and impose the
pattern that he has decided upon. Every episode reflects
this attitude and is reinforced by a liberal use of heroic
epithets designed to exalt human endeavour and make it
admirable in its own right — 'tant de belles executions &
d'extraordinaires prodiges de vaillance,' 'les grands prodiges,
les merveilles extraordinaires,' 'des merveilles incroyables &
des grandeurs infinies,' etc. The reader is presented with a
series of illustrations of human action at its highest and is
invited to applaud an incarnation of all the best qualities
in man.

Hotman de Latour was not gifted as a novelist: he did not
know how to present his material, how to highlight the
points necessary to give movement and tension to a story;
but he succeeded in delineating a more positive heroic figure

than any that had gone before. Most of the features to be found later in Oroondate and Cyrus were already present in Palingène, appealing to a public increasingly interested in men of grandeur and will-power who obey the imperatives of sublimity and exaltation, the public that responded so readily to *Le Cid*.

CHAPTER VIII

POLEXANDRE

Polexandre, chronologically the first of the major heroic novels, is of particular interest because the definitive version of 1637 was preceded by three earlier versions[1] in which Gomberville accorded an increasing importance to the part played by a central hero and which consequently provide a useful confirmation of the trend indicated in other novels such as *Ariane* and *l'Histoire celtique*.

When he first turned his mind to the adventures of Polexandre, Gomberville was apparently only nineteen years old. His reading up to that age must have included a fair number of examples of the *roman sentimental* in vogue at the time, since most of his first venture, *L'Exil de Polexandre et d'Ericlée*, is made up of a series of loosely interconnected love adventures in which young couples are prevented from achieving happiness by the attempts of their parents to marry them off to others.[2] The world in which these characters move is an everyday world, with innkeepers, *archers* and sailors playing central rôles. In the fifth and last chapter, the characters find and read a book entitled *L'Exil de Polexandre et d'Ericlée* which tells the story of Polexandre, how he came to the court of Henri II as a boy, fell in love with Ericlée, was exiled for killing a rival who had challenged him, met a hermit who turned out to be his mother and himself became a hermit.[3] The work is in most respects an absurd concoction, fully justifying its author's self-deprecating references to 'la vaine confusion de cette nouvelle histoire'.[4]

There are indications, however, in the pages devoted to Polexandre's period at court that Gomberville was trying to create a type of hero somewhat more outstanding than the bourgeois characters of the *roman sentimental*. Polexandre is intended to be a paragon of chivalry, 'de qui le nom & les incomparables vertus sont espanduës par tout le monde',[5] who, while still a youth, 'se persuadoit que les choses les plus difficiles se devoient rendre aysées par la grandeur de son courage'.[6] Few words are devoted to the joust and the duel in which he is involved[7] but this is compensated for by the spectacle he provides as he arrives for a tournament, announcing himself as 'l'Amour' and heading an extraordinary procession of allegorical figures representing the four elements, the twelve signs of the zodiac, and so on.[8] These same pages reveal the beginnings of Gomberville's cult of the superlative which was to develop over the succeeding editions of his work.[9]

Ten years later, when a new version, entitled *L'Exil de Polexandre*, appeared, Polexandre was still only an embryonic hero. His story here is broadly similar to that of the 1619 prototype — he is a young nobleman at the court of Henri II who falls in love with Olimpe, heads a procession of allegorical figures, fights against the Huguenots in the Religious Wars, is banished from court for a year over an incident with the royal favourite, and goes to Denmark to fight Phélismond whose love for Olimpe has offended her.[10] He does not appear until over half-way through the work and for much of the time is subordinate to other chracters, such as Montmorency during the Religious Wars, or Bajazet, the pirate chief, for whom he captains a vessel. Feats of individual prowess are secondary to military actions and naval battles, viewed from afar with little concern for heroic contributions. The tone of the work sinks at times to a low level in the story of Sinas, an ordinary sea-captain, and in a description of the pirates' drunken revels.[11]

That the 1629 version represented an attempt to depict a more heroic kind of Polexandre is, however, affirmed by Gomberville: 'ne luy trouvant ny la qualité ny le merite que je luy aurois souhaité, je voulus me rendre le maistre de sa fortune et de sa condition, et . . . le porter aussi haut que mon imagination pouvoit aller'.[12] What strikes the reader is the emphasis given to the quality of the relationships between the central characters, Polexandre, Bajazet, and Zelmatide, an Inca prince. They are all members of the same superior caste, having more in common with each other than with the men they command. Their contacts with one another are always conducted at a high level of *courtoisie* and they converse in the language of heroic *générosité*. Bajazet, though chief of a band of pirates who acknowledge no law but their own, constantly refers to *gloire*, *vertu*, and *valeur* and implies that for him such qualities are always associated with altruistic morality. The relationship between Polexandre and Phélismond provides an example of the heroic outlook in action. Though Olimpe had ordered Polexandre to challenge Phélismond, their mutual *générosité* draws them together and they become close friends: when they eventually fight, the combat is thus one of the highest *vertu* rather than of belligerent enemies.[13]

It was this latter aspect of the novel which Gomberville developed and refined for the 1632 version, now simply called *Polexandre*. Many of the episodes and descriptions have been retained, sometimes verbatim, but the tone of the work has been raised still further by the excision of the baser elements. The main emphasis has now moved to the glory of individual action. All the major characters are endowed with superhuman strength and martial skill, and each is given the chance to impress both his companions and the reader in a battle-scene or duel, but their feats are executed with such concern for the tenets of courtesy that they have little in common with the butcherings described in *Amadis*. When Polexandre, here metamorphosed into Charles Martel, fights the duc d'Aquitaine, he knocks him off his horse but immediately jumps to the ground to help him '& fit cette action avec une si grande generosité, que mesme la pensée ne luy vint pas de se servir de son advantage'.[14] The Phélismond episode has been extended to accommodate a greater amount of *généreux* behaviour, with Polexandre and Phélismond each offering to die for the other. All the valiant characters admire each other's prowess and pay fulsome compliments on it.[15]

The 1632 version is distinguished from its predecessors primarily by the fact that the characters no longer exist merely as actors in a series of incidents: the incidents are now created as a means of allowing the characters to display their *vertu*. They exist in their own right, which Gomberville conceded had not been the case with Polexandre in the first two versions of the novel.[16] Once the emphasis had been moved in this way to an idealized form of behaviour, heroism could emerge in its complete form.

When the final version of *Polexandre* appeared in 1637, Gomberville had reached maturity as a novelist. Of the preceding versions, certain episodes were retained which contributed either to the heroic tone or to the exotic atmosphere, but the work as a whole shows a completeness of conception that is entirely new. The construction is skilful if at times confusing to the modern reader and reveals an imaginative scope which surpasses most of the other novels of the time. Having none of the inhibitions that beset those novelists who saw themselves as writers of prose epics, Gomberville eagerly takes his reader through Mexico, Senegal, Denmark, and the Congo as well as the more traditional Mediterranean lands. In each, he tries to introduce the flavour of the society in question and, though the major protagonists tend to share the same cosmopolitan attitudes, there is a range of secondary characters whose features are quite clearly differentiated. In particular, the analysis of love is remarkably subtle for the period, with an awareness, not found elsewhere in his day, of the implications of the *je ne sais quoi* element, expressed not in long abstract discussions but through the reactions of lovers.

Gomberville had in fact succeeded in creating a new kind of novel based on a heroic view of man, affirming with confidence elements only sketched out in *Ariane* and *l'Histoire celtique* and in the earlier versions of *Polexandre*. There are features which suggest links with earlier forms of novel, but they are in general peripheral and do not affect the central action (e.g. an occasional giant or a supernatural intervention of the sort found in *Amadis*, an episode or two worthy of Camus' *Spectacles d'horreur*).[17] Though there is a wide range of incidents, they all relate directly to the overriding theme of the glorification of man's capabilities as embodied in a small number of exceptional beings who rise above the ordinary run of mortals.

At the summit of the pyramid is Polexandre himself, universally acknowledged to be the greatest of men. In this, the fourth and final of his metamorphoses, he is king of the

Canary Islands, a descendant of Charles d'Anjou and son of the heiress of the Palaeologue line. He is visually arresting and impresses other people both by his appearance and his personality as semi-divine: 'il vint au monde avec ces excellentes qualitez que l'aage, l'estude & l'experience vendent bien cherement aux hommes ordinaires. Son ame en descendant du Ciel en terre se conserva tout ce qu'elle avoit receu au lieu de son origine.'[18] The idea that he has a link with heaven is reinforced by his strong religious convictions (a feature he shares with the other heroes in his world, even though their beliefs may be pagan): he always gives thanks after a victory and works actively to spread Christianity, preaching the word in Africa and persuading the inhabitants of l'Isle du Soleil to give up human sacrifice.[19] His mind turns naturally to helping others, so that he 'sembloit estre choisi par le Ciel, pour estre le consolateur de tous les affligez'.[20] Those in trouble recognize at once his special destiny as a saviour: 'D'abord que je vous ay vû, il m'a semblé que vous m'apportiez le remede que le Ciel reserve pour la guerison de mes maux.'[21]

Polexandre's altruism and that of the other major characters is reflected in the meaning given to the heroic epithets which abound in the text. *Générosité*, by far the most frequently used, invariably has an altruistic sense:

la compassion que sa haute generosité l'obligeoit d'avoir des personnes affligées . . .[22]

vostre generosité vous faisant compâtir à ses horribles souffrances, . . .[23]

Sa generosité s'irritant à l'objet d'un si noir assassinat, il se jetta au milieu de ces combattans.[24]

Combats reflect the same interpretation of the values of heroism. Battles and duels are described only in so far as they contribute to an appreciation of the hero's noble qualities. If an encounter does no more than further the plot, it is usually dismissed very quickly, sometimes with the suggestion that mere aggression is of no real interest: 'Vous sçavez bien de quelle sorte un homme fort vaillant se démesle de semblables occasions; c'est pourquoy je ne vous ennuiray point de ce qui se passa en celle-cy. Le Roy de Thombut y fit tout ce qu'un homme qui se fait nommer l'Indomptable peut faire.'[25] Combats between morally comparable individuals are accorded more space, but here too it is not so much the valour which merits attention as the magnanimity shown when valour has proved itself. The author is fond of producing a general impression of enormous skill and courage by the use of quasi-Homeric evocations which provide the requisite heroic flavour without committing him to any great detail.[26]

If Bajazet and Zelmatide are capable of heroic actions and attitudes, Polexandre is something of a superhero, so far superior to other men that he exists in moral solitude despite his concern for their welfare. Experience has taught him that he will never be able to fit in to ordinary life even as a king, and, depending on his mood, he considers himself destined for the greatest glory or damned to spiritual isolation and unheard-of tribulations. It is experience, too, which prompts his *confident* Alcippe to declare 'vous ne seriez pas ce que vous estes, si les choses ne vous arrivoient autrement qu'au reste des hommes'.[27] While his friends seem to come to terms with opposing circumstances and manage to settle down in peace, Polexandre is pursued by fortune and feels that he will never be allowed to find happiness. His life takes the form of a quest for a goal which he comes close to considering unattainable at a number of points, that of finding Alcidiane. He has no other aim and his conscience raises no objection to his leaving his kingdom for long periods in the care of a viceroy: he returns from time to time to attend to any problems that may have arisen but becomes less and less interested in his subjects and eventually leaves for good, vowing never to return and never willingly to set foot in any kingdom other than Alcidiane's.[28] When he is offered the throne of Zahara, he accepts to the great acclamations of the people but promptly appoints a viceroy and leaves again.[29]

The love that drives Polexandre on is different from that enjoyed by the other heroic characters. His friends, notably Zelmatide and Bajazet, have normal relationships with the women they love, within the terms of *galanterie*. They make a declaration and are accepted for a probationary period during which they are kept at a distance; the woman eventually

makes her own declaration and the two are married in due
course.[30] Other characters experience a much less happy
form of love, being possessed by a demonic desire for another
person; they lose all consideration for their status and reputation and usually come to a tragic end, a warning to others
of the devastating effects of passion.[31]

Polexandre's relationship with Alcidiane is unique in the
novel. Alcidiane is in an entirely different category from the
other female characters, and in fact has no predecessor in
the seventeenth-century novel. She has many of the attributes
of a mystical ideal, suggesting the rose in the *Roman de la
Rose*. She inhabits an almost unreal world, an island which is
all but inaccessible, so fertile that it enjoys two harvests a
year and fruits at all seasons: gold, silver, and diamonds
abound and the inhabitants are so vigorous that at the age
of eighty they still seem young.[32] Alcidiane keeps herself
away from public gaze except for state occasions and makes
her will known through her 'slaves', ministers who wear
golden chains as a mark of their servitude. The unreality is
extended into the outside world, for no one objects when she
forbids a tournament taking place in Morocco or calls on all
knights to avenge her upon Phélismond, who has been
declaring in Denmark that he alone is worthy of her.[33] Very
little detail is given of her appearance, since this would
detract from the quasi-divine aura that surrounds her.[34]

The semi-religious aspect is emphasized by the way Alcidiane is approached by those who love her. Her beauty is so
perfect that many feel themselves obliged to serve her, but
they are by no means all of the same type. Pisandre is socially
much lower than Polexandre or Phélismond; Abdelmélec is
généreux only in the sense of 'courageous' and does not live
by the rules of *courtoisie*. Almanzor falls in love with Alcidiane's portrait and dies, never having seen her, calling out
in a pseudo-religious ecstasy:

puisque comme les Dieux, ô Alcidiane, . . . tu regnes absolument sur
l'esprit de ceux qui ne t'ont jamais veuë, je me persuade que comme eux
aussi, tu vois nos actions & lis mesme dans nos pensées. Tourne donc les
yeux sur Almanzor & reçoy pour marque de son eternelle fidelité la
vie qu'il abandonne sans regret, puisque c'est à toy seule qu'elle est
sacrifiée.[35]

Almanzor-Bajazet on the other hand honours her but does not feel drawn towards her service: 'Je la trouve digne des vœux de tous les cœurs qui sont capables d'amour. Mais je ne suis pas assez honneste homme pour pretendre à la gloire de la servir.'[36] She appears therefore to act as an ideal for those who need to prostrate themselves before a wrathful divinity. Certainly Polexandre's approach to her is at times that of a man who considers himself damned, impelled towards her but knowing that death awaits him if ever he comes near her.[37]

The relationship between Polexandre and Alcidiane is by no means an abstract one, however. Gomberville has produced a study in ambivalence which makes Polexandre both an archetypal hero and a strongly characterized individual, an ambivalence which emerges in his dual approach to Alcidiane, as a hero and as a lover.

As a hero, he is obliged to seek for the ideal and, having identified it, to devote all his energies to trying to reach it. His holy grail is Alcidiane on her elusive island and nothing is allowed to prevent him from moving towards her. If ever the quest became hopeless, life would end: 'que tu sçavois bien, ô grand Almanzor!' he cries, 'qu'Alcidiane estoit la seule felicité que les Heros avoient à rechercher sur la Terre; & que tu fis bien de perdre la vie, quand tu perdis l'esperance d'arriver à cette Beatitude.'[38] Whatever obstacles fortune puts in his way will therefore be overcome or he will die in the attempt. Maintaining a forward impetus is an essential concomitant of his heroic status.[39]

On occasion, when it looks as though fortune may have succeeded in cutting him off from success, he almost gives in to despair, but his will-power and devotion to his quest invariably win through. If he is left alive after a shipwreck or a battle, he takes it as a sign that he is intended to carry on his search.[40] The striving is an end in itself, a destiny which he cannot escape and which must not be affected by his own weariness:

Je suis resolu de consumer toute ma vie apres une entreprise qui ne me sera pas moins glorieuse que je la treuve impossible; . . . je vay sans rien attendre, ny de la Fortune ny de l'Amour, m'acquitter de ce que je dois à vostre incomparable merite, à la necessité de ma condition,

& à mes propres sentimens.[41]

Il faut que j'obeïsse à mes destinées, & que sans craindre l'orage, ny esperer le calme, j'acheve le voyage qu'elles m'ont fait entreprendre. Je sçay que cette timidité qu'on appelle raison voudroit bien par ses considerations specieuses me faire perdre l'envie, apres m'avoir osté l'esperance. Mais ses conseils sont trop lasches pour estre escoutez, & la grande Alcidiane ne seroit pas ce qu'elle est, si la raison ou la fortune se pouvoient opposer à ce qu'elle a resolu.[42]

It follows that no threats or conditions, even from Alcidiane, can influence his resolve. When Alcidiane proclaims that Polexandre will be put to death if he tries to see her, it is simply a statement of what will befall him after he has fulfilled his destiny: whether he lives or dies afterwards is immaterial provided he has achieved his goal: 'Je cherche Alcidiane, je soûpire apres elle, & ne souhaitte que le bonheur de sa veuë, encore que . . . elle m'ait declaré criminel, & que par un Arrest irrevocable, elle vueïlle que je sois immolé sur les Autels du Dieu des vangeances.'[43]

Polexandre's destiny as a hero is therefore not to obey the will of Alcidiane, as Cyrus was to see his destiny in obedience to Mandane, but to strive to attain the ideal that she represents without regard to her feelings on the matter. The demands of heroism have an absolute validity. Though the other major characters have more normal relationships than Polexandre, there is a general agreement amongst the men that female values must not be allowed to intrude into the world of heroic energy. The men may be subject to the wishes of their ladies in certain matters but the ladies must accept the supremacy of heroic criteria. When Bajazet, supported by Polexandre and Iphidamante, is besieging the capital of Morocco in order to recover a portrait of Cydarie (whom he has with him), the ladies, Almanzaïre, Cydarie, and Mélicerte, suggest that such an action is excessive, but Bajazet's father rejects their arguments as 'des preuves de la timidité du sexe', and Polexandre and Iphidamante 'n'ayant garde de desapprouver une pensée si conforme aux leurs, conjurerent Bajazet de ne se pas laisser vaincre aux persuasions des Dames'.[44]

As a lover rather than as a hero, that is, when considering Alcidiane as a person with whom he has a relationship rather than as an ideal he must strive to attain, Polexandre has no will of his own. If ever his mind begins to form the idea that he has any kind of right or claim where Alcidiane is concerned, he suppresses it ruthlessly:

que je suis lâche & perfide, dit-il, de me considerer plustost que l'incomparable beauté pour qui je souffre! Au lieu de benir les peines qu'elle veut que j'endure, & courir au trespas puisque je ne sçaurois luy rendre d'autres preuves de la tres-humble servitude, je veux composer avec elle, trouver des modifications en ses arrests, n'accomplir sa volonté que conditionnellement, choisir moy-mesme le genre de mon supplice, bref ne me presenter au martyre qu'apres estre asseuré de la Couronne. Loin, bien loin de moy cette amour propre.[45]

Despoüillons-nous donc de toute sorte de volonté, & demeurant dans une indifference generale pour nous-mesme, allons apprendre de la bouche de nostre Juge, s'il nous faut ou vivre ou mourir.[46]

He is filled with a conviction of his own inadequacy and refuses to believe that he has the slightest prospect of happiness with Alcidiane, even when he is confronted with evidence from reliable observers: 'à peine se fut-il arresté un moment sur un si agreable sujet que le desepoir & l'incredulité luy osterent de l'esprit toutes ces belles idées. Il rentra dans les deffiances qu'il avoit tousjours euës de soy-mesme.'[47] When the name of Alcidiane is mentioned, he trembles and grows pale.[48]

Gomberville makes it plain that this attitude is peculiar to Polexandre and is caused by his underestimation of himself rather than because it is a necessary element in a heroic love relationship. The other characters do not share his attitude, limiting themselves to a sufficient degree of modesty and deference, and disinterested persons point out to him that he is doing himself an injustice by treating himself as so unworthy: 'vostre esprit ne cessera jamais d'estre ingenieux à vous persecuter,' says the faithful Dicée. 'Il doute eternellement de la verité des biens qui vous arrivent; & les seules apparences du mal passent aupres de luy pour de tres-certaines realitez.'[49] There is even the suggestion that Polexandre's reactions are somewhat ridiculous. When a meeting is finally arranged between Alcidiane and Polexandre, he trembles so much that he loses control of his limbs and can only stumble down the stairs leading to her chamber. Amynthe, the *confidente*, chokes with laughter and asks him if he knows where he is. 'Comment le sçaurois-je? luy respondit serieusement ce Prince, si mesme je ne sçay pas ce que je suis.'[50]

This is in keeping with a certain ironic detachment on Gomberville's part which manifests itself at times. He suggests that lovers are incapable of seeing their situation clearly: they exaggerate the beauty and qualities of the one they love,[51] and he does not always make it plain whether the view of a character he is giving is his own objective view or that of an infatuated lover. It is an ambivalence which applies to Alcidiane: the reality is different from Polexandre's idealized view of her. Far from being an allegorical abstraction, she is an individual with complex emotions, though the extent of their complexity does not emerge until Volume V, since for most of the novel she remains at a distance, issuing edicts for others to obey.

All that she feels revolves around an overriding need for emotional freedom. 'Je suis née libre', she cries[52] when the prospect of having to marry against her will threatens, as though this were enough to cancel out all other obligations, and 'je luy offre ma liberté'[53] is the ultimate statement she can make about her love for Polexandre. Though she is attracted to him, she finds the idea that she might be beholden to him impossible to accept and is led into ungenerous thoughts as a result, imputing the victories he has won on her behalf to a desire on his part to erode 'la liberté de laquelle nous nous vantons'. She is capable of tortuous reasoning in opposition to the evidence: 'je m'imagine encore que les extrémes humilitez de Polexandre ne sont point sans orgueil; & qu'il met toute sa vanité à ne la point faire paroistre'.[54] The crime for which Polexandre is forbidden to return to her island is that he had not regarded her 'avec toute la terreur & toute la reverence que l'on doit avoir pour les choses sainctes'.[55]

By the final stage of the novel, when Polexandre is presumed dead, her feelings have clarified themselves sufficiently to allow her to acknowledge that she had loved him; a dream in which the wounded Polexandre calls to her for help reveals the truth behind her pride: 'en cette extremité mon affection m'a fait oublier ce que j'estois'.[56] As soon as she suspects that she is being manipulated or tricked, however, her pride reasserts itself and she angrily assumes that Polexandre merely wishes to boast how he had made her fall in love with him.[57]

The basis for this sensitivity and fear of humiliation is a belief that love is a weakness which leads to complete subjection to the will of another. Being a queen, Alcidiane has to maintain her moral status, and there is ample evidence in *Polexandre* of the disasters that can ensue when love is allowed to rule the reason. Her resistance to love and marriage arises from a fear of derogating from her supreme position, and her submission to Polexandre at the end of the novel is an acknowledgment that the passivity associated with woman must give way to the active values of heroism, to a man, as she tells her people, 'qui par la merveille de ses actions a merité d'estre vostre Maistre & le mien'.[58]

The *sévérité* of Alcidiane, though eventually overcome, adumbrates the attitudes characteristic of *préciosité* some years later, and Adam was no doubt correct in describing her as 'la première en date des précieuses',[59] but it should be remembered that Gomberville does not concern himself with the kind of intellectual analysis of love that was to be such an important feature of *Clelie*; still less does he reduce love to the level of a society game. He constantly stresses the fact that love is a force which can swamp all the other faculties and pervert normal moral and social standards. It brings disaster and death in some cases to ordinary people. In this respect, Gomberville is closer to Racine than to the *précieuses*.

From a technical point of view, the relationship between Polexandre and Alcidiane represents an important innovation in that the tension between the lovers has become the main source of the impetus of the plot, giving it a self-contained momentum, rather as one spring in a clock works against another. Though *L'Astrée* had depended to a certain extent on a similar tension between hero and heroine, the majority of seventeenth-century novels before *Polexandre* had depicted hero and heroine reacting together against the external and unpredictable onslaughts of fate. Gomberville showed that the interplay of psychological forces arising from the nature of love offered a much richer basis for the construction of a novel, and his lead was to be followed by most of the writers of heroic novels.

For Gomberville, heroism is a destiny visited upon certain individuals, comparable in some ways with the religious concept of grace. It is not a destiny that can be chosen or created by the individual himself, however great his will-power. It makes the recipient aware of an ideal which he then exerts himself to the utmost to attain: his devotion to the ideal becomes the sole purpose of his life and takes precedence over other responsibilities, such as the duties of kingship. Though he is normally a king or a prince, his position does not bring any privileges which he has not deserved by his own merits.

The life he leads is one of action. Since he belongs to the small group of men who can stand up to fortune, he has an obligation to alleviate the misfortunes of others, an obligation which he accepts naturally and completely. Others look to him for help, aware that he can bring qualities to bear which are outside their capacity. The standards of *générosité* according to which he conducts his life are not the same as those of ordinary *honnêteté* which operate in the society of lesser mortals, but represent a higher concept of behaviour which can only be admired by the majority.

His destiny is not simply one of self-fulfilment, as it was to be for the heroes in *Cassandre*. Sometimes it brings him into situations which are the very opposite of *jouissance*. He is not concerned with the acquisition of *gloire*, though his actions bring him immense fame. As he helps his fellows, so he rises above them. He responds to imperatives applicable only to supermen and follows a path through life which leads him morally away from the rest of mankind. The more heroic he proves himself to be, the more isolated he becomes from his fellow beings, even those who can claim to share some of his aspirations: 'le héros devient une sorte de statue, un monument que tout le monde peut visiter et qui doit éblouir tout le monde'.[60]

By his clear depiction of a superior kind of human being devoted to furthering the good of mankind, Gomberville has a strong claim to be considered the founder of the heroic novel. There has been a tendency amongst modern literary historians, however, to place *Polexandre* outside the heroic novel proper because its author did not subscribe to the theory that the novel was a prose epic with fixed rules as to its construction and subject-matter.[61] In fact, Gomberville concerned himself a good deal with history. He had written a *Discours des vertus et des vices de l'histoire* (1620), and *Polexandre* is firmly set in a period he knew well, the late fifteenth century: references in the text to Vasco da Gama's return from India, Boabdil's withdrawal from Granada, the reigns of Louis XII and Henry VII of England,[62] etc. enable the events of the novel to be dated between 1492 and 1499. There is also a certain concern for verisimilitude in matters involving the differences between nations. Several languages have to be tried on strangers to find out which one they know, and new languages have to be learnt. Arriving in Denmark, Polexandre is careful to land away from big towns and takes precautions to dress in the local style so that he is not noticed.[63]

These are minor elements, however, in a work which derives its impact primarily from its imaginative scope. Certainly, Gomberville had no time for theories about the structure of the novel. He admitted that he lacked the patience to organize his work properly: 'l'irregularité de mon esprit ne peut souffrir ces importunes & perpetuelles justesses. Il se plaist en la confusion. Il aime les déreiglemens.'[64] But his achievement was to create a truly heroic figure whose exploits and fame covered the whole world and who could embody the highest aspirations of mankind. Questions of form and construction only became of any real importance after the publication in 1641 of *Ibrahim*, in which Scudéry demonstrated how the heroic novel could be put into a more realistic framework. It is equally significant, however, that within the new framework, Scudéry offered an alternative definition of heroism to that embodied in *Polexandre*.

CHAPTER IX

IBRAHIM

The preface to *Ibrahim*[1] makes it plain that its author does not consider the novel to have made any progress since *L'Astrée*. There is evidently a general lack of awareness of the nature and purpose of the novel: reform is necessary, to be carried out by the formulation and application of the rules of the genre, 'qui par des moyens infaillibles meinent à la fin que l'on se propose'. The rules according to which the successful novelist should operate can, he claims, be deduced from the Greek romances: for instance, they limited the plot to one central theme to which all the episodes were attached, they began their story *in medias res* and obeyed a unity of time of one year. The most important rule, according to Scudéry, is that of verisimilitude, without which the novel is merely grotesque: 'cette fauceté grossiere ne fait aucune impression en l'ame & ne donne aucun plaisir'. To ensure truth to life in his own novel, Scudéry has provided details of the religion, customs, and laws of the nations of which he treats; his chief characters are historical; he has limited the number of shipwrecks to which they are subjected.[2]

Verisimilitude, however, means much more than just local colour. It involves the way in which the author approaches his hero (and as a result, the concept of heroism). Nothing is more important, Scudéry declares, than to impress strongly upon the reader the idea or the image of heroes, 'mais en façon qu'ils soyent comme de sa connoissance', for this is what interests the reader in their adventures. Unlike those authors who described superhuman activities and left the reader to assume that they derived from a superhuman mentality, Scudéry wants to analyse the workings of the hero's mind. Heroism lies not in the action but in the motivation and the reasoning behind it, and if the reader is not shown what these are, how is he to know that fortune has not contributed as much as the hero, that his valour is not 'une valeur brutale', and that he has suffered his misfortunes as an *honnête homme*?: 'ce n'est point par les choses de dehors; ce n'est point par les caprices du destin, que je veux juger de luy; c'est par les mouvemens de son ame, & par les choses qu'il dit'.

Such an approach was a step forward in the theory of the novel but in practice its effect was to reduce the scale of the hero and bring him much closer to the everyday world of the 1640s. The world of heroism in *Ibrahim* is not a miraculous region inhabited by exceptional people, but an extension of ordinary experience, only just beyond the reach of the educated and imaginative reader who would have found himself introduced into a world in which he could almost feel at home, in which the social norms were the same as his own though adhered to more punctiliously. The picture of a leisured class moving in surroundings of great opulence is held out to tempt the dreams of Parisian aristocratic and bourgeois society. When an important scene is to take place, the setting is carefully described with particular reference to furnishings, clothes, jewellery, etc.; details of fashion are introduced, no doubt with the aim of allowing the female reader to compare them with those of her own day. Even when the Turkish army is drawn up for battle, there is a description of the materials of which their tents are made, together with the decorations and patterns of colours.[3] The degree of opulence is urged upon the reader as something that he is expected to be able to appreciate, if only in financial terms: on one occasion, when a basket of precious stones is described as being 'd'une valeur si excessive, qu'il y avoit à huict cens mille francs de perles',[4] the mention of their specific value is presumably meant to be the ultimate means of impressing the reader. There is, indeed, in *Ibrahim* an awareness of the importance of money not found in any other heroic novel.[5]

The concern for this kind of *vraisemblance* is based on a belief that the reader will be of a particular type and will have certain tastes. It is assumed that he will be interested in long accounts of the history of Turkey and in descriptions of palaces (though those who are not interested in architecture and 'ces belles choses, pour lesquelles j'ay tant de passion' are invited to ignore the description of Ibrahim's palace).[6] He is encouraged to believe that *Ibrahim* represents a new departure in the concept of the novel in that it derives directly from history and in fact provides information unknown to the historians.[7] Other novelists are mocked for their *naïveté* in endowing their heroes with prodigious memories.[8]

The characters who inhabit this world reinforce the impression that it is only slightly removed from the polite society known to the reader. The tone is set by a group of friends of the hero and heroine, the cream of Genoese society: they sympathize with Justinian and Isabelle, sometimes act as a chorus, discussing whether they have acted correctly or not,[9] but mainly spend their time in conversation and *badinage*. Serious topics are specifically excluded from the gatherings of 'cette belle Troupe, qui n'avoit autre pensée, que celle de se divertir':[10] 'il estoit defendu de parler en ces occasions, ny de la guerre, ny des affaires generales: ... les Vers, la Peinture, la Musique, l'Amour, la Vertu, & toutes les choses qui dependent du bel esprit, estoient les seules dont on pouvoit s'entretenir.'[11] Whole sections of the novel are given over to their discussions on the lighter aspects of love and they take their rather trivial preoccupations with them wherever they go. When they are caught in a storm and become the slaves of the Moroccan royal family, they soon transfer the same salon atmosphere to the Moroccan court and establish the principles of *galanterie* there; a month or so later, they are to be found in the seraglio in Constantinople, still behaving as though they had never left Genoa.[12]

The men of the group are portrayed in such a way that their courage and *générosité* are taken for granted but are felt to be of less importance than their skill in conversation, their wit, and their ability to turn a compliment. The social virtues are given more prominence than the martial ones and are what makes a man admirable. The comte de Lavagne, ambitious and active enough to organize a *coup d'état* in Genoa, is described in terms which call to mind Faret's *honnête homme*: 'Sa beauté, sa bonne mine, sa conversation, sa complaisance, son humeur guaye & enjoüée, l'addresse qu'il avoit à dancer, à joüer du Luth, à chanter, à monter à cheval, & à toutes les choses qui peuvent donner quelque agréement, le rendoient incomparable.'[13] The Marquis français, who had left France for reasons that sufficiently indicate his courage and self-reliance, is greatly in demand, but it is because of his carefree attitude rather than any heroic qualities; in the episodes devoted to him, the only attribute that emerges is his skill in handling a complicated situation and turning it to his advantage.[14]

The hero and heroine, Justinian and Isabelle, are fully integrated members of this group. Though each of them is descended from illustrious ancestors (Justinian from the line of the Palaeologues and Isabelle from the Princes of Monaco), they are for practical purposes members of the Genoese nobility. Justinian is a typical product of that society with the normal accomplishments expected of a young nobleman, but he had not shown any signs of being egregious by the time he left his home town. He sets off on his travels, not in answer to an irrepressible urge for greatness but, like Mélinte in *Ariane*, because of 'l'extreme envie que j'avois tousjours euë, d'aller admirer les pompeuses ruines de l'ancienne Rome, & les grandeurs de la nouvelle'.[15] He learns the art of war as a profession rather than accepting it as a destiny.[16] His skill in fighting is considerable but he is by no means invincible.[17]

It is after he has been sold as a slave in Turkey that his heroic qualities really begin to reveal themselves. The initial impetus is provided by his despair at having, as he thinks, lost Isabelle, but there is obviously also an underlying urge to achieve some kind of distinction, even if the outcome is death. The combination of sorrow at finding himself 'dans une oysiveté honteuse'[18] and the desire to seek some way of dying nobly makes Ibrahim transcend his forced rôle as a foot-soldier and take on that of an inspired leader in the capture of a town. This is the beginning of his success: the Sultan treats him 'comme si j'eusse esté cent degrez au dessus de luy, & par ma naissance, & par mon merite, & par ma valeur',[19] and makes him Grand Vizir. In subsequent wars, his heroic status is accepted without question but it is in keeping with the tone of the novel that relatively little space is devoted to accounts of his skill and courage, equal import-ance being attached to his political acumen in the preliminaries and aftermath of war.[20] Indeed, the reader in 1641 might well have imagined Ibrahim to be an oriental version of Richelieu when told that 'c'estoit luy qui commandoit les armées; c'estoit luy qui faisoit les Sangiacs & qui leur donnoit les gouvernemens des Provinces. C'estoit luy qui presidoit au conseil d'Estat, & qui seul en formoit la resolution, dans le cabinet du Sultan. Enfin Ibrahim estoit si puissant, qu'il ne luy manquoit que le seul nom d'Empereur, pour estre le premier de tout l'Orient.'[21] With his sober manner, he lacks the panache of Polexandre or Oroondate and gives the impression that the *gloire* he has achieved is somewhat accidental, the product of circumstances rather than his own *élan*.

Nor does the nature of Ibrahim's position lend itself to the level of glory associated with these rival heroes. He has been raised to the eminence he occupies because he has gained the favour of a mighty ruler. He had not aspired to any level of eminence at all and fulfils his functions merely because it is required of him, though he is extremely gifted as a minister. However favoured he may be, he is always subordinate to the Sultan, however, a man whom he believes to be 'un des meilleurs Princes du monde' but who has no claims to being classed as heroic, for he is capable of great cruelty and on several occasions allows himself to be dominated by passions which bring out all his latent unjust and self-interested instinct. Despite his emotional dependence on Ibrahim and his professed inability to live without him, he is prepared to betray his friend by taking Isabelle from him and installing her in his harem, and ultimately by planning to kill him. This is the man at whose feet Ibrahim throws himself, 'pour qui il sacrifieroit sa vie avec joye; qui regnoit dans son coeur, bien plus absolument que sur ses peuples'.[22]

Ibrahim's attitude towards the Sultan is a mixture of genuine respect, devotion, and a measure of caution and fear. His will has of necessity to take account of the Sultan's wishes and the immediate responses characteristic of most heroes have to be tempered to fit the circumstances. Though the Sultan had made it possible for him to remain a Christian in private while appearing as a Muslim in public, the privilege could not be taken too far. When the Sultan had sent a series

of paintings to help furnish his palace, including some showing Turkish victories over the Christians, Ibrahim had been
troubled in his conscience but 'enfin il n'avoit osé ne les y pas
mettre'.[23] When he is considering whether to abandon
Isabelle and return to Constantinople as he had promised, it
is not only honour which weighs in his decision but the
possibility that the Sultan might come with an army and lay
waste his country.[24] At the end of the novel, when it is
apparent that the Sultan is a complete slave to his passion for
Isabelle, Ibrahim can only resort to flight together with
Isabelle and her friends and, when that expedient fails, he is
powerless before the Sultan's rage: he has no chance to take
the initiative and must face death with as much fortitude as
possible. It is in fact only a change of heart on the part of the
Sultan that saves the situation.

It is evident that Ibrahim is not the kind of hero portrayed
in novels such as *Cassandre*, *Scanderberg*, or *Alcide*. He is
prepared to lead an existence in which his moral freedom is
at times severely restricted: he does not strive to surpass his
fellow men in physical prowess or constantly measure his
status against that of rivals. Similarly, the love-relationship
he has with Isabelle has no superhuman side to it. It is
comparable with those depicted in the Greek romances and
their French derivatives: once the couple have established
that their love is mutual, there is a bond of affection and
unselfishness between them which strikes the modern reader
as more normal than the abject self-abasement of Polexandre
or the *gloire*-centred emotions in *Cassandre*.

The element of pride and tension between them is almost
entirely lacking. For the sake of the plot, it is necessary that
Justinian should believe that Isabelle has been obliged to
marry a foreign prince so that he goes away in despair,
accepts slavery, and exposes himself recklessly to death in
battle, but there are never any recriminations between them.
Isabelle is not a semi-divine creature like Alcidiane but very
much a woman of flesh and blood. She is described in detail
(hair, complexion, eyes, teeth, etc.)[25] in such a way that
female readers could imagine and appreciate her perfectly in
terms of their own world, just as she fits in with the world
of Genoese society.

The love she feels for Justinian is one in which she makes no secret of her commitment to him. He means more to her than her principality and possessions, or even her freedom: 'Je puis ... vivre malheureuse, infortunée, chargée de chaisnes, exilée de mon pays, sans biens & sans liberté: mais je ne puis vivre sans honneur & sans Justinian.'[26] She is over-joyed to be with him in Constantinople despite the threat to her honour and retains no pride where he is concerned:

Apprenez-moy donc ce que je dois attendre de ma fortune; avec prom-esse, s'il est vray que je n'aye plus de part en vostre souvenir, de ne murmurer plus de mon malheur; d'accuser mes deffauts de vostre changement; & ne pouvant vivre pour vous, de n'estre jamais à personne, et de mourir dans un Cloistre.[27]

He is similarly ready to sacrifice all his hopes of happiness if it is necessary for her sake. Such emotions are intended by the author to be readily accessible to the reader, who is invited on occasion to call on his own experience to provide confirmation of their force. The reader, it is implied, shares a heightened sensibility with the hero and heroine and, if he had the misfortune to be treated as they were, he would suffer the same reactions.

Ibrahim is not a heroic novel if by that is meant an account of the exploits of a quasi-divine figure fulfilling or achieving his destiny as a ruler in the face of constant threats and dangers. By virtue of its general conception, the areas that lend themselves to such an interpretation are limited. The circumstances in which Justinian is required to act out his life, the nature of the supporting characters, the type of relationship he enjoys with Isabelle, all tend to pull him back into the ordinary world rather than thrust him up into the rarefied atmosphere inhabited by demi-gods. *Ibrahim* is none the less a heroic novel in that it presents a picture of a man closer to perfection than the majority of mankind, but it contains an alternative concept of heroism to that based on 'les choses de dehors' and 'les caprices du destin'.

Instead of identifying the will as the instrument whereby the individual can impose himself on circumstances and on other men to achieve *gloire*, Scudéry sees the will (or the reason, since the two are identical) as the means whereby internal control can be exercised over the passions and the energy associated with them properly directed. *Gloire* may be the result, but only as a by-product: self-advancement is not an aim but a possible benefit. The fact that Ibrahim is politically subservient to the Sultan is thus no reflection on his true worth. He is in fact morally greater than the Sultan because he orders his passions better.[28] He is aware of the supremacy of the will and always applies it in the cause of virtue. When the Marquis français, the apologist of inconstancy, argues that the individual is strongly influenced by his temperament which in its turn is dependent on his humours, to the point where it is almost impossible to establish 'la veritable raison de toutes choses', Justinian is moved to counter that it is only our inclinations which are affected by the stars or by our humours and that reason can correct them all. Animals can only follow their instinct, 'mais pour l'homme, il n'en est pas ainsi: il est maistre absolu de ses sentimens & de ses actions; rien ne le force, rien ne le violente'; suicide provides proof of the supremacy of the will since man's natural impulse is to live.[29]

Such a view calls to mind the theories of Descartes. *Ibrahim* postulates the same relationship between reason and the passions as Descartes does when he urges that all men are capable of controlling their passions if they take the trouble to learn to direct their inclinations.[30] Successful control brings freedom from the tyranny of the passions and enables the individual to fulfil his potential. The outcome of such liberation in *Ibrahim*, however, is not the aristocratic urge to *gloire*, 'l'orgueil qui se donne en spectacle', as defined by Bénichou,[31] but internal fulfilment aiming at much less spectacular results such as contentment and a happy marriage. The *jouissance* at which Justinian aims is modest, the maintenance of certain standards representing perhaps less aristocratic values: 'comme il n'avoit pas tant d'ambition que de desir d'estre aimé, l'Empire de toute la terre n'auroit pu luy donner une joye aussi sensible que celuy du cœur d'Isabelle'.[32] Those characters on the other hand who pursue *jouissance* at the expense of others are shown to be inferior and in many cases come to grief.[33]

The Sultan is described as having only ever been overcome

by one passion, but that the noblest of all, i.e. love, or in his
case merely a weakness for women.[34] He falls in love with
Axiamire simply through seeing her portrait, and is soon
consumed by a feeling against which his reason is powerless:
'je suis forcé à cette inclination par une puissance superieure,
qui ne me permet pas de m'opposer à moy-mesme. Ce n'est
pas que je ne connoisse bien encor la raison, mais c'est qu'en
cette rencontre je ne la puis suivre.'[35] Having fallen in love
with Isabelle later on, he conducts a debate with himself,
knowing that he should suppress his passion but realizing that
he is incapable of doing so.[36] Isabelle lectures him on the
need to apply his will:

> toutes les personnes qui ont l'ame grande comme ta Hautesse ne peuvent
> jamais faire de fautes que volontairement. Il n'est rien qui puisse forcer
> la raison quand on s'en veut servir: & les passions les plus violentes ne
> sont sans doute que le pretexte des foibles, lors qu'ils veulent excuser
> les mauvaises actions qu'ils font: estant certain qu'il n'est point impos-
> sible de les surmonter.[37]

Many of the intercalated episodes deal with the dire effects
of uncontrolled passions, in which innocent people are
involved. On occasion, reason can reassert itself and rectify
the situation, such as when Arsalon is so impressed by the
générosité of his daughter and son-in-law that he forgets his
desire for revenge, or when the Sultan is filled with remorse
at the (false) news that Axiamire has been killed as the result
of his attempt to have her abducted.[38] In other cases, there
is no such happy solution, as when Soliman's sons, Mustapha
and Giangir, both die as a result of the hatred and jealousy
of the Sultan's wife, Roxelane.[39]

What emerges is a clear division between those who can
control their passions and thus liberate their natural *générosité*
and those who are incapable of rising above their irrational
impulses. Fortunately, the Sultan's reason manages to reassert itself at the crucial moment at the end of the novel
because he is inherently virtuous and can call on reserves
of moral strength:

> ceux qui ont les inclinations vertueuses & qui ne sont meschans que
> par une violente passion, ou par les conseils d'autruy, n'ont besoin que
> d'un moment pour se porter au bien. Leur raison n'est pas si tost
> esclairée qu'ils trouvent un puissant secours en eux-mesmes.[40]

Moral strength is the essence of heroism in Scudéry's view rather than courage or pride, and when it manifests itself in suitably impressive circumstances it marks the individual out as admirable, but this sort of heroism is not an aureole of grandeur available only to a tiny few, condemned to live almost beyond the comprehension of other men. The heroism shown in *Ibrahim* leads not to solitude but to a greater solidarity with the rest of mankind. It thus aligns itself with the Cartesian definition of *générosité* as the firm and constant resolution to use the will to do what is right. Scudéry's hero and heroine live out the precepts to be formulated by Descartes:

les plus généreux ont coutume d'être les plus humbles.

pour ce qu'ils n'estiment rien de plus grand que de faire du bien aux autres hommes et de mépriser son propre intérêt, pour ce sujet ils sont toujours parfaitement courtois, affables et officieux envers un chacun. Et avec cela ils sont entièrement maîtres de leurs passions.[41]

They lack the self-interest that formed the character-base of so many contemporary heroes. The virtues for which Justinian is praised are devoid of pride: 'un air haut sans estre superbe, une galanterie sans affectation, une propreté negligée, une franchise sans artifice, une civilité sans contrainte'.[42] They are social virtues, associated with the heroism of universality rather than the heroism of singularity found, for example, in *Cassandre*.[43]

What is under consideration here is effectively a refined version of the *honnêteté* which was establishing itself as the social ideal in Parisian society, an extension of the social norms which the reader might be expected to obey. By implication, any person of sensitivity with a sufficient level of *générosité* and moral strength might well be able to gain heroic status given propitious circumstances and a willingness to exercise the will-power necessary to break out of the restrictions of ordinary life. A world in which such things happen is being held out to the reader for him to grasp: the prerequisites for heroism are present all around him and within him.

It is for that reason that the links between the world of Justinian and Isabelle and that of Paris in 1641 are so strong. Corneille's criticism of Racine's *Bajazet*, that the characters 'ont tous, sous un habit turc, le sentiment qu'on a au milieu de la France', might well have been taken as a compliment if it had been applied to *Ibrahim*, since the *honnêteté* and *galanterie* depicted by Scudéry are shown to be not simply ephemeral French fashions but modes of behaviour dictated by reason and therefore found universally wherever reason is allowed to fulfil its proper function.[44] Scudéry's idea of heroism, unlike Gomberville's, is based on optimism about the human condition and the power of social virtues to produce a better world.

CHAPTER X

CASSANDRE

If *Ibrahim* brings heroism into the everyday world, *Cassandre*[1] sets out to take the reader right away into a world he could never know. Not only is the action set around Babylon in the time of Alexander the Great, but the characters are almost without exception royal and concern themselves solely with the noble pursuits of love and war. There is much stress on the heroes' physical strength and dexterity, particularly in and after Volume V, at the beginning of which La Calprenède declares that he is moving away from the style of Plutarch, Curtius, and Justinus, the sources of his story, and adopting the manner of Homer, Virgil and Tasso; the narrative will concentrate on the actions and reputations of the heroes themselves rather than on the fate of the nations with whom they are connected.

The influence of the romances of chivalry can be felt in the descriptions of battles in which men are cut in half with a single blow and arms raised to strike are lopped off.[2] The same clichés occur, with blows on the head so strong that the recipient 'crût estre accablé des ruines d'une tour' or is made to 'baisser la teste jusques sur l'arçon de la selle'.[3] The heroes themselves, however, belong to a special caste of superhuman beings who have nothing in common with ordinary mortals, very different from the heroes of the earlier romances. They feel drawn to each other regardless of the interests they might supposedly be representing and change sides freely if they think their status as *généreux* and free men is in any way threatened. Politics in the broadest sense is anathema to them. They are concerned primarily with action supporting their own interests and have no time for questions of national profit. The whole of Alexander's conquest of Asia as well as the opposition to him is depicted as the search by a group of individuals for greater and greater glory.

The essence of the heroic code in *Cassandre* lies in being true to oneself. Duty is an aspect of self-interest: the only responsibility acknowledged is that of ensuring that the external image corresponds to the ideal of personal greatness. At an early age, the hero senses that his destiny is to lead him beyond the prescriptions of the morality he can learn from other men. From then on, he is aware in an almost mystical way of the ideal to which he must be true, and each one of his actions is referred to it, either consciously or unconsciously.

The case of Oroondate, the main character in the novel, is illustrative. He leads the Scythian army on behalf of his father, the king, against the Persians and during the battle has occasion to rescue the women of the Persian royal family from the threat of capture by his own soldiers. He falls in love with the Persian princess, Statira, and abandons his own army to stay at the Persian court under an assumed name. Having rescued a knight, with whom he feels an instant affinity, from a group of Scythian soldiers, he discovers that it is Artaxerxe, Statira's brother, and becomes his dearest friend, so that when a second battle between the Scythians and Persians takes place, Oroondate's filial and patriotic duty gives way to love and friendship: 'Je n'apprehenderay point d'estre fils desnaturé pour estre loyal Amant & amy irreproch-able, ny ne feray conscience de combattre contre un Pere qui vient renverser la fortune que mon amy m'a establie.'[4] Artaxerxe is naturally somewhat reluctant to kill the fellow-countrymen of his friend and holds back in the battle, but Oroondate throws himself into the thick of the fight, slaughtering the Scythians in order to oblige Artaxerxe to fight with and for him.[5]

Oroondate subsequently makes his way back to Scythia and presents himself at court. His reaction when his father, outraged that his son should have fought against his own country, orders him to be thrown into prison, is one of injured pride which seemingly meets with the approval of the narrator: 'mon Prince se leva de devant luy, & croyant avoir satisfaict à ce qu'il devoit à son Pere, il luy sçeut si mauvais gré d'un accueil si inhumain apres une absence si longue, qu'il ne daigna luy dire une seule parole pour sa justification.'[6] After two years, the king relents and asks

Oroondate to lead an army against Zopirion, one of Alexander's lieutenants. Oroondate agrees, not from any desire to atone for his earlier actions but because he is moved by a 'desir de gloire' and 'l'amour des belles actions'.[7] Having defeated Zopirion, he again abandons his army to go off to Persia and this time does not return until he has himself become king. Hearing at one stage that his father has attempted to kill Artaxerxe, he disowns him, crying out, 'ah tigre inhumain, je te desavoüe, ... je tiens ma naissance plus honteuse que si je la tenois du plus bas de tous les hommes'.[8]

Oroondate's attitude, though presented in greater detail, is shared by the other heroic individuals in the novel. They insist on retaining their liberty of action at all costs, and obligations accepted as binding by lesser mortals, such as patriotism, are strictly subordinated to the expression of personal aspirations.[9] The loss of freedom on a physical level is more hateful than death, but captivity, if unavoidable, can never affect the spirit. Oroondate, finding himself isolated in an attack on Babylon, almost despairs at the prospect of being taken prisoner,[10] but faced with his enemy he declares: 'Je suis prisonnier ... mais cette captivité du corps ne s'estend point jusqu'à l'ame.'[11] After being arrested, Lisimachus tells his friends: 'C'est aux ames lasches à craindre en esclaves, je suis né libre & Prince, & je ne feray jamais de lascheté qui vous fasse rougir pour moy, ny qui me rende indigne de la gloire de mes Ancestres.'[12]

The desire for liberty prompts an energetic response to threats and oppression, the expression of a positive approach to life very different from the passivity displayed by the heroes of the Greek romances. Confronted by danger, La Calprenède's heroes will always strike out in their own defence and never entertain the possibility of being killed except as an expression of their moral freedom. When Arsace is sent poison and a dagger and told to choose his own method of dying, he chooses the dagger but uses it to stab his guards and escape,[13] a striking contrast to Ibrahim in a similar situation waiting for the Sultan's mutes to come and strangle him. However shattering the blows that fate has dealt out to them, these heroes always retain enough fighting spirit to want to hit back; however welcome death may seem, it can always be delayed sufficiently to make one final mark on the world.[14]

The hero's relationships with other people are governed by the code of *générosité*. It manifests itself externally in the form of actions which appear to indicate that the hero is not vindictive, vengeful, or cowardly but can moderate his desire for success or even postpone the fulfilment of his aims by showing mercy or doing favours for enemies. In reality, the motivation behind these acts is not altruistic: *générosité* is another aspect of the self-centred principle on which all the major characters operate. It ensures that onlookers provide the degree of admiration and approval necessary to maintain the heroic image at its highest level and, if there are no onlookers present, it confirms the hero's own view of himself. It depends on a carefully graded system of moral assessments in which the amount of moral advantage to be gained from a *généreux* act has to be weighed against the difference in moral status between the hero and the beneficiary of his act. To be the recipient of *générosité* has the equivalent effect of lowering the moral status.

Oroondate is brought before Alexander as a prisoner and released by him, and the memory of this act remains with Oroondate for some time as 'le déplaisir qu'il receut de se voir vaincu en generosité'.[15] Conversely, when Arbate, a traitor who has been the cause of most of his misfortunes, is found in the camp and brought before Oroondate, thoughts of revenge enter the hero's mind but he rejects them and tells Arbate to go, not because he wishes to show mercy towards him but because to exercise vengeance on such a man would suggest that there was some moral comparability between them: 'Vis, desloyal, luy dit-il, vis, puis que tu es indigne de la mort que je te pourrois donner, & que tu es destiné sans doute à une fin plus honteuse que celle que tu recevrois d'Oroondate.'[16] The way in which revenge is taken is all-important: it must be carried out in accordance with the requirements of *gloire*, never as an end in itself. Oroondate discovers his mortal enemy, Perdicas, lying wounded but cannot bring himself to dispatch him. He lets him live so that he can be killed in the right way: 'je ne luy pardonne point une offense, qui n'est point de nature à esperer de pardon;

mais je differe sa peine jusques à ce que je la luy puisse donner sans honte & que je puisse mourir sans repentir.'[17] It is *gloire*, too, which requires Arsace to give up his ideas of revenge upon his beloved's father who has greatly wronged him and makes him decide to sacrifice his own life instead: 'il est vray', he tells himself, 'qu'il faut que tu meures, mais il faut que tu meures comme tu as vescu, & que dans ta mort, tu ne dementes, ny ton amour, ny toutes tes actions passées'.[18]

The essence of *générosité* in La Calprenède's system of values and its dependence on the ego are made clear by Oroondate after he has rescued Alexander, his rival, from drowning, placed him at the feet of Statira and disappeared again, unrecognized and unrewarded. In reply to Araxe, his astounded *confident*, who protests that such a deed goes beyond the demands of honour since Alexander could hardly have complained if his worst enemy had not made an effort to save him, he points out that Alexander's feelings have nothing to do with the matter:

Si Alexandre n'avoit point subjet de se plaindre de moy, j'en avois beaucoup moy-mesme, & comme ma satisfaction m'est plus chere que la sienne, le reproche que je me pouvois faire (pour avoir manqué à faire une bonne action; ou par quelque crainte de peril, ou par quelque consideration d'interest) m'eust esté bien plus sensible que celuy que je pourrois recevoir de luy, de qui je ne pretends, ny de recompenses, ny de remercimens.[19]

Générosité is a self-centred virtue, its main function being to confirm the hero's assessment of himself.

The relationships between heroes and heroines in love involve many of the features mentioned above. The element of pride is strong on both sides and neither partner readily admits dependence on the other. The relationship has to be monitored constantly and pressure applied appropriately if one feels that the other is not responding sufficiently. The resulting union is therefore different from both the utter devotion shown by Polexandre and the calm confidence experienced most of the time by Ibrahim: it is a stormy affair in which a good deal of the tension is provided by the claims and self-assertion of one or other of the lovers.

The man's approach is relatively simple. He sets out to win his lady by doing service for her and, although he would not claim that in themselves his actions give him any rights, he certainly feels that they entitle him to some consideration and becomes angry if he thinks they are not being sufficiently recognized.[20] He will persist in his pursuit until the woman gives some kind of indication that she is not averse to him and he will then consider himself to have a link with her which cannot be broken without his consent. If he feels he has been wronged by her, her sex will prevent him from taking any form of direct revenge such as treachery on the part of a man would demand, but his pride will remain strong and he is perfectly capable of reviling the woman he loves, calling her 'infidèle', 'lâche', 'ingrate', and 'indigne'.[21] Far from seeking to explain the beloved's hostility as something that he must have deserved, as Polexandre would have done, La Calprenède's hero experiences a rush of blood to the head and an urge to strike back. Thus, when Statira, tricked into thinking that Oroondate no longer loves her, rejects him coldly, his first impulse to kill himself quickly gives way to a more aggressive reaction:

venant à considerer l'indignité du traittement qu'il recevoit d'une personne à qui il avoit donné tant & de si belles preuves de son amour, pour qui il avoit faict tant de remarquables actions, & qu'il avoit tant de fois obligée par son salut propre & celuy de tous les siens, il fit succeder le depart à la douleur, & se levant tout à coup apres l'avoir regardée quelque temps d'un oeil d'amour & d'indignation tout ensemble; Il est vray, Madame, luy dit-il, que je suis traistre, lasche & desloyal: mais si je le suis, c'est envers mon Pere & mon Roy, envers mes parens & mon pays que j'ay trahis & abandonnez pour vous, & pour les vostres, . . . cette lascheté de laquelle vous m'accusez se trouve veritablement en vous & vous feignez que je vous abandonne dans vos disgraces, pour avoir un pretexte de m'abandonner vous-mesme lors que je vous avois des-ja delivrée des mains de cet ennemy que vous me preferez laschement. C'est là la veritable bassesse . . .[22]

It is consonant with this attitude that male values are never allowed to be contaminated by female tendencies towards passivity and acceptance. The natural desire is to want to kill any rival who seems to be preferred by the lady; the idea of conceding defeat is unthinkable. The fact that she may have married another man makes no difference to the hero's pursuit of her and he never considers himself bound by the constraints of duty which she may propound.[23] Having married Alexander to spite Oroondate and having then discovered that Oroondate was innocent, Statira writes to him regretting what has happened and promising to pray to heaven that he will receive the reward for what he has done for her. Oroondate considers this cold consolation: 'non, non, Statira, . . . vous n'en serez pas quitte à ce prix, on ne se deffait pas de moy avec cette facilité: & ce n'est pas si legerement qu'on repare des pertes semblables à celles que j'ay faites'.[24] Her proposal is that he should live and suffer like her in the hope that the gods will bring about some change in his fortune or in his inclinations; Oroondate's response is to swear to kill Alexander, despite Statira's explicit command to the contrary.[25]

With this constant drive towards possessing the woman he loves, it is natural that the hero should feel that she is not responding with the same degree of affection and contributing as much to the relationship as he is. He requires constant reassurance and quite frequently reproaches her for her inaction, interpreting it as coldness. Recriminations are never very far below the surface and are used as a weapon in the struggle to establish emotional domination, for La Calprenède's heroes treat love much in the same way as they treat war. Just as a duel may be fought against an honourable opponent, even a friend, for the purpose of establishing who has the greater *gloire*, so it may be necessary to clarify the moral relationship between two lovers by a sort of verbal duel in which certain statements are made and demanded and a joint position reached which satisfies the honour of both parties. At the darkest moments of the novel, for instance, when Oroondate has been captured by Perdicas, who already holds Statira prisoner, the two are allowed to meet, for all they know for the last time. Almost the first words uttered by Oroondate are reproaches that Statira had not revealed herself when she had found herself in the same house as Oroondate who had thought her dead: 'ma presence vous fut si odieuse . . .' he complains, 'ma vie si peu chere que vous ne voulustes pas l'asseurer par la simple connoissance de la vostre'. Statira justifies herself by referring to the need to guard her reputation at a time when her husband had only just died; Oroondate apologizes for having doubted her motives and Statira declares that she loves him sufficiently to prefer him dead rather than unfaithful.[26] The honour of both is satisfied: they have each made a declaration of love while reserving their rights as independent beings.

For the woman, maintaining her freedom is quite as important as for the man, but she has necessarily to use other methods. Unless she is an Amazon like Talestris and can adopt male methods of upholding her *gloire*, she can only defend her honour and oblige others to accept her will by moral pressure, where a man could use either moral or physical force. Her independence therefore frequently manifests itself in negative responses, particularly in the form of severity towards her suitors. She is slow to make any sort of declaration to a man who loves her and each step has to be carefully delimited with precise terminology. After several years of service, Lisimachus is overjoyed to receive from Parisatis a few words which scarcely go beyond the terms of ordinary civility.[27] Some time later she concedes 'Je vous estime beaucoup' and again 'j'ay une bienveillance pour vous qui va au delà de l'estime', but immediately there is a proviso: 'mais je n'ay pas une si forte affection pour vous qu'elle me fasse oublier ce que je me dois à moy mesme & me porte à faire des fautes qui blesseroient ma reputation & offenceroient mortellement le sang illustre d'où je suis sortie'.[28]

The constant appeals to duty made by these women suggest that they are motivated by filial obedience or submission to the demands of the state, and it is true that they have no means of avoiding such obedience other than by putting themselves to death. There is none the less a certain element of personal decision involved. Statira has been under pressure to marry Alexander for some time before she agrees to do so and then it is in order to avenge herself on Oroondate. Moreover, her father Darius had previously made it known that he wished her to marry Oroondate. Parisatis informs Lisimachus that she has married Ephestion because of the gods, her mother, her duty, *and* 'le merite de ses services'.[29] Déidamie has sworn to be true to Agis even though her father has rejected him in favour of another suitor for political reasons.[30]

The duty to which these ladies refer is in fact primarily a

duty towards themselves, the same responsibility to ensure the maintenance of their heroic image as is found with the men. Their pride is just as lively: it is only in the courses of action available to their wounded pride that the difference is discernible. When Statira is made to believe that Oroondate is unfaithful to her, she falls ill with the shock and comes close to death, but her pride produces an identical reaction to that evinced by Oroondate:

Non, je ne mourray point pour luy, j'ay faict assez sans mourir, & ce seroit là ma derniere honte & sa derniere vanité, il en seroit trop glorieux, le traistre, & se vanteroit avec trop d'insolence d'avoir faict mourir d'amour la Princesse de Perse & la fille de l'ennemi de son Pere, je veux plustost vivre pour le haïr & pour le mespriser.[31]

Talestris' response when she discovers how much Oronte has suffered for her sake is to call to mind all the sufferings she has experienced for him.[32] Barsine loves and is loved by Memnon but she is also loved by Oxiarte, brother of King Darius, who eventually falls ill because of his passion. Seeing himself as the cause of the impending death of his king's brother, Memnon renounces his claim to Barsine and leaves the court, but Barsine is outraged that he should think that his duty to his king could take precedence over his obligations to her. Only she could release him from his bond and decide the nature of the duties to which he is subject.[33]

It is important therefore that the terms of a relationship should be as acceptable to the heroine as to the hero, for the mere fact that both desire the relationship is not enough to guarantee her moral independence. Men tend to assume that, since they are the ones who can produce rapid and decisive changes in circumstances by direct physical action, it is their solutions which are the best. Oroondate's sister, Bérénice, speaks for all the other heroic women in *Cassandre*, however, when she imposes her will on an extraordinary situation. Her father has ordered her to marry Arsacome and she has declared that she will kill herself if she is obliged to do so, in order to remain true to Arsace. Hearing of the projected marriage, Arsace storms the town and carries Bérénice off to the safety of his own camp, only to be met by the question: 'Arsace, ... qu'avez-vous fait?' 'J'ay fait', he replies, 'ce que vous deviez attendre de mon amour; & je vous ay retirée des bras de cét indigne mari qu'on vous destinoit.' To him, this is self-evident, but Bérénice adds another element which completely alters the situation as far as she is concerned: 'Ouy, reprit Berenice, mais vous m'avez arrachée de ceux de mon pere,' and she asks him to give her back her freedom. Arsace does not understand: she *is* free and if she thinks otherwise, it must be because her affections have changed and she wishes to be with Arsacome. Bérénice has to explain her standpoint:

> Je vous ay promis que j'espouserois la mort plustost qu'Arsacome; mais je ne vous ay fait esperer, ny par mes discours, ny par mes actions, que je fuyrois des bras de mon pere pour vous suivre, & que je me licencierois en vostre faveur à des actions honteuses & indignes d'une Princesse.'

She had not asked to be rescued and if she is made to marry Arsacome, she will kill herself, a way of escape less cruel than the shame Arsace is offering her. Furious, Arsace can only accede to her demand and returns her into her father's keeping, while she reaffirms her love for him: 'si je prefere mon devoir à vostre satisfaction, à tout autre qu'à vous, je prefereray le tombeau'.[34]

Where Arsace and Bérénice differ is in their interpretation of freedom. Arsace, typically male, assumes that Bérénice wishes to be free of constraints preventing her from being with him and, if his strength can remove the constraints, then she must welcome the new situation he has created. Her female view sees this as morally no different from being forced to marry Arsacome. It is simply a question of one male imposing his will on her rather than another. Freedom for her means imposing her own will and, unless her father releases her from her filial obedience, the only way she has of doing that is by killing herself.

In *Cassandre*, there is moral equality between male and female because they all value their moral freedom more highly than anything else. Love and marriage can only be entered into if neither partner feels that moral subjection is being demanded of them. While the relationship is developing, the men try to interpret every situation as one that can be solved by direct action; the women see the same situation as subject to the moral forces of which they are possessed. When a union is finally arranged, the interests of both parties have been secured. Oroondate can claim that his marriage to Statira is possible because his courage and fidelity have removed all the obstacles to it; Statira can argue that it is possible because her courage and fidelity are such that she is prepared to risk criticisms of her reputation and suggestions that she is 'légère', to her a threat every bit as serious as a battle is to Oroondate because she has no way of overcoming it.[35]

This is not to say that all the male or all the female characters are replicas of one another. Oroondate is quicker in his reactions, Lisimachus more self-effacing, Démétrius more susceptible to sudden and violent attacks of passion;[36] Statira is warmer in her declarations, Parisatis more reserved and controlled. The feature they all share is a strong sense of pride, manifesting itself in an overriding concern for *gloire*. The other heroic qualities are interpreted in terms of it — *vertu* is strength, either physical or moral, applied in the maintenance of *gloire*, *générosité* is the urge to allow pride its free expression.

The heroism depicted in *Cassandre* is totally aristocratic, firstly in the sense that all the characters are from the very highest nobility, if not from long established royal lines,[37] and are keenly aware of their position; but more important is the fact that the qualities that make them heroic draw them out of the normal world into an area of moral isolation. They are only capable of communicating with the relatively few individuals who inhabit this same area with them.[38] Being committed to total self-reliance, they make no contribution to the rest of society. Their actions are judged solely in terms of their own advantage and there is never any question of justifying the position they hold: nobility of the sword is acknowledged by all to be the highest order of mankind. What they are justifies what they do. Members of the lower orders are expendable[39] and they accept that a man with sublime *vertu* is entitled to rule over others without necessarily having any commitment to their welfare.[40] The three major male characters — Oroondate, Artaxerxe and Lisimachus — are only potential rulers who do not come into their kingdoms until the end of the novel and could therefore claim not yet to have any responsibility towards their peoples, but, to judge by the rulers we are shown, notably Alexander, the King of Scythia, and Darius, kingship is merely a state which provides greater opportunities for the display of *gloire* (which is why Oroondate at one point wishes he already had his father's crown, to face Alexander on equal terms).[41] It imposes no limitations, no duties, no responsibilities.

An aristocratic ethic of this sort presents obvious similarities with Cornelian heroism as defined by several modern scholars: 'l'amour emphatique des grandeurs', 'le penchant à se célébrer soi-même',[42] 'l'âme attentive à ne pas se trahir'[43] are all part of the framework of La Calprenède's heroism as of Corneille's, based on a belief that the will can direct the passions in such a way that man can transcend his limitations and achieve sublimity.[44] Neither La Calprenède nor any other writer of heroic novels ever suggests, however, that the pursuit of *gloire* might lead into an area where it could produce an 'admirable' crime, such as Corneille depicted in *Rodogune* and *Théodore*. If they were aware that the ethic of self-fulfilment contained such an implication, they preferred not to pursue it. La Calprenède's characters exist in a world where good and evil are clearly differentiated and the heroic characters act entirely on the side of good, though the good in question is not altruistic. It consists in being true to the ideal of *gloire*: virtues such as clemency, justice, and magnanimity may benefit others but they are exercised because *gloire* demands it. The giver receives as much as if not more than the recipient.

What La Calprenède offers the reader in *Cassandre* is an unwavering affirmation of human greatness on the terms specified above. The values recognized as those on which the French *noblesse d'épée* based their class-myth are approved of, applauded, held up for universal admiration as the only true aspiration for men with noble ideals, and a society that had just seen the first victories of the young duc d'Enghien and was experiencing a resurgence of aristocratic individualism after the death of Richelieu responded with enthusiasm, and saw these values as the evocation of their own dreams of grandeur.

CHAPTER XI

CLEOPATRE

The success of *Cassandre* made it almost inevitable that La Calprenède would write another novel of the same kind. The formula of historical and pseudo-historical characters fired by ambition and love battling their way through to eventual success and happiness was one that could be repeated and extended indefinitely, given the public's willingness to accept plots dependent for their momentum on abductions, misunderstandings caused by traitors, and chance encounters between knights. As soon as the last part of *Cassandre* was published, La Calprenède started work on *Cleopatre*. In 1646, he received 3000 *livres* from Sommaville for the manuscripts of Parts II and III, each part to consist of four books of forty or fifty *feuillets* each. The first volume was published in 1647 (though the *achevé d'imprimer* is given as 17 April 1646) and all the major publishers at the Palais were involved with the production of the novel at some stage, suggesting that they anticipated a similar success to that of *Cassandre*. Moreover, the work was dedicated to the duc d'Enghien, then enjoying considerable esteem for his continuing series of victories over the Spaniards and an obvious model for the hero of a novel.

The first few volumes of *Cleopatre*[1] indicate that La Calprenède was indeed intending to follow the pattern he had established in *Cassandre*. The central male characters (Coriolan, son of Juba, King of Mauretania, Césarion, son of Julius Caesar and Cleopatra, and Artaban) are charismatic individuals, able to inspire courage in those who follow them and terror in their enemies. They have a fearsome strength and a remarkable skill in delivering the great blows that appealed so much to Madame de Sévigné.[2] Their moral courage allows them to face all opponents without flinching, and a confrontation with a moral equal provides the opportunity for great self-assertion. The apparent success of a rival brings out in them a determination to overcome the opposition he represents.[3] The women also reveal a healthy self-reliance and an ability to support their own interests, though none of the major female characters shares the Amazonian prowess of Talestris.[4]

Some elements of the plot of *Cassandre* (presumably those which had been admired by readers or perhaps those which appealed most to the author) were picked out and developed in *Cleopatre*. In *Cassandre*, the young Démétrius, an impulsive and passionate youth, falls violently in love with Hermione whom he has inadvertently wounded in battle. When she dies, he falls ill and himself comes dangerously close to dying. Having recovered, he erects a monument to Hermione where he spends his days in solitary sorrow, though later on he falls equally violently in love with Déidamie and eventually marries her. In *Cleopatre*, the same strain of sensibility is expanded and dwelt on at length in the episode of Tyridate and Mariamne. Tyridate, a refugee at the court of Herod, had adored Mariamne but had always been aware that her feelings for him would never lead her into the slightest impropriety. When the news comes to him in Alexandria that she has been put to death, his heart breaks. He faints while the story of her death is being recounted; then, when there is no more to learn, 'la douleur faisant ses derniers efforts, luy serra le cœur de telle sorte, que ceste partie la premiere animée & la derniere mourante, ne fut plus capable de soustenir les fonctions necessaires à la conservation de la vie'.[5] Many pages are devoted to his emotions before he dies and to those of others who visit his tomb and read the inscription on it. Again, in *Cassandre*, the relationship between Bérénice and Arsace is affected by her resentment at being approached by what she assumes to be a man of inferior birth. When she realizes his worth, she is still troubled by the social difference between them: 'pleust aux Dieux qu'il fut né Prince, . . . & s'il ne luy manquoit que des Empires, sa vertu suppleeroit à ce deffaut ou elle le mettroit bientost dans les voyes d'en acquerir,'[6] though it is not long before Arsace's true identity is revealed. The same theme of nobility and *vertu* runs throughout *Cléopâtre* in the relationship between Elise and Artaban, who feels very strongly that his *vertu* entitles him to the power and glory denied to him by his social origins.[7]

Despite the inclusion of these well-tested features, the public's response to *Cleopatre* does not appear to have been entirely favourable. In the *Au lecteur* of Volume IV (1648), La Calprenède begs the reader to suspend comparisons with *Cassandre* until more of the work has appeared, assuring him that 'dans ce que tu as veu de Cleopatre, tu n'es pas encore entré en matiere, que c'est un champ plus estendu que tu ne te l'estois imaginé' and promising a lot of stories, written with 'assez de vray-semblance' and 'avec un ordre qui n'est possible pas commun'. We are told, too, that *vaudevilles* appeared, making fun of the Tyridate-Mariamne episode and suggesting that Mariamne had been sent to the *Feuillantines* by a jealous Herod.[8] One such satire calls on the novel as evidence that she was a coquette who could not live without a lover:

> Et d'elle on a pris la methode
> de faire enrager les maris
> Alors qu'ils sont vieux comme Herode.[9]

Whether the public's reaction influenced it or not, the publication of *Cleopatre* did not follow the steady pattern established by *Cassandre*. The first five volumes appeared regularly in 1647 and 1648. A revised *privilège* dated 21 February 1648 states that Cardin Besongne who had published Parts I–III now wished to publish Parts IV and V, 'dans laquelle doit estre la Conclusion dudit Ouvrage'. There are no indications in the text that it was due to be concluded after Volume V, and Volume VI followed soon afterwards in 1649. There was then, however, a break in publication until 1653 when two further volumes appeared, and the final four volumes were published in 1657. The breaks in publication may have been due to the economic difficulties caused by the Fronde,[10] though it should be remembered that it was precisely during the years 1649–53 that *Le Grand Cyrus* established its considerable reputation.

The effect of this extended period of creation and publication is visible both in the construction of the work and in the type of character offered for the reader's admiration. *Cassandre* had been planned with a good deal of thought. The five parts of the novel provide the life-stories of the main characters as *tiroirs* while the main plot continues to develop, the action crystallizing round the two battles of Babylon. The threads of the sub-plots are all brought together in the last part and only resolved with a good deal of suspense after the final battle. There is evidence that the work was conceived as a whole: for instance, in volume II Oroondate returns home and is imprisoned by his father for two years; he is not allowed to see his sister Bérénice and is eventually released on condition that he leaves immediately to take charge of the army, the reasons for which do not become apparent until volume VII. *Cleopatre*, on the other hand, develops haphazardly. Some of the episodes trail off into *invraisemblance*.[11] The main plot is thin for the weight of sub-plots it is required to carry. It contains no battles or physical action other than hand-to-hand skirmishes, and it has to be artificially extended by the abduction of Cléopâtre in volume V and the attempted abduction of Elise in volume VII. Even these *peripeteiae* do not provide much impetus, for the suspense is allowed to ebb slowly away: the worst of the villains have been eliminated by the end of volume IX, the major misunderstanding between Cléopâtre and Coriolan is already well on the way to being resolved by the time the truth is revealed in volume X and a large proportion of the last few volumes is spent on the avoidance of action in *badinage* and *galanterie*.[12]

The static and rather lax nature of the plot, acting as a framework for the kind of idealized conversation that was so popular in the novels of the 1650s, is paralleled by a corresponding change in the type of character presented. Even from the publication of volume I, there had been indications that La Calprenède's inspiration was moving in a somewhat different direction. Whereas the first hundred pages of *Cassandre* had plunged straight into the heroic medium, showing supermen at war, jousting and performing acts of outstanding *générosité* of which only a few individuals would be capable, the first volume of *Cleopatre* moves slowly. Most of it is given over to the story of Tyridate, a man capable of deep emotion who loved Mariamne with a disinterested love — 'je pouvois dire avec verité que j'aimois Mariamne pour l'amour d'elle seule, & que dans tout le cours de ma passion je ne consideray jamais Tyridate'[13] — and to the history of Julius Caesar's relationship with Cleopatre,[14] in which the great conqueror, regarded as a god by the ordinary people, becomes a lovelorn suitor, declaring from her *ruelle*: 'je meurs si par pitié vous ne me retirez du tombeau, & je vous proteste par ces beaux yeux que j'adore avec toute sorte de respect, qu'il est impossible que ma vie soit d'une plus longue durée si vous ne la prolongez par vostre bonté.'[15]

A reduction in the heroes' fierceness and pride is noticeable. They are less aggressive, less concerned to impose themselves on the world by force of character. Césarion has 'l'esprit tres-docile' and is noted for his 'douces inclinations'.[16] His step-brother, Alexandre, 'eust pû passer, si les habits de l'autre sexe l'y eussent favorisé, pour une des plus belles Dames de la terre', though we are assured that 'dans la douceur de ses yeux on voyoit briller aussi quelque chose de tres-fier & de tres-martial'.[17] They are naturally susceptible to love and, unlike the heroes of preceding novels, fall irretrievably in love *before* they have proved themselves in battle.[18] As a result, the commitment to ambition and *gloire* which had always been inherent in the hero is subordinated to love. It is considered entirely laudable that they should scorn all external manifestations of glory and give up 'toutes les choses dans la possession desquelles les personnes ambitieuses establissent leur felicité'[19] for the sake of their love. Nor are their declarations to this effect hollow: Coriolan reconquers the kingdom his father had lost in order to be able to offer Cléopâtre a crown but, when she rejects him, he loses interest in it and allows it to fall into the hands of the Romans again.

Love having become the dominant theme, the point of focus for the narration has shifted in *Cleopatre*. *Cassandre* had depicted the events it portrayed from the central point of the action, the house near Babylon where Oroondate and his companions assemble and from which they attack their enemies. The stories recounting past events range over wide areas, following the heroes as they travel, taking in duels and

battles and occasional visits to courts. The experiences of the
heroines, Statira and Parisatis, are not accorded any great
amount of space while they are outside the main area of
action. In *Cleopatre*, however, the story is attached at all
points to a number of 'social bases', places away from wars
and violent activities (other than sudden abductions and
the skirmishes they provoke) where life can be lived in a
leisurely and graceful way. The most important of these is
in Alexandria, at the houses of Tyridate and the Roman
governor, Cornelius Gallus. It is peopled mainly by the
female characters until the men begin to return one by one
from their various adventures, and gradually takes on the
appearance of a court, completed when Augustus arrives
from Rome.[20]

Most of the subsidiary episodes start from the court of
a kingdom and treat it as the point of reference so that
battles and great deeds are of importance only for the effect
they have on the situation at the base, where they are assessed
by a group. The story of Césarion and Candace, for example,
is related from the point of view of the Ethiopian court,
with reports of Césarion's victories brought in from the
provinces.[21] Ariobarzane's military successes are viewed
with wonder from the distance of the Thracian court.[22] The
imperial court of Rome is the starting-point for a number of
such episodes, and the size of the court leads to more complex, interacting relationships. The story of Coriolan and
Cléopâtre is played out against the background of a large
group of aristocrats in Rome and their relationship depends
on the influence and intrigue of many other people.[23] The
Emperor's all-powerful position and his support of Coriolan's
rival, Tibère, interferes with the hero's natural urge to impose
his will on the situation. When Coriolan and Tibère go off to
war determined to outdo each other in valour for the service
of Cléopâtre, the *gloire* they achieve still has to be validated
by the Emperor, who is himself not entirely made up of
heroic virtues. Towards the end of the novel, he again disturbs
the free play of heroic natural selection by supporting the
claims of the worthy but not outstanding Roman, Agrippa,
in his suit for the hand of Elise against the entirely heroic
Artaban, this time for the political reason that he wishes to

subject Elise's kingdom of Parthia to Rome.[24] The hero, wandering free across the world, has here been tamed and made to fit in with the restrictions of the civil order. From being a figure on a personal quest, following his ideal wherever destiny may lead him, he has become a member of a social group sharing common ideals, to which he returns whenever possible.

The relationship between hero and heroine is also to a certain extent shared with the group in that their love develops almost in public, with others offering advice, sometimes taking sides in differences, arranging meetings and so on, to the point where the collective attitude threatens to become more important than the individual's. Antonia, noted for her reserve, is wooed by an unknown knight who arranges extravagant public displays of his affection, such as a trip in an illuminated boat worked with her name and symbols of love. At a tournament, he enters as her champion, again with much evidence of his love for her.[25] When it is eventually revealed that he is Drusus, the Emperor's son, he apologizes to Antonia's brothers for having approached her in this unusual way. They approve his endeavours and take him to see the Emperor and Empress, at the same time urging Antonia to receive him into her service. 'Toute l'Assemblée éclatta en applaudissemens à la veuë & à la connoissance de Drusus: & comme il estoit aymé de tout le monde, il n'y eut personne qui n'apprist avec joye que c'estoit luy, qui avoit fait des choses si galantes pour Antonia, qui ne criast qu'ils estoient dignes l'un de l'autre & que c'estoit le couple du monde le mieux assorty.' The Emperor and Empress join the others in begging Antonia to accept Drusus and to allow him to attack 'par la guerre ouverte ce cœur qu'il avoit voulu surprendre par artifice'. As a result, Antonia's own reactions are pre-empted: even though she feels 'quelque dépit de la tromperie qu'il luy avoit faite', she has to suppress it and accept the general will.[26] Similarly, Lentulus' love for Tullia becomes the preoccupation of most of the court, including the imperial family: 'Ils plaignoient tous mon infortune qui leur estoit connuë en partie, & faisoient tous leurs efforts pour me retirer de cette fatale passion qui m'avoit perdu.'[27]

It is only a short step from this emphasis on the attitudes

of the social group to the point where conversations about general aspects of *galanterie* are substituted for individual manifestations of love, as happened in *Le Grand Cyrus*, *Clélie*, and other novels of the 1650s. The later volumes of *Cléopâtre* include a few such discussions, on how a suitor should approach the woman he loves and the kind of favour she can legitimately bestow on him,[28] but in general La Calprenède does not offer the reader analyses of the metaphysics of love so much as an impression of a glittering court in which individual characteristics are submerged in collective activities. Increasingly as the novel progresses, the heroic characters are mere ornaments for a round of entertainments, participating in the pleasures Parisian high society enjoyed and the bourgeoisie dreamed of, 'une superbe collation, le divertiseement de la Comedie, de la Musique, & de la promenade'.[29]

The distance separating *Cleopatre* from *Cassandre* is illustrated by the episode of Alcamène and Ménalippe in volume VIII of *Cleopatre* which seems as though it might well have been left over from *Cassandre*, so great is the similarity to the earlier conception of heroism. Alcamène is, like Oroondate, a prince of Scythia who wins magnificent victories at the head of his father's army and then, 'pressé d'un ardent desir de faire quelques voyages & de visiter inconnu les Cours estrangeres',[30] leaves his troops and travels incognito to the neighbouring kingdom of the Dacians, the enemies of his father. Here, he falls in love with Princess Ménalippe, is suspected of infidelity and, after the most extraordinarily complex series of adventures, is united with her at last.[31] It is not the events, however, which recall *Cassandre* so much as the place accorded to stirring actions and moral liberty. The battle between the Scythians and the Dacians occupies a central position: lists are given of the provinces from which the troops come, the preparations are described in detail, the fighting itself is covered from many different angles, giving an impression of movement and energy.[32] Alcamène is a man who accepts no limitations on his freedom of action: he relies on direct confrontation to overcome opposition. His pride asserts itself even when Ménalippe has declared her hatred for him and he refuses to give in to his rivals: 's'il faut perdre une vie également odieuse à Menalippe & à Alcamene, je la perdray plus glorieusement aux pieds de Menalippe par la main d'Alcamene que dans la place de Serica par celle de Phratapherne ou de Merodate.'[33] Ménalippe is a fiery woman who can fight with men on equal terms, defies her captors, disobeys her mother rather than betray her love and stabs the man she thinks has caused her irreparable loss. The relationship between the two lovers matches their approach to life. They are drawn immediately towards one another and acknowledge the fact quite readily. There is deference on the part of Alcamène but no undue reserve in Ménalippe, no fear of his advances, no withdrawal behind a protective screen of *bienséance*. Above all, they have no interest in the reactions of the courtiers around them, for they rely on their inclinations and have no need to submit them for approval to a norm established by a group. They are free individuals.

The kind of relationship existing between Alcamène and Ménalippe is not found elsewhere in *Cleopatre*. The other male–female relationships are affected by a significant change in the concept of love which altered the moral balance between the sexes. In *Cassandre*, love had been an extension of the pride by which the hero and heroine ordered their lives.[34] Both of them welcomed the emotion provided their moral liberty was guaranteed and each had specific ways of preventing any attempt, real or imagined, to suppress that liberty. In *Cleopatre*, the male's pride has virtually disappeared as far as love is concerned. Service must be offered to the lady, but not with any pretensions to earning a reward: 'on peut esperer de sa bonté . . . ce qu'il luy plaira de nous accorder, mais ce seroit estre temeraire beaucoup plustost que hardy, que de pretendre comme des choses qu'on peut meriter ce qu'on ne doit attendre que par une pure grace.'[35] Submission must be complete, and must eradicate all personal desires: the aim is threefold, 'de luy rendre ce que nous devons aux Dieux avec une soubmission beaucoup plus entiere que celle que nous avons pour eux, . . . de ne rien faire & de ne rien penser que pour sa gloire, & . . . ou de passer ma vie ou de treuver ma mort dans les occasions de la servir.'[36] When the lady, through a misunderstanding, rejects her suitor, the new hero has no access of pride urging him to strike back. Oroondate is uncouth compared with Coriolan, who never dreams of suggesting that Cléopâtre might be ungrateful but, like Polexandre, assumes that he must have incurred her justifiable wrath for something of which he is not aware.

Pride on the part of the male would be misplaced in *Cleopatre* if it ever found its way in because of the assumption throughout the novel that the male is morally inferior to the female owing to his propensity for passion. The neoplatonic theory that love is subject to the will, still found in *Polexandre* and *Ibrahim*, has gone: *l'amour d'élection* has been replaced by *l'amour d'inclination.* Love is an overwhelming force which renders the will powerless and forces itself upon the unsuspecting individual. Once it has taken hold, it rapidly becomes dominant and may well pervert established moral responses. Adallas develops an incestuous passion for his sister and tells her 'j'y suis porté par une puissance à laquelle je ne puis resister & attaché par une nécessité qui me forcera de vous aimer jusqu'au tombeau'.[37] Philadelphe, carried away by his passion for Délie, informs her that she cannot expect morality from 'celuy que vous ne laissés pas en estat de recognoistre ce qu'il doit à la nature, à la vertu & à vos volontés.[38] Often the lover can appreciate the course of action he ought to take to throw off his passion and can give good advice to others, but is incapable of following it himself.[39]

There are women who react in the same way to love, generally marginal characters. Eurinoé is determined to take revenge on Césarion but is struck with love for him, being possessed of 'un cœur qu'une puissance superieure ou une estrange fatalité firent passer d'une extremité à une autre'.[40] Olimpie finds herself falling in love with a man she hardly knows, though she tells herself she is being 'peu raisonnable'.[41] Woman's greater moral strength saves them, however. Eurinoé and Tullia throw off their passion and follow the inclination dictated by reason;[42] Olimpie hides her feelings until she is sure that the man she loves is worthy of her and it is safe to reveal her affection.[43] With most of the female characters, reason never allows love to reach the point at which it is out of control. Women act as a moderating influence on the more violent emotions of the men and exercise the restraint which their lovers are incapable of showing. A contrast is made, for instance, between the constancy, patience, and 'prodigieuse force de son esprit' shown by Mariamne and the violent excesses of her husband, and indeed, though in a different category, of Tyridate, at whose extravagances she sometimes laughs.[44] Ovid is guided by Cipassis: 'quand je m'y laissois emporter [i.e. aux violences de mon amour], elle me sçavoit fort bien remettre dans la moderation qu'elle desiroit de moy & me reduire sous l'empire de la raison'.[45] Arminius, dissatisifed with the 'complaisance' he gets from Isménie, wants her to share his passion, but 'comme elle se rendoit aisément à la raison, elle resistoit fortement à ce qu'elle jugeoit déraisonnable, ou tant soit peu éloigné d'une severe honnesteté'.[46]

In the grip of their involuntary impulses, the men are tempted to interpret such rational attitudes as indifference. Arminius is offended that Isménie repays his passion 'd'une simple bienveillance, & d'une bienveillance qui ne trouble pas pour un seul moment la tranquillité de vostre ame!'[47] Tyridate protests that no duty could 'raisonnablement' oblige Mariamne to reject him but only a lack of affection, to which she replies: 'L'affection que je dois avoir pour vous . . . ne me pouvoit pas raisonnablement obliger à ce que j'ay faict pour vous complaire.[48] Since the men cannot appreciate the distinction between their own disordered passions and the finer sentiments experienced by their mistresses, other terms have to be brought in to differentiate the various levels and forms of emotion involved. *Estime*, *affection*, *bienveillance* — these terms, much used in the salons of the 1650s, allow La Calprenède to define the moral gap which has developed between his heroes and heroines.[49]

Although he does not devote much space to analyses of the emotions and is not concerned to specify the precise limits of each of these terms, La Calprenède has clearly been influenced by the concept of *honnête amitié* evolved by Madeleine de Scudéry and her circle. Whereas in *Cassandre* male and female values had maintained their respective validities and had found a level at which both could exist, the male in *Cleopatre* is aware that he has much to learn about the emotions and that what he considers natural may in fact be potentially dangerous. With his energetic and straightforward approach to life, he is basically rather an unsophisticated being. He needs the civilizing influence of woman with her innate sense of *bienséance* and her knowledge of the channels through which emotion should properly be directed. He therefore accepts her moral superiority and subjects himself to the social norms she has established, behaving with *galanterie*, suppressing his self-interest, and endeavouring to achieve that 'amitié parfaite, qui est l'union des Cœurs, la joye des Ames, l'assortissement de tous les plaisirs humains, & la souveraine felicité de cette vie'.[50]

The hero as depicted in *Cleopatre* is outwardly similar to the type of individual found in most of the heroic novels of the 1640s. He has the same strength, the same courage, the same direct and immediate responses. His moral autonomy, however, has been reduced. He is aware that the driving force that makes him invincible on the battlefield is a weakness when it comes to emotional relationships with the opposite sex: the energy that enables him to besiege and capture a town is of no use in besieging a mistress. His inability to control his passions means that he cannot claim to be entirely in control of his own destiny.

The hero is now therefore a man who can impose his will on other men but who appreciates that he must bow before the superior moral power of woman. Coriolan, Césarion, Artaban, Philadelphe, Ariobarzane, and Arminius have no difficulty in coming to terms with other men but they are at a disadvantage with women, for it is the latter with their stronger rational faculty who establish what is right and wrong. If the male could guarantee control over his emotions, he could retain his freedom, but as soon as he becomes the victim of a violent passion, which is likely to happen at any time, he is obliged to adopt the woman's terms. (Men who refuse to acknowledge their inferiority and insist on following their crude male impulses are criminals, like Tigrane and Adallas.) He must submerge all self-interest in the service of the lady; he must accept unquestioningly the course that she has decided he is to follow; he must put aside all other aspirations.

Though most of the virtuous male characters are created in this new mould, *Cleopatre* also includes two important variations on the kind of hero mentioned above. With Tyridate, La Calprenède has created the hero of sensibility whose supernormal qualities are animated entirely by love. His courage is stimulated by love, his patience is inexhaustible in the cause of love; he is disinterested, unselfish, and sincere, and as soon as love gives way completely to grief, the life flows out of him.

The second variation is represented by the Roman, Agrippa. He is courageous and noble but he belongs to a different category from Coriolan, Césarion, and Artaban since his virtues are primarily civic. He has a place in the state and guarantees order, not as a law-maker such as a military hero might become but as an interpreter of the law. He belongs to a kind of Roman *noblesse de robe*, having no charisma himself but reflecting the glory of Caesar under whose authority he operates. In a sense, therefore, he represents an infusion of female values into the world of heroism, substituting debate for physical combat and mature reflection for spontaneity. The three men who love Elise provide an interesting example of contrasting levels of reaction. Tigrane, the victim of uncontrollable passions, tries to abduct Elise; Artaban, the traditional hero, rescues her and defeats Tigrane; Agrippa, 'qu'aucune passion ne pouvoit faire sortir des bornes de son devoir',[51] tells Tigrane to plead his case before Caesar who is due to arrive shortly. Later, Agrippa considers his feelings. He knows that Elise favours Artaban but, 'comme toutes ses pensées estoient conformes à l'honneur & à la generosité', he does not want to use the authority he wields in his own interest; instead he tries to find a compromise 'pour concilier son Amour avec sa vertu'.[52] He falls ill from the effort of trying to effect such a reconciliation, but when Elise writes to him to say that she is being persecuted because of his love for her he is dismayed by the thought that he should have made someone else suffer. He decides that 'il falloit faire sur cette passion qui avoit produit de si mauvais effets un effort aussi grand que les maux qu'elle avoit causés'.[53] He emerges triumphant from the struggle and urges the Emperor to unite Elise with Artaban: 'il a combattu cette passion, ennemie de sa gloire & de son devoir, & par le secours de son courage il l'a mise en estat de ne troubler plus sa vertu'.[54] By this victory over his passion, Agrippa stands apart from the traditional heroes in the novel and perhaps represents the beginning of a new form of hero, one who displays some of the female virtues of moderation and emotional discipline.

The difference discernible in the kind of hero depicted by La Calprenède between 1642 and 1657 can no doubt be explained by reference to the changes in the society for which he was writing. *Cassandre* had appeared during the first years of the Regency when an atmosphere of aristocratic exuberance pervaded Parisian society and the martial qualities which the *noblesse d'épée* felt were their special preserve were being demonstrated in the campaigns of the Thirty Years War. Much of *Cleopatre*, on the other hand, reflects the less warlike atmosphere of the period following the end of the Fronde, when the virtues of the warrior were coming to be less highly regarded and when strongly feminist views were being heard in the salons. After the success of *Le Grand Cyrus*, La Calprenède had to take account of the new fashion for novels reflecting closely the preoccupations of these new salons and circles.

It has been suggested[55] that there is a more obvious link with contemporary events in volume XII, when Coriolan and Césarion are imprisoned by the Emperor and are liberated by a popular uprising, calling to mind the imprisonment of the princes in 1650 and their subsequent release after an anti-Mazarin uprising. It seems unlikely that La Calprenède was intending to draw a direct parallel with the events of the Fronde since he has gone out of his way to show the Emperor as a man capable of great injustice, vengeance and cruelty:[56] in 1657 it would have been unwise to suggest such things of the king. This episode is of importance, however, for the light it throws on La Calprenède's commitment to the idea of a morally independent aristocracy, subject to the ruler in certain matters but protecting its own values to the point of death if necessary. While Augustus is applying his power unjustly, seeking revenge on Coriolan and Césarion and trying to coerce Cléopâtre and Elise into marriage, the princes display their *générosité*: Alcamène plans to use his Scythian troops to free the prisoners, Artaban heads an uprising and storms the fortress where they are held.

Throughout the whole finale, Augustus' self-interest and lack of principle are contrasted with the heroic virtues of the princes. When matters have reached deadlock, Coriolan presents himself unarmed before Augustus 'avec une asseurance digne de la grandeur de son courage, accompagnée d'une modestie qui luy estoit naturelle'[57] and offers his life provided Cléopâtre and Marcel are spared. This is the act of a true *généreux*, but it meets with an unheroic response from the Emperor who intends to take the opportunity to execute Coriolan: there is no clemency in La Calprenède's Augustus, whereas Coriolan had always shown mercy to his enemies.[58] It then emerges that Coriolan had prevented Césarion from striking the Emperor down during one of the skirmishes outside the fortress. Caesar is amazed at his enemy's virtue, though Coriolan declares that he acted out of friendship for Marcel: 'sans le respect que j'ay pour tout ce qui est aimé de Marcel, je n'eusse pas eu ce soin pour la vie d'un si cruel ennemy'.[59] Even now, Augustus is incapable of rising above the limitations of politics to impose a magnanimous solution and it is only when the problem of Tibère's claim to Cléopâtre is resolved that he can bring himself to unite Coriolan and Cléopâtre. Consequently, Coriolan's declaration of submission strikes a hollow note; 'c'est maintenant que je sens la douleur & le repentir de vous avoir offencé, & que par cette bonté, plustost que par tous les effects de vostre puissance, je vous reconnois pour mon Seigneur & mon Empereur.'[60] There is no doubt who has emerged as the hero. To La Calprenède, the *noblesse d'épée* were evidently still the guardians of the heroic virtues, however they might have become modified by changing social circumstances and however much the royal power might have increased.

CHAPTER XII

LE GRAND CYRUS

After the publication of *Ibrahim*, Georges and Madeleine de Scudéry had left Paris in 1644 for Provence where they stayed until 1647. By the time they returned to the capital, the novel was dominated by La Calprenède whose *Cleopatre* had just started appearing. His formula of aristocratic individualism and love rooted in pride, established with *Cassandre*, had been used for a number of novels including *Scanderberg* and *Berenger*, and it was this formula that the Scudérys adopted for their new novel. The general framework of *Artamene ou le Grand Cyrus*[1] reproduces many of the features of *Cassandre* — the setting in ancient Persia, the hero who appears in another country under an assumed name and falls in love with the king's daughter, the efforts he makes to rescue his beloved from her abductors.

During the period when he is known as Artamène (volumes I and II), Cyrus is very much a self-centred hero, concerned above all to increase his *gloire*. His attitude towards others is conditioned by the same need to maintain his status as that experienced by Oroondate. Sparing the life of a villain, for instance, is not so much an act of magnanimity as of self-esteem, because 'il y auroit trop peu d'honneur à te l'oster'.[2] He throws himself into physical combat, either as one of an army or singly, rushing ahead of the rest of his comrades,[3] revelling in the triumph over his opponents, shouting 'j'ay vaincu' with undisguised pride.[4] He gains a tremendous pleasure from defying overwhelming odds. There is in these early volumes a continuous series of battles, skirmishes, and duels from which Cyrus emerges victorious and which absorb most of his energy. He has no responsibility for the overall progress of affairs in that he is subject to King Ciaxare and can therefore devote all his efforts to the furtherance of his *gloire*. It is Scudéry's version of the *Cyropaedia*, emphasizing his hero's *fougue* and youthful pride.

At this early stage, Cyrus has no time for love: war is the only activity worthy of his attention, the only path to heroic glory.[5] After he has seen Princess Mandane in the temple, however, he is disturbed by a new emotion which disputes with *gloire* for pre-eminence in his mind,[6] but the love that establishes itself there is dependent to a large extent on self-esteem. When Mandane urges him to be less conspicuous in battle by wearing less striking armour, he refuses because war is one area where her wishes are secondary to heroic self-proclamation.[7] Similarly, though she is angry that Cyrus has fought with his rival against her express wishes, Mandane is worried that she may offend him if she objects too strongly where his honour is in question.[8] His respect for her does not go as far as self-effacement and he is capable of complaining about the treatment he receives: 'si j'estois dans vostre esprit de la façon dont j'y pourrois estre, vous auriez un peu plus d'indulgence pour mon amour.'[9] In the face of such an insistent and self-centred passion, Mandane, like Statira and Bérénice in *Cassandre*, has to ensure that her own position is secure. Love threatens to overcome her *gloire* and must therefore be reduced to a less intense level: what she offers Cyrus is esteem and gratitude, or at the most 'une tendresse infinie' and 'une fidelité inesbranlable'.[10]

The concept of heroism which permeates the early volumes of *Cyrus* is thus based on the same egocentric, aristocratic ethic of personal fulfilment as that in *Cassandre*. Hero and heroine work their way towards an emotional understanding while carefully maintaining their own moral independence. As the novel progresses, however, the way in which Cyrus is depicted changes. The tension between Cyrus and Mandane is replaced as the driving force behind the plot by the *roman-esque* device of abduction, used repeatedly until the end of the novel. The plot settles down into a series of attempts by Cyrus to rescue Mandane. The king whose interests he had been representing fades from the scene and Cyrus conquers one country after another in his own name as he relentlessly pursues those who have abducted Mandane.[11] His stature increases: he is known throughout the world for his exploits but, more important, he is esteemed by all for his equity and

magnanimity. He is less concerned with acquiring *gloire* than
with dispensing justice to those who need it: 'il avoit l'ame
si Grande, qu'il estoit incapable de manquer jamais à rien de
ce qu'il estoit obligé de faire'.[12] He turns into a superhero
like Polexandre, presiding over a crowd of heroic individuals,
all admirable but lacking his supreme charisma. He helps
them to solve their problems and in some cases sends them
home united with their beloved but, again like Polexandre,
he comes to feel that, though he can bring happiness to
others, he himself is doomed to unhappiness.[13]

The changing flavour of the work is reflected in the *tiroirs*.
Some of those in the early volumes recount heroic adventures
and build up impressive pictures of extraordinary individuals
in the traditional manner,[14] but a greater number offer
nouvelles in which unexceptional characters, closely identified
with a group attached to a 'social base', usually a court,
involve themselves in and extricate themselves from emotional
entanglements.

From volume V onwards, the pattern of the work has
taken on a markedly different form from that of the original
formula. The main plot continues steadily on, with Cyrus
moving from one country to another tracking down the third
and fourth abductors of Mandane. As he goes, he collects
around him a crowd of lesser heroes and heroines whose
stories are told in the intercalated episodes and who fill out
the areas of the plot not occupied with military action. There
are battles between Cyrus' army and those of his rivals,
based closely, as Victor Cousin demonstrated, on the campaigns of the Prince de Condé,[15] and the confrontations with
Thomiris in volume X add movement and suspense but, for
the rest, the main plot largely takes the form of a series of
conversations dealing with *galanterie*. The princes and princesses accompanying Cyrus and Mandane behave as though
they were in a travelling salon, making few concessions to
the conditions they are required to live in. They compose
'cette belle Cour errante',[16] passing the time in exactly the
same way as they would in Sardis or Susa:

ce grand nombre d'Honnestes Gens, que la familiarité du voyage unissoit
encore davantage, faisoit un si agreable meslange de Gens de toutes
sortes de conditions, d'humeurs, & de Nations differentes, qu'il eust

falu estre fort stupide, ou fort chagrin, pour s'ennuyer en un lieu où il y avoit tant de Personnes divertissantes.[17]

The war which was the original occasion of the expedition consequently tends to be relegated to second place. *Galanterie* is the primary occupation in life and war can at times be something of an intrusion:

pour faire voir combien Cyrus estoit aymé de tous ceux qui le connoissoient, il ne faut que sçavoir que Ligdamis, Thrasimede, Menecrate, Parmenide & Philistion, quoy qu'ils fussent encore Amans de leurs Femmes, les quitterent pour suivre ce Prince à la guerre, bien qu'il voulust les en dispenser.[18]

Main plot and *tiroirs* alike turn into a vehicle for the kind of analysis of the passions, the emotional casuistry which was to be recognized as the distinctive mark of *preciosité*. Some of the episodes are no more than accounts of conversations between Madeleine de Scudéry and her friends in which any genuine appreciation of feeling is smothered beneath the refinements of *galanterie*. Some, however, reveal an insight into the complexities of human emotion which, in comparison with the earlier heroic novels, is startling. The idea (still found in *Mitridate*, *Alcide*, and *Berenger* amongst others) that love is a simple passion which can be associated with other simple passions such as *gloire* but which by definition is quite separate from hatred or jealousy has given way to an awareness that love embraces a large number of conflicting emotions and that the way in which these emotions interact is a mystery to the person suffering them. Their effects can be noted but their cause cannot be explained: they are outside the area of rational control, though any person who falls victim to them is tempted to rationalize the behaviour they force upon him. The analysis of love in those few episodes in which Madeleine de Scudéry has resisted the urge to make concessions to the salon is a worthy adumbration of Madame de La Fayette and Racine.[19]

Love as it is represented establishes itself before the lover is aware of any emotional attachment on his part. It has nothing to do with reason or a response towards particular qualities in another person: 'l'Amour . . . se vante d'estre au dessus de la raison, de naistre plustost dans le cœur que dans l'esprit, & de naistre mesme sans le consentement de

ceux dans le cœur desquels il naist'.[20] It makes no difference
what conscious defences are prepared, 'dés que nous craignons
d'aimer quelqu'un, nous l'aimons desja',[21] and emotions are
formed and fade without reference to the will of the person
concerned. Jealousy mingles itself as a wellnigh inevitable
ingredient of love, confusing the victim's attempts to understand his situation: in the more violent characters, love can
produce reactions indistinguishable from those of hatred.[22]
As their passions pull them one way and another, they are
prepared, like Racine's characters, to accept as second best
a relationship based on any sort of positive response, even
hatred or anger, if they are denied the love they crave.
Indifference is worse than hatred:

je pensois du moins n'estre que haï, . . . mais par ce cruel oubli où vous
estes de tout ce qui me regarde, je voy bien que je suis encore en un
estat plus deplorable que je ne croyois, puis qu'assurément je suis
mesprisé: . . . Il y a du moins quelque sentiment dans une ame qui
hait: & il n'est pas absolument impossible que l'amour naisse parmy le
feu de la colere. Mais d'un esprit froid & insensible, qui ne conserve
nul souvenir de tout ce que l'on a fait pour l'obliger: le moyen d'en
esperer de la tendresse & de la reconnoissance?[23]

There is a suggestion too that love brings out in some of
those it affects an urge to dominate rather than a desire
to serve.

The story of Cléobuline[24] illustrates many of the aspects
of love mentioned above. As Queen of Corinth, Cléobuline is
naturally concerned with her *gloire* and status but finds to
her horror that she has fallen in love with Myrinthe, a worthy
man but socially inferior to her. All her efforts to reason
away her passion are useless and she concludes that all she
can hope to do is conceal it. Her feelings are complicated,
however, by the fact that Myrinthe loves Philimène and she
is unable to prevent herself from revealing to her *confidente*,
Stésilée, the mixture of love, pride, and jealousy that is
torturing her:

j'aime sans estre aimée; j'aime sans qu'on le sçache; & j'aime une
Personne qui aime ailleurs. Et cependant je l'aime de telle sorte, que je
ne puis cesser de l'aimer, ny souffrir qu'il en aime une autre: quoy que
je ne voulusse pas qu'il sçeust que je l'aime, ny qu'il me dist jamais
qu'il m'aimast, quand mesme il pourroit arriver qu'il m'aimeroit.[25]

She even confesses eventually who the man is and how violently her emotions are affecting her whole view of the world, including her self-respect: 'je sens que l'amour que j'ay pour Myrinthe devient haine contre moy-mesme: & que la jalousie que j'ay pour Philimene devient fureur contre ma propre raison.'[26] Like the Princesse de Clèves suffering from comparable emotions, she recalls the lessons she has received, 'que la tranquilité de l'esprit estoit le plus grand de tous les biens, & que cette tranquilité estoit à l'ame ce que la santé est au corps: c'est à dire que sans elle, on ne peut joüir de nulle sorte de plaisir'.[27] Faced with her own weakness, she finally decides that she must marry Myrinthe to Philimène and this move brings about a radical change in the emotional balance. Myrinthe, married to Philimène but aware that the queen loves him, loses interest in his wife and falls in love with Cléobuline: she, however, reacts in the opposite way: 'plus elle connoist que Myrinthe est amoureux d'elle, plus elle s'en esloigne.'[28]

The sort of emotional veracity evident in the story of Cléobuline casts an entirely new light on the heroic ethic. *Gloire*, *générosité*, and *vertu* stand out as the façade that a person of eminence is expected to maintain: they are not necessarily a guarantee of superhuman forces behind. Cléobuline's regal status makes certain demands on her which she is not entirely convinced she needs to obey. She seriously considers marrying Myrinthe, feeling she has the same right to happiness as any other woman, and *gloire* only just wins the contest for supremacy in her heart.[29] It has sufficient force to prevent her transgressing the external requirements of kingship — 'si la gloire ne venoit à mon secours, je retomberois dans ma premiere foiblesse'[30] — but she realizes that her own *vertu* is not strong enough to maintain her at a level where she is morally matched to her status: 'il ne faut point te fier à ta propre vertu: car avec toute ta gloire, il y auroit de la folie à te confier à tes propres forces.'[31] Her decision to marry Myrinthe to Philimène is a desperate attempt to do something irrevocable before her resolve to maintain her *gloire* collapses. She begs Philiste to convince her that she has done the right thing, that 'il y a plus de Grandeur de courage à faire ce que je fais, qu'il n'y a eu de foiblesse à me laisser vaincre'.[32] From being the natural expression of a heroic will to impose a personal order on the world, *gloire* has become an obligation to be fulfilled, in opposition to the natural desires of the heart.

A similar analysis of love and its relationship with heroic emotions is found in certain other episodes, notably 'Histoire de Belesis, d'Hermogene, de Cleodore et de Leonise'[33] and 'Histoire d'Aglatidas et d'Amestris'.[34] The interaction of pride, jealousy, and love is followed through with few concessions to the demands of the *romanesque*. The discrepancy between the reality of a lover's feelings and the rational account he tries to give of them is made clear. Bélésis tells his friend, Hermogène, 'je ne pourrois jamais recevoir un plus sensible déplaisir que de vous voir aimé de Cleodore, quoy que j'aime tousjours Leonise', though it is evident he still loved Cléodore.[35] Cléodore triumphs when she tells Bélésis she is going to marry Hermogène, experiencing 'une assez grande joye d'avoir connu avec certitude dans les yeux de Belesis qu'il estoit encore pour elle ce qu'il avoit esté autrefois. Ce ne fut pourtant pas dans le dessein de luy pardonner, mais seulement parce qu'elle espera le rendre plus malheureux', and she cannot understand why she subsequently suffers feelings of regret over Bélésis.[36]

The concept of human nature embodied in episodes such as these is basically deterministic. The passions are formed involuntarily by 'une génération perpétuelle . . . , en sorte que la ruine de l'une est presque toujours l'établissement d'une autre', as La Rochefoucauld was to put it.[37] The victim of love finds himself behaving in a way he did not intend and has to try to come to terms with an aspect of his being over which he has little, if any, control. He will almost certainly experience jealousy and possibly hatred as well. The people who are shown suffering these emotions are not depicted as abnormal or despicable, as they would have been in *Polexandre*: on the contrary, they are generally admirable. Cléobuline, for instance, is heroic 'par la Grandeur de son ame, par la noblesse de ses inclinations, par la generosité de son cœur, & par l'estenduë de son esprit';[38] she practises liberality in a noble and heroic manner and combines the severity of justice with the gentleness of clemency.[39]

The contrast is all the greater, therefore, when the main plot continues to postulate the freedom of the individual to direct his passions towards the end that he considers the best. Cyrus is shown as a man who experiences strong emotions but who never allows them to force him into performing an unheroic deed or harbouring an ungenerous thought. His reason is his constant guide. He lectures Aryante, the last of the abductors of Mandane, a naturally virtuous man who 'sentoit une repugnance estrange toutes les fois que son amour le forçoit à s'esloigner des sentimens que la vertu inspire',[40] asserting that love had never made him do anything of which he needed to repent or which could be held as a reproach against him. Aryante murmurs that it is so easy to be equitable when one is fortunate, so difficult not to be unjust when one is wretched, but Cyrus will not accept any excuses: 'Puis que vous ne voulez pas que je vous considere . . . comme un homme qui soit obligé à escouter ny la raison, ny la justice, ny la generosité, ny la reconnoissance, mais seulement comme un homme que l'amour dispense de tous les devoirs de la societé raisonnable . . .'.[41] To Cyrus, anyone who suggests that his emotions excuse his actions has admitted his inferiority.

The power of love is not entirely subject to reason, even in Cyrus and Mandane, for each of them falls victim to jealousy. Cyrus is perturbed that his greatest rival might be the one to rescue Mandane: 'la fureur s'empare de mon esprit; la jalousie que je ne connoissois presques point, trouble ma raison'.[42] When his fears prove groundless and Mandane remains undelivered, he feels almost as much joy as sorrow 'par un bizarre sentiment d'amour & de jalousie tout ensemble'.[43] Mandane acknowledges to herself that her own jealousy is a weakness but does not like to admit to it publicly.[44] Thomiris, the Queen of the Massagètes, who plays an important rôle in the sequence of events at the end of the novel, is a violent, passionate women whose love for Cyrus manifests itself as hatred, jealousy, and rage. The comparable figures in *Cassandre*, Roxane and Perdicas, had appeared as villains because their passions were out of control: it was in fact the gods themselves who made them slaves to their passions so that they lost their judgement and received their due punishment as a result.[45] Thomiris on the other hand is treated with a degree of sympathy because the power of her passions is recognized as being outside her control.

In general, however, a distinction is noticeable between the main plot, in which reason is the central principle behind the heroic actions, and many of the subsidiary episodes in which externally noble and striking characters prove to be motivated by emotions over which they have no control. The distinction is accentuated by the development in the subsidiary episodes of an alternative interpretation of the values of heroism, redefined in accordance with the kind of world in which the stories are set, namely a refined circle of courtiers, dominated by the female characters, in which the encounters are verbal and emotional rather than physical. Social graces are here more important than a martial air.

The redefinition of the heroic virtues is the more evident because of Madeleine de Scudéry's practice of providing portraits of the major characters introduced into the episodes, in which their heroic qualities are enumerated and explained.[46] *Gloire* and *générosité* are attributed to male and female characters alike but are very different from the virtues Oroondate would have understood. Cléonisbe loves *gloire* more than herself, she is *généreuse*, 'de la derniere generosité' and has 'le coeur Grand, ferme & tout à fait Heroïque', but the major feature of her heroic nature is her great sense of pity and her tender kindness.[47] Onésile's qualities are all overshadowed by her *générosité* which makes her render services to all those of *vertu*, beyond anything expected of her: 'qui que ce soit n'a jamais sçeu obliger d'une maniere plus noble, plus desinteressée, ny plus Heroïque'.[48] Philoxène loves her *gloire* and is noted for her tenderness and her loyalty towards her friends: she is sociable and her virtue is 'ny sauvage, ny austere'.[49]

The *générosité* of which these ladies are possessed is a concern for the welfare and the happiness of others. Their *gloire* is a concern for their reputation, not the reputation to be gained by seeking out danger but the one that accompanies a virtuous life and is subject to attack by slander. It cannot be fought for except by the constant repelling of any threat that might give slander a chance, by the maintenance of a strict *bienséance* and *honnêteté*.[50]

The emphasis has shifted from those virtues in the heroic spectrum that raise the hero above his fellow men to those that bind him more closely to them — kindness, loyalty to friends, sympathy. There are two which were scarcely relevant to the novels committed to endless military actions and duels but which are here particularly emphasized, viz. liberality and modesty. Modesty fulfils a special function in that it prevents the person of superior qualities from losing sight of the obligations that bind all men together. It is a corrective to the natural tendency to develop an inflated view of one's own capacity which in its turn breaks down the solidarity on which society should be based. Péranius is an outstanding man, valiant, jealous of his *gloire*, liberal, and *généreux*, but his greatest quality is that he prefers to praise others rather than be praised himself, possessing to a high degree 'cette modestie qui est une marque infaillible de la valeur heroïque'.[51] Pisistrate on the other hand, despite being loyal, liberal, courageous, and *généreux*, is somewhat too attached to his own opinions and falls short of heroic status.[52] In women, modesty reveals itself in the opinion they have of their beauty or, with women like Alcionide and Sapho, of their wit and learning.[53]

Where modesty serves to maintain homogeneity in a society, liberality, mentioned as a virtue in connection with all the major characters in the novel, helps to set apart within the group those who possess supreme qualities. By showing generosity towards his friends and acquaintances, the hero brings them nearer to him but at the same time raises himself morally above them, having the same effect as clemency in the military hero. Liberality is a heroic virtue, according to Parthénie.[54] 'Qui n'est point liberal, n'est point genereux', declares Doralise and she explains that valour, kindness, prudence, and wisdom can be found in all sorts of men but, for liberality, 'je ne voy que cette vertu toute seule, par où les Grands puissent raisonnablement s'eslever au dessus des autres'.[55]

The effect of this new interpretation of heroism on the subject-matter of the novel can be seen in several of the episodes, such as the 'Histoire d'Elise'.[56] Élise herself has the same charismatic quality as the great military heroes, striking those who see her with her quasi-divine air, so that they are drawn to her: 'elle a si bien sçeu accorder la fierté & la modestie dans son cœur, qu'il en resulte je ne sçay quoy de Grand & de Divin dans tous ses mouvemens, qui la rend infiniment aimable'.[57] She does not of course use her charisma to inspire men in battle, but it has the same effect of setting her apart from those around: it is 'je ne sçay quoy de divin, qui separe celles qui l'ont du reste du monde: qui les fait craindre & respecter de ceux qui les aiment: & qui sans faire incivilité à personne, fait toutesfois qu'on ne se familiarise jamais trop avec celles qui ont cette aimable fierté'.[58]

It is *fierté* she has, not *orgueil*. On the contrary, 'elle n'a pas seulement de l'humilité, elle a encore de la modestie'.[59] Her heroic manner hides a heart full of goodness and tenderness, especially towards her friends to whom she is absolutely loyal. She resists any threat to her *gloire* as firmly as any male hero, not by direct action but by reacting sharply to any suggestion that might affect her reputation as a virtuous woman.[60] Throughout the episode, she is a model of heroic virtue, admired by others and displaying 'une fermeté incroyable' in the face of affliction.[61] As she lies dying, the whole court treats her as the moral power in their society. She comforts her sorrowing friends with 'une tendresse genereuse, qui ne s'exprima point par des larmes, & qui ne l'obligea pas à donner aucune marque de foiblesse'.[62] She counsels the king, 'l'exhortant à estre juste; à estre clement; à estre liberal; à aimer ses Peuples; & à ne se laisser jamais gouverner par ses passions'.[63]

Élise and other characters like her are the incarnation of a heroic ideal offered to the polite society of the Fronde period as an alternative to the militaristic heroes of earlier novels. Élise is not inferior to Cyrus, 'dont les Conquestes sont encore plus grandes que celles d'Elise':[64] she is different. She is heroic because she has the qualities that enable her to stand out as a moral force in the society in which she lives, to champion and exemplify the standards of *bienséance* and self-control necessary in a compact group such as a court. In short, she is heroic because she is a model of *honnêteté*.

The heroic novel had been propagating the ideals of *honnêteté* throughout its existence and had reflected closely the increasing influence of feminism.[65] In *Antiope*[66] and *Rosane*,[67] it had been possible for characters to discuss the need for *honnêteté*: is the apparent dissimulation involved in civility not fundamentally dishonest and therefore unheroic? why whould we be modest about something we know to be praiseworthy? In *Le Grand Cyrus*, such questions are assumed to have been answered. The hero accepts the rules of society unhesitatingly while never losing sight of the reasons why they are necessary. Since his heroic status depends partly on his impeccable behaviour in society, however, he ceases to be a man apart in the tradition of earlier heroes. Pacore in *Alcide*, Cyrus in *Axiane*, Pyrrhus in *Mitridate* — these had all been brought up away from civilization, developing the simple heroic virtues with which nature had endowed them and which allowed them to move naturally into a position of authority when they were eventually introduced into society. The world of courtiers had tended to be depicted as an unheroic place, the haunt of devious favourites and dangerous courtesans, often hostile to the hero's straightforward values. The new hero is expected not only to live in a society of (virtuous) courtiers but to excel in it by his 'air galant', a 'je ne sçay quoy . . . qui naist de cent choses differentes'. This is something that can only partially be a gift of nature, for 'il faut de plus que le grand commerce du monde, & du monde de la Cour, aide encore à le donner: & il faut aussi que la conversation des Femmes le donne aux hommes'.[68] Not everyone born with great qualities will achieve it[69] and no man can acquire it without cultivating the opposite sex. He must show that he responds with sensibility to their charms and at some stage of his life should fall in love. The rugged virtues of 'ces hommes de fer & de sang, qui passent toute leur vie à la guerre: ou de ces Chasseurs determinez, qui sont tousjours dans des forests'[70] are no longer sufficient. They need to be made sociable by love and brought back from the rarefied atmosphere in which the ethic of aristocratic individualism had set them. The heroic aureole is now reserved for the man who fits best into society rather than the one who stands above it. He needs to be 'aimable' and 'honnête': his charisma is his 'air galant':

> ce je ne sçay quoy galant, qui est respandu en toute la personne qui le possede, soit en son esprit, en ses paroles, en ses actions, ou mesme en ses habillemens, est ce qui acheve les honnestes Gens, ce qui les rend aimables, & ce qui les fait aimer.[71]

The love he is required to experience is not the confused passion that takes away all moral sense. Such emotions are to be avoided as far as possible by following the precepts of *amitié tendre* (or *amitié héroïque*),[72] a relationship which retains the pleasures of conversation and *galanterie* while stopping short of any involvement that might upset the emotional equilibrium of the couple. At the court of Cyprus, where the laws of Venus Urania are observed,

> les amours permises sont des amours si pures, si innocentes, si détachées des sens, & si esloignées du crime, qu'il semble qu'elle n'ait permis d'aimer les autres, que pour se rendre plus aimable soy-mesme, par le soing que l'on apporte à meriter la veritable gloire, à acquerir la politesse, & à tascher d'avoir cet air galant & agreable dans la conversation, que l'amour seulement peut inspirer.[73]

No demands are made of the loved one, no pain is felt from jealousy. Yet *amitié tendre* brings with it a level of disinterested feeling which can nullify the extremes of emotion to which man is subject and leave him free to exploit his heroic potential. It is 'la chose du monde la plus innocente, la plus juste, la plus douce, & ... la plus Heroïque ... C'est sans doute l'amitié qui adoucit toutes les douleurs, qui redouble tous les plaisirs, qui fait que dans les plus grandes infortunes, on trouve de la consolation & du secours: & c'est elle enfin, qui a fait faire mille actions Heroïques par toute la Terre'.[74] It does not demand grand gestures and enormous sacrifices. It is a relationship which needs the stability of a settled society and thrives on day-to-day attentiveness: 'ce sont les petites choses qui font les grandes amitiez'.[75]

The heroic ideal that Madeleine de Scudéry formulates in *Le Grand Cyrus* thus negates many of the features previously considered essential in the hero. The moral freedom that the hero had striven to maintain has been rendered nugatory by the fact that the passions are now seen to be stronger than the will. To be separated from the rest of mankind is no longer required of him. He needs to be a full member of society and indeed cannot become properly heroic unless he has absorbed the manners and attitudes of the group to which he belongs. He is admirable because he reinforces the social norms, not because he transcends them. Great love and devotion for a lady, one of the most important aspects of the traditional heroic ideal, is now suspect since the passions are potentially dangerous and can lead to situations beyond the control of even the most heroic person. Preference is given to alternative kinds of relationship, based on *tendresse*, *estime*, and 'les petits soins & tous les petits devoirs de l'amitié'.[76]

Much of this new heroic ideal is expounded in a tentative way, becoming increasingly affirmative as the novel progresses. The result is an ambivalence running throughout the work. On the one hand, Cyrus perpetuates much of the received tradition, being a man of insuperable will-power, devoting all his energies to the heroic service of Mandane, recognized by all as specially marked out among men to live and love in an incomparable way: on the other hand, many characters are depicted as heroic according to the ideal formulated by *préciosité*, stressing the virtues necessary in a refined society, concerned with what makes men more alike rather than with what distinguishes them. The ambivalence is left unresolved although clearly, if the *précieux* view of the individual is accepted, the traditional ideal cannot be held to be valid since its premises are incompatible with those of *préciosité*.

Le Grand Cyrus represents the final metamorphosis of the heroic novel. The prose-epic form ostensibly recounting the heroic deeds of a great figure is here used as a framework on which to hang a large number of subsidiary episodes reflecting a concept of man and an ideal very different from those for which the form was created. In *Clelie*, the process is completed: the form is still retained but little attempt is made to hide the fact that the heroic element has become an empty convention: 'sous des apparences semblables, le roman héroïque était devenu un roman bourgeois'.[77]

PART III

The analysis of the major heroic novels in Part II shows that any attempt to establish a definition of heroism covering the whole corpus of heroic novels between 1630 and 1660 risks masking as many important aspects as it illuminates. The heroic ideal embodied in the major novels changed so radically that the only features that can be seen as constants are the more obvious ones, such as a commitment to love.

Polexandre, the first of the major novels, reflects a very personal concept of heroism, based on a largely pessimistic view of human nature, in opposition to that of the majority of such authors. In Gomberville's vision, man as a species is subject to the tyranny of the passions. Love in particular can be a disastrous experience, striking him down like a plague: there is nothing that can be done to prevent its attacks or, in the main, to cure them. There are, however, certain individuals who have been endowed with a will strong enough to overcome the passions and who can therefore succeed in living according to the *généreux* precepts of altruistic heroism, to be admired by the majority of mankind. Within this group of specially favoured beings, there are some whose heroism is even more refined. They are the elect: they have had a heroic destiny visited upon them and must respond to the call, regardless of whether they feel adequate to it or not. Everything with them is subordinated to the pursuit of the highest virtue.

Heroic destiny in *Polexandre* is thus not dependent on the individual's own wishes. However hard he tries, he will not be able to reach heroic status unless he is blessed with the requisite 'grace'. *Ibrahim*, in contrast, holds out to everyone the chance to achieve heroism. The world from which Justinian emerges is only a short way removed from that in which the average reader would have felt at home. His virtues are those to which all could aspire — loyalty, a strong sense of honour, firmness, fairness. His is essentially an imitable form of heroism, inspiring the reader to adopt the same standards of *honnêteté* and altruism.

Cassandre ignores questions of ultimate moral responsibility, depicting an ideal of absolute individual freedom, such as the *noblesse d'épée* claimed as their own. Everything the hero does is assessed in terms of his fidelity to his image of himself: all other obligations, including those towards his king and country, are secondary to it. Even love has to be subordinated to self-interest and can only be acknowledged when the demands of *gloire* have been satisfied. In him, pride and self-reliance are admirable, the urge to self-aggrandizement is glorious, but the moral dangers inherent in such an attitude are assumed not to exist.

In *Cleopatre*, however, a moral contradiction becomes apparent. The heroic characters still see themselves as responsible only to their private image, but they have in fact lost the power to control their own destiny because their will can no longer be relied upon to direct their passions. Since they cannot guarantee to impose themselves on every situation that confronts them, they have lost the moral autonomy so prized by Oroondate. The moral leadership has passed to the women who, with their strong sense of *bienséance*, are more capable of controlling their passions. The hero/heroine relationship is no longer one of moral equality with each partner ensuring that his or her own pride is satisfied. The deference and service that the hero had previously devoted to his lady as an indication of his honest intentions have been replaced by subjection. He has no rights, can make no claims but can only hope that he will not be considered too unworthy of her.

Le Grand Cyrus confirms that the passions can oblige even heroic individuals to act against their reason and illustrates the complexities of emotion with which men and women have to struggle. The possibility that a being might exist whose will could control his passions is not excluded, though a comparison with *Clelie* suggests that Cyrus is depicted as such a being because he was originally envisaged by the author as a reincarnation of Oroondate, rather than because Scudéry shared Gomberville's belief in a 'chosen' heroic few, exempt from the weaknesses found in other men.

Le Grand Cyrus offers an ideal of restrained social behaviour and *amitié tendre* as a defence against the potential tyranny of the passions.

Heroism as it appeared in the major novels was the product of the society for which it was created. The readers expected to find confirmed in these novels the pattern of behaviour that they imagined as their ideal, and novelists consequently offered an increasingly *bourgeois* interpretation of heroism to match the change from aristocratic individualism in 1640 to the world of the financiers and their wives in 1655. Having demonstrated its ability to keep pace with the changing ethos during the period of the Fronde, the heroic novel none the less declined rapidly around 1660. The possible reasons for its eclipse will be considered in the following chapter.

CHAPTER XIII

DECLINE

The heroic novel fell from popularity with remarkable rapidity. During the 1650s, Scudéry and La Calprenède had produced some of their most successful works and looked ready to continue well into the 1660s, but *Almahide* (1660-3) and *Faramond* (1661-3) were their last efforts respectively in this style,[1] and observers were already noting a change in fashion. In a letter dated 15 December 1663, Chapelain commented that the public's taste had forsaken novels 'qui sont tombés avec La Calprenède' and now favoured 'les voyages'.[2] One of the characters in *La Promenade de Saint-Cloud* (1669), boasting that he had never read a novel, declares 'je me réjouis tous les jours de ce que le siècle commence à s'en dégoûter'.[3] The abbé de Villars, writing admiringly of Madame de La Fayette's *Princesse de Montpensier* (1662), remarked 'on a veu cesser tout à coup cette ardeur qu'on avoit pour les Romans'.[4] In 1683, Du Plaisir commented that 'les petites Histoires ont entièrement détruit les grands Romans'.[5] Some sixty years later, Lenglet du Fresnoy affirmed that the writing, though not the reading, of these long novels had ceased about 1660.[6]

A glance at the bibliographies will confirm that the fall in the number of heroic novels published at this time corresponded to an increase in the number of *nouvelles*, a form which became strikingly popular. Such an apparently straightforward replacement of the novel by the *nouvelle* in the public's affections has encouraged explanations of the change in terms of simple substitution. The novel was long and complex, the *nouvelle* short and concentrated: therefore, it is argued, the public must have welcomed the *nouvelle* because it had grown tired of the length and complexity of the heroic novel. Seventeenth-century commentators had already formulated such an argument, but it was reaffirmed authoritatively in the eighteenth century by the *Bibliothèque universelle des romans*: 'Lorsqu'on s'apperçut que les longs Romans fatiguoient la patience des Lecteurs François, on imagina les Nouvelles historiques; & leur succès a été si complet, qu'elles ont fait disparoître les grands Romans.'[7] It has been restated in various forms regularly since then.[8]

As supporting evidence for this explanation, reference is often made to satirical comments found in Scarron, Sorel, and others about the lack of everyday realism in heroic novels, and to the vogue for burlesque verse that developed after the publication of Scarron's *Typhon* in 1644, reaching a peak in about 1650. The assumption is that these reflect a dissatisfaction with the idealism of the heroic novel and that it was a concern for greater realism that was responsible for its sudden decline. It is probably true that the reading public was growing a little tired of the way each new novel repeated the same stereotyped situations and indulged in conventionalized sentiments, but we must be wary of assuming the existence of a strain of anti-heroic realism or subversive parody strong enough to turn the public against the heroic novel. A study of 'realistic' prose fiction and the burlesque shows that they did not really represent a negative approach towards heroism.

Throughout the period of its vitality, the heroic novel coexisted with two other forms of prose fiction, relatively more realistic than it. One such form related adventures not dissimilar to those found in the heroic novel, but made no attempt to raise the characters to a higher moral plane than that on which the reader might be expected to exist. Such works, frequently inspired by Spanish originals, therefore depended on the interest aroused by the episodes of the plot rather than on the moral quality of the characters. *Le Roman véritable*,[9] for instance, is made up of a series of stories linked by the appearance of the main characters in each one. The settings are realistic in so far as they are Spanish rather than taken from far-off lands and ages. The characters are sufficiently noble to know the correct way to behave but are not preoccupied with *générosité* or with *galanterie*. They are direct and forthright; they become involved in brawls and have to hide from the law; they avoid

over-refined concepts of love. Particularly noticeable is the
fact that the style is not inflated as it so often was in the
heroic novel. It contains no unnecessary superlatives, no
overloaded sentence structures, no involved compliments.
The anonymous author is concerned to tell a story and
considers his task accomplished if the story is transmitted
as directly and as economically as possible. The four stories
published by Boisrobert in 1657[10] offer the same combination of *romanesque* incidents and 'realistic' characters,
containing, despite their collective title, nothing heroic in
the sense implied in the heroic novel. Segrais' *Nouvelles
françoises* are likewise based on incidents very similar to
those found in the heroic novels — abductions, chance
meetings, etc. — but avoid the worst of the conventions
associated with the latter.

The other form of more realistic novel took its subject-
matter from ordinary life and depicted entirely contemporary
characters in recognizable settings. *Polyandre* deals with
financiers, rowdy aristocrats, *précieuses*, arguments over the
function of poetry, and the difficulty in finding patrons,
Le Romant comique with the realities of life in the provinces,
the problems besetting travelling actors, brawls in taverns.[11]

The heroic novel occasionally ventured into this less
idealized area and devoted an episode or two to a more
recognizably real world, stripped of magnificence and exotic
trappings. The story of the Marquis français (le Feint Astrologue) in *Ibrahim*[12] makes no attempt to hold up a mode
of behaviour for the reader's admiration or to show the
workings of the human emotions, but merely relates the
amusing consequences of a white lie. Bonnet breaks the
heroic atmosphere of *Berenger* at one point by including
a pirate who regales the company with earthy stories and
sings a drinking-song.[13] The first volume of *Le Toledan*[14]
is suffused with a picaresque tone which prevents a genuinely
heroic aura being built up around the central character. The
author apologized for it in volume II, blaming it on his
Spanish source, and promised that subsequent volumes
would contain far less of it.

If some of the writers of heroic novels felt free to move
away from the traditional heroic material and introduce a

more realistic element into their works from time to time, the writers of 'realistic' novels did not see their primary function as the negative one of satirizing the more cumbersome long novels. Neither Sorel nor Scarron wrote specifically to parody the heroic novel in the way in which Sorel had set out to ridicule the pastoral in *Le Berger extravagant* or Du Verdier the romance of chivalry in *Le Chevalier hypocondriaque*. To a certain extent, Sorel had a polemic intention in writing *Polyandre*, since he was opposed to those who maintained that only the adventures of kings and queens were of any interest,[15] but apart from a number of satirical remarks about high-flown declarations of love,[16] he does not attempt to score points at the expense of the heroic novel. Scarron certainly made explicit his impatience with the clichés of character and plot associated with the heroic novel,[17] and the brawls in *Le Romant comique* are no doubt intended as satirical comments on the heroic encounters described by La Calprenède and Scudéry, but there is no attempt to offer a 'realistic' alternative to *romanesque* conventions. Indeed, the *Romant comique* is dependent on many of the same conventions as the heroic novel.[18]

Equally, it is not possible to categorize the vogue for burlesque verse as primarily an anti-heroic phenomenon, for the majority of burlesque versions of heroic works published around 1650 left their subject-matter substantially untouched and concentrated on the form of expression. As the titles of many of them suggest, the burlesque was normally concerned with travesty rather than with parody, that is to say, it related the deeds and words of ostensibly great and dignified personages in the lowest form of everyday speech rather than inventing different circumstances for the personages to appear in, as parody would have done.[19]

Most burlesque writers took an established heroic or legendary theme and travestied it by replacing the more elevated verse form with an octosyllabic line, using large numbers of archaisms, neologisms, popular and lewd expressions, and academic words used in an incongruous context. Beneath the layer of ribaldry and linguistic inventiveness, Dassoucy's *Ovide en belle humeur* straightforwardly recounts the *Metamorphoses*. His *Poesies et lettres* contain a large number of *vers héroïques*, couched in superlatives and addressed to the great military leaders of the day, followed by a number of *vers burlesques*, flattering the same noble figures but using everyday language in octosyllables instead of alexandrines.[20] Lengthy passages of the *Arioste travesty*[21] contain nothing that could not be taken for a genuine rendering of the original with a little ribaldry added. Picou, in his *Odyssée d'Homere*, makes only the occasional reference to everyday objects and includes little that seems intended to make the reader laugh: his only ambition would appear to be to recount the fidelity of Penelope while avoiding the poetic diction usually employed for this sort of work, in the belief that 'souvent une simplicité naifve n'a pas moins d'agréement qu'un langage poly & des termes bien choisis'.[22]

The admiration accorded to Scarron was earned largely by his skill in manipulating the verse-form and vocabulary associated with the burlesque. Those who praised him did not suggest that he had demolished the heroes of the ancient world in his *Virgile travesty*, but merely that he had made them more accessible, providing 'des graces folâtres & goguenardes' in place of Virgil's 'beautez graves & serieuses'.[23] Some observers made the point explicitly that the subject-matter of travestied works was not affected, since 'les Vers Burlesques different seulement en façons de parler & de langage, de ceux dont les phrases & stances sont hautes, graves & serieuses: car le mesme Poëme peut estre grave ou burlesque, en changeant seulement les façons de parler.'[24] Writers of burlesque works, moreover, sometimes declared their intention of not interfering with the subject-matter of the heroic material they had borrowed. Scarron, for example, promised to demonstrate to the Prince of Orange that his burlesque muse could 'traiter comiquement un sujet heroïque sans le prophaner',[25] and Nouguier openly stated his aim of relating his chosen epic theme without any attempt at parody, restricting any burlesque comments to the level of digressions. He manipulated his epic material skilfully, retaining an obvious affection for it.[26]

It is evident that the heroic novel did not fall victim to a concerted onslaught mounted by dedicated opponents. Though satirical comments about its lack of verisimilitude

may have helped to reduce its momentum to a certain
extent, we need to look inside the novel to find the causes
of its decline, for a reading of the heroic novels published
in the late 1640s and the 1650s shows that many authors,
while continuing to use the forms and conventions established
in the 1630s, had lost much of their interest in the heroic
subject-matter. They would construct a skeletal plot around
a set of historical incidents and allow it to develop very
slowly, but the greater part of the novel would be devoted
to episodes of *galanterie* or discussions on abstract points of
love. Sorel, as usual, was aware of the change:

Toutes leurs avantures ne sont pas Heroyques ny guerrieres; entre
plusieurs Tomes d'un Roman, on en void quelques-uns de tres gros
qui ne contiennent pas trois feuilles où il soit parlé du Heros principal,
n'estant employez qu'à des Histoires destachées lesquelles ne sont
aucunement du sujet, & ne sont remplies que de folles amourettes & de
cageolleries ou galanteries assez basses, . . . Cela est fort indigne de ce
stile Heroyque que les Autheurs se proposent.[27]

In some cases, the major characters taken from ancient
history were glimpsed only occasionally, while a totally
different crowd of characters, barely disguised *habitués* of
the salons of the Marais, populated the episodes. *Le Grand
Cyrus* is an example of how the main plot could lose contact
with the *tiroirs*, which were supposed to depend on it.[28]
Similarly, *Hermiogene* ostensibly relates the events leading
up to the assassination of Julius Caesar, but the main interest
is in the depiction of Roman society as a world in which
civility and form are more important than power and politics.
Clorinde has virtually no main plot;[29] the episodes are set
against a background of military action (Pompey's wars
against Mithridates and the Roman campaigns in Judaea),
but no individuals emerge and incidents involving fighting are
passed over quickly. On the other hand, the emotional
subjugation of men by women is detailed in numerous forms,
with the strictest severity as the norm.[30]

   In other cases, the world of social sophistication spread
from the episodes to the main plot as well. In *Le Toledan*,
what heroics there are are restricted to a few of the subsidiary
episodes and contrast so noticeably with the overall tone of
restraint and refinement that at times it seems almost as

though the author is parodying the heroic style.[31] *Clelie*
goes even further. The portraits of the authoress's friends
and the discussions on the metaphysics of love have left no
scope for heroic material: the figures intended to justify the
epic structure are reduced to the size of courtiers, 'Caton
galant et Brutus dameret'. Indeed, the argument put forward
in volume VIII for a moral concept of the novel is an attempt
to justify retaining the form of the heroic novel while jettison-
ing the breadth of vision and imaginative power that had
established that form. The list of essential features in a novel
given by Anacréon is such that it does not require an author
to include any heroic incidents or glorify human endeavour
at all in his work.[32]

Novelists and those for whom they wrote were rapidly
losing interest in the mythology of heroism. To understand
why, we need only look at the radical changes — ideological,
social, and political — that had taken place in France during
the ministries of Richelieu and Mazarin. On the ideological
side, the factor that had the greatest effect as far as the novel
was concerned was the erosion of the assumptions about the
nature of man necessary for a belief in heroism. As we have
seen in Parts I and II above, the prose-epic form of the novel
had emerged in the 1630s as a vehicle for the depiction of an
ideal man, capable of transcending the limitations of human
nature: unlike the mass of mankind, he could maintain a
clear distinction between his will or reason and his emotions,
and guarantee to follow the path of virtue. By the 1650s,
however, the concept of free will was well on the way to being
superseded by a deterministic view, according to which man
was conditioned by forces over which he had no control,
notably his emotions.

The result was not, as was once thought, a simple 'demolition' of the concept of heroism, with an aristocratic ideal
being systematically dismantled by Jansenist pessimism.
Every society or social grouping creates an ideal, to which it
hopes its members will aspire, and the ideological ferment
into which France was thrown during the period in question
produced a metamorphosis, or perhaps rather a fragmentation,
of the concept of heroism. Sections of society far removed
from the *noblesse d'épée* and with no particular affinities

with Jansenism formulated their own versions of the heroic ideal, which might be achieved through service to the state, charity, rebellion, self-abnegation, or even renunciation of the world. Yet the search for man's moral identity necessarily involved a questioning of the very premises of the ideal proposed, and it can be argued that every move towards the affirmation of heroism raised a corresponding question about its validity.[33] The modern reader of the novels of the mid-seventeenth century is indeed struck by the fact that they reflect an increasing awareness of a moral ambiguity underlying all human behaviour, which brought into question the nature, and even the existence, of virtue, since actions were no guarantee that the motive behind them was virtuous.[34]

The society that both produced this questioning and at the same time was affected by it had undergone a number of significant political and social transformations. The 1630s had seen the *noblesse d'épée*, or at least some of its more extreme elements, ready to commit treason in an attempt to stop the movement towards centralized monarchical control. By 1660, the nobles' position had been so eroded that they were only too glad to accept their subordinate status under an all-powerful king. In the 1630s, the wealth of the nation was being increasingly directed into the state's coffers, and by the 1650s those who manipulated the state finances had emerged as the dominant class, the major force behind the establishment of a new bourgeoisie which would control the developing capitalist economy. The influence exerted by women in the 1630s in the area of social behaviour had become so strong by the 1650s that it was rapidly imposing a new set of social virtues. The ideal man imagined by the generation of 1660 had lost the self-assertion and the prickly pride that had characterized the heroes of Louis XIII's reign: he displayed instead a depth of sensitivity, a responsiveness to the feelings of others, and an ability to show restraint and delicacy in social situations that were entirely new.

In response to the changes taking place, the writers of heroic novels offered their public a new depiction of love as an overwhelming, irrational force afflicting characters who moved in circles similar to their own. As we have seen, the novels of the 1630s and early 1640s had, on the whole, embodied the assumption that man had free will and that the pursuit of virtue raised no problems for those who were prepared to allow their will to operate unimpeded. Novels such as *Histoire celtique*, *Ibrahim*, *Scanderberg*, and *Antiope* are in a sense hymns to the potential of human will-power, showing the greatest of men harnessing the energy released by their passions and directing it towards the goal dictated by reason. Villains are those in whom the passions are stronger than the will and who are thus driven on by irrational forces.

Cassandre and the novels inspired by it, such as *Alcide* and *Berenger*, already offer an alternative view. Here love is shown to be an extension of *amour de soi*, ultimately dependent like *gloire* on self-interest, and the *vertu* which is the hero's object is dissociated from the idea of altruism to become an embodiment of the urge to self-aggrandizement. This suggestion that heroism was not necessarily linked to virtue represents the first stage in the weakening of heroism, for it struck at its moral basis. It implies that self-aggrandizement is an end in itself, and thereby allows the possibility of a form of heroism that condoned anti-social or immoral acts. It is curious, however, that the novel never in fact went on to investigate the corollary, as Corneille did in *Rodogune* and *Théodore*, that the pursuit of personal ideals could be heroic, even if it led into crime. The novel always assumed the existence of moral imperatives based on the aristocratic interpretation of Christian morality. Killing is permissible, but only in certain very specific circumstances: the poisoning of rivals or the obsessive pursuit of vengeance by any means are the actions of individuals whom the hero steadfastly opposes and over whom he finally triumphs.

From *Cleopatre* onwards, the heroic novel is almost entirely given over to the adventures of characters whose will is subordinate to the passion of love with its irrational inclinations and its propensity to jealousy and despair. Since love had become, practically speaking, the sole motivating factor in the plot, much of the traditional material became irrelevant. Battles, duels, and confrontations of *générosité* had been a necessary ingredient in the earlier novels because they provided an excellent method of demonstrating how the man of will-power with his moral freedom could impose himself on any set of circumstances and create his own destiny. The pursuit of love was itself subordinate to the maintenance of moral independence. After the Fronde, the novelist was more concerned to analyse the effects of the irresistible force of love on his characters, with particular reference to the differences in the responses made to it by the sexes. Manifestations of physical prowess were of no use in furthering this aim and consequently faded from the central position they had occupied, though, because of the epic structure of the heroic novel and its commitment to the great military leaders of the past, they could not be discarded completely. *Clorinde*, *Clelie*, and similar novels manage with only a perfunctory acknowledgment of this aspect of heroism, however.

Within thirty years, therefore, the form of the heroic novel, developed as a vehicle for an optimistic affirmation of human greatness centred on a major heroic figure, was having to serve as the framework for an investigation of the affective side of human nature, coloured by a deterministic view of the passions. The subordinate episodes, which had previously existed as a support for the main plot, had taken on a primary rôle as quasi-independent short stories, dealing with particular aspects of the metaphysics of love. Heroism as understood by the generation of 1630 had ceased to correspond to the realities of life experienced by the post-Fronde generation, who in general were coming to share La Rochefoucauld's attitude, 'qu'à une grande vanité près, les héros sont faits comme les autres hommes', and the part of the novel linked with the older concept of heroism became less and less important. Madeleine de Scudéry's recognizable portraits of contemporary figures in *Le Grand Cyrus* and *Clelie* allowed the epic form to maintain a certain momentum, thanks to their novelty, but, as was inevitable, the cumbersome framework was eventually seen to be redundant and was abandoned, allowing the episodes to emerge as free-standing *nouvelles* in their own right.

The triumph of the *nouvelle* in the 1660s was not a victory at the expense of a totally different form of prose fiction, but rather part of a progression, one which can be seen already working its way out in the 1640s and 1650s.

Madeleine de Scudéry's venture into the *nouvelle* with
Celinte (1661) was simply the logical extension of the major
modifications she had already brought to the heroic novel in
the 1650s.[35] A form as substantial as that of the prose-epic
novel was bound to create its own inertia; none the less, its
eclipse in the 1660s is perhaps less remarkable than the fact
that it had managed to dominate prose fiction for so long
after it had ceased to fulfil any necessary function.

CONCLUSION

'Des centaines de romans qui, de l'*Astrée*, nous mènent à la *Princesse de Clèves*, que reste-t-il que l'on puisse lire aujourd' hui?' asked Marcel Arland, offering an answer with which it is difficult to disagree: 'Quatre ou cinq œuvres, pas davantage.'[1] The heroic novel cannot pretend to stand with the great novels of French literature. As I have tried to show, its importance lies rather in the help it gives in understanding the movement of ideas in mid-seventeenth-century France. Works written by philosophers, moralists, or theologians may provide the most direct expression of the way in which new explanations of the world and of man's place in it were being formulated, but it is very often in the humbler form of the novel that we find the best indication of how the various interpretations of the human condition affected the attitudes — perhaps subconscious — of the mass of the reading public.

It is not, I think, an overstatement to talk of an obsession with the heroic potential in man during the first half of the seventeenth century. To explain why that particular society should have been so concerned with heroism is no doubt as much the province of the psychologist or the anthropologist as of the literary historian, but it is none the less worth looking for factors that might have acted as stimuli towards the emphasizing of heroic virtues. Attempts have been made to explain the emergence of the heroic novel in France as a response to the political circumstances of the 1630s. The *Bibliothèque universelle des romans* asserts that 'on aimoit tout ce cliquetis, parce qu'une fermentation générale agitoit tous les cerveaux, & que les guerres civiles allumoient dans toutes les têtes des volcans secrets'.[2] Wadsworth suggests that the progress of war in Europe caused Gomberville to increase the heroic element in each subsequent version of *Polexandre.*[3] Arland refers to the war against the Protestants, the nobles' resentment towards Richelieu, and the threat from the House of Austria as factors in the public's preference for the heroic over the pastoral.[4] Others have indicated sociological forces, the rise of the bourgeoisie with their desire to participate vicariously in an aristocratic ideal:

L'idéal de vie qui inspirait ces romans, ce mélange d'héroïsme et de galanterie répondaient aux rêves non seulement de la jeune noblesse et des officiers de nos armées, mais aussi de tant de petits bourgeois et de bourgeoises qui se représentaient sous cette forme les séductions d'une vie plus libre, plus intense et plus brillante.[5]

I would suggest, however, that, of the major factors that made up the ethical climate of the time, the one to which the heroic novel was primarily a response was the concern to identify the nature of human liberty and the form of society that would best allow it to flourish. France in the first half of the seventeenth century was balanced between the old order, rooted in feudalism and felt by many to be the 'natural' order, and the new structure of society based on absolutist principles, limiting the moral freedom of the individual but offering a new sense of national solidarity. The conflict of interests produced particularly rapid changes during the period 1630–60. In 1630, the old order was still recognizable, still awaiting the most radical changes to be effected by Richelieu. By 1645, major sections of society, including the *noblesse d'épée* and the *noblesse de robe*, were having to reassess their values in an attempt to maintain their position. By 1660, a society had emerged which, despite its external grandeur, was essentially bourgeois.

While these changes were taking place, literature was reflecting a search for man's moral identity, so much so that it is difficult to find any form of literature which did not concern itself, at least to some extent, with the question of how human liberty could legitimately be expressed, and the novel in particular embodied some of the complexities involved. What all writers of heroic novels offered was a statement of their belief in human liberty, but they by no means shared the same notion of the nature of that liberty. In *Cassandre*, *Scanderberg*, *Alcide*, and *Mitridate*, liberty is to be found in the old ideal of self-assertion, the aspiration to sublimity; in *Ibrahim*, *Le Grand Cyrus*, *Le Toledan*, and *Clorinde*, it resides in the acceptance of ethical imperatives imposed by a refined society. Some, like Gomberville, used the heroic novel to project a dream of escape from 'les miseres' and 'les foiblesses de la condition humaine';[6] for others, like Hotman de Latour, it was a lament for passing greatness; for yet others, like Guérin de Bouscal, it was an assertion that greatness could still exist, provided the realities of the world were faced up to. In many cases, it reflected a desire to reconcile the urge to self-aggrandizement character-istic of the old order with the need for self-limitation in the new.[7]

These various ideals of liberty had ultimately to give way before the realization that man's freedom was in fact restricted by his own nature. A suspicion that moral values were not absolute after all was the beginning of an investigation into the complexity of the emotions, an investigation which was carried out much more radically in other forms of literature. Many of La Rochefoucauld's maxims on the nature of the passions[8] are a statement in precise terms of what the novel had been trying to express somewhat confusedly for some time. The heroic novel itself never reached the point of explicitly questioning the existence of a heroic element in man. Before it reached that stage, it had been eclipsed, though the works of Gomberville, La Calprenède, and Scudéry continued to be read by the generation for which they had been a statement of faith.

NOTES

INTRODUCTION

1. M. Lever, 'État preśent des études sur le roman français au XVIIe siècle (1973-1977)', *XVIIe Siècle* XXX, 4, p. 309.
2. R. Picard, 'Remises en question', *RHLF* 77 (1977), pp. 355-8.
3. H. Coulet, *Le Roman jusqu'à la Révolution*, 2 vols. (Paris, 1967); A. Adam, *Histoire de la littérature française au XVIIe siècle*, 5 vols. (Paris, 1948-56), each volume of which gives substantial coverage to the novel.
4. M. Lever, *La Fiction narrative en prose au XVIIe siècle* (Paris, 1976); R. C. Williams, *Bibliography of the Seventeenth-century Novel in France* (New York, 1931); R. W. Baldner, *Bibliography of Seventeenth-century French Prose Fiction* (New York, 1967).
5. One of the most encouraging features of recent work in this area is the effort made by scholars such as R. Francillon (*L'Œuvre romanesque de Madame de La Fayette*, Paris, 1973) and M.-T. Hipp (*Mythes et réalités. Enquête sur le roman et les mémoires, 1660-1700*, Paris, 1976) to demolish the iron curtain often erected between the pre-1660 novel and the works of Mme de La Fayette and her successors.
6. F. Deloffre, *La Nouvelle en France à l'âge classique* (Paris, 1967); R. Godenne, *Histoire de la nouvelle française aux XVIIe et XVIIIe siècles* (Geneva, 1970).
7. Lever's 'État présent' (see above, note 1) lists Sorel and Scarron as holding second and third places respectively in the list of subjects of scholarly analyses. Camus has been the object particularly of critical editions.
8. *Nouvelle bibliotheque de campagne, ou choix d'episodes intéressans et curieux, tiré des meilleurs romans, tant anciens que nouveaux*, 3 vols. (Amsterdam and Paris, 1769), Avertissement, v, vi.
9. Körting, *Geschichte des französischen Romans im XVII Jahrhundert*, 3 parts in one vol. (Leipzig, 1885), I, 361. See his remarks on Gomberville (I, 217-18) for an indication of his lack of sympathy for this kind of novel.
10. Saintsbury, *A History of the French Novel to the Close of the Nineteenth Century*, 2 vols. (London, 1917), vol. I.
11. Morillot, *Le Roman en France depuis 1610 jusqu'à nos jours* (Paris, s.d.), p. 7.
12. See Coulet, op. cit., I, 165-6; S. Kévorkian, *Le Thème de l'amour dans l'œuvre romanesque de Gomberville* (Paris, 1972), p. 232; Lever, 'État présent . . .', *loc. cit.*, p. 311.

13. Of the numerous works dealing with this area, the following are of particular importance: F. E. Sutcliffe, *Guez de Balzac et son temps: littérature et politique* (Paris, 1959); A. Levi, *French Moralists. The Theory of the Passions, 1585 to 1649* (Oxford, 1964); A. Stegmann, *L'Héroïsme cornélien. Genèse et signification*, 2 vols. (Paris, 1968); *Héroïsme et création littéraire sous les règnes d'Henri IV et de Louis XIII*, ed. N. Hepp and G. Livet (Paris, 1974).

14. Adam, *Histoire de la littérature française*, II, 400.

15. Sorel, *La Maison des jeux*, 2 vols. (Paris, 1657), II, 419; *La Bibliotheque françoise*, 2nd edn. (Paris, 1667), pp. 183 et seq.; *De la connoissance des bons livres, ou examen de plusieurs autheurs* (Paris, 1671), p. 8.

16. Lenglet du Fresnoy, *De l'usage des romans*, 2 vols. (Amsterdam, 1734), II, 35-67.

17. *Bibliothèque universelle des romans, ouvrage périodique dans lequel on donne l'analyse raisonnée des romans anciens et modernes, françois, ou traduits dans notre langue*, 224 vols. (Paris, 1775-89), Part II, chaps. 6-9.

18. Green, *French Novelists, Manners and Ideas from the Renaissance to the Revolution* (London and Toronto, 1928), pp. 15-22.

19. Saintsbury, op. cit., I, 176, n. 1.

20. Magendie, op. cit., pp. 181-95.

21. Adam, *L'Âge classique 1624-1660* (Paris, 1968), pp. 145-7.

22. Coulet, op. cit., I, 160.

23. H.-J. Martin has identified more than ten editions of Part I of *L'Astrée* and has estimated that its readers must have been numbered in tens of thousands, a remarkable figure for the time (*Livre, pouvoirs et société à Paris au XVIIe siècle (1598-1701)*, 2 vols. (Geneva, 1969), I, 295).

24. Sorel, *La Bibliotheque françoise*, ed. cit., p. 176.

25. Op. cit., p. 96; cf. Adam, *Histoire . . .* , vol. 1, 399.

26. It is interesting to note, however, how frequently defenders of inconstancy in the manner of Hylas appear in novels otherwise committed to an ideal of heroic constancy: Palamède in *Ariane*, Le Marquis français in *Ibrahim*, Elgazaïr in *Polexandre*, Démocarez in *Berenice*.

27. Langlois (*Le Tombeau des romans*, Paris, 1626) mentions only *L'Astrée* and Barclay's *Argenis* as evidence in his defence of the novel.

28. See Tallemant des Réaux, *Historiettes*, ed. Adam, 2 vols. (Paris, 1960), I, 554-5. A 'Satyre du temps' indicates an awareness that Gombauld was attempting something new: 'Gombauld, embrassant la façon d'Italie, Par son Endymion a delaissé Thalie' (*Les Satires françaises du XVIIe siècle*, ed. Fleuret and Perceau, 2 vols., Paris, 1923, I, 120).

29. Boisrobert, *Histoire indienne d'Anaxandre et d'Orazie* (Paris, 1629), Advis au lecteur qui servira de preface.

30. Hotman de Latour, *Histoire celtique*, 3 vols. (Paris, 1634), Adver-
    tissement.
31. The editions of these works to which I shall make reference are:
    a) Gomberville, *La Premiere (-Cinquiesme) Partie de Polexandre*, 5
       vols. (Paris, 1637).
    b) La Calprenède, *Cassandre*, 10 vols. (Paris, 1642-5).
    c) La Calprenède, *Cleopatre*, 12 vols. (Leiden, 1648-58).
    d) Scudéry, *Ibrahim ou l'Illustre Bassa*, 4 vols. (Paris, 1641). Two
       four-volume editions of *Ibrahim* were published in 1641 by
       Sommaville, both in-8°, with identical dedications, *privilèges*,
       and *achevé d'imprimer* but from different type settings and with
       different pagination. In one, the volumes contain Premiere
       Partie, Suite de la premiere partie, Seconde Partie, Suite de la
       seconde partie respectively, each part consisting of ten books;
       in the other, Premiere Partie, Deuxiesme Partie, Troisiesme
       Partie, Quatriesme Partie respectively, each part consisting of
       five books. References are made to the former edition.
    e) Scudéry, *Artamene ou le Grand Cyrus*, 10 vols. (Paris, 1649-53).
       References are given as *le Grand Cyrus* or *Cyrus*. The question
       of the relative contributions of Georges and Madeleine de
       Scudéry to the composition of *Ibrahim* and *Cyrus* is likely to
       remain unresolved. For these two novels, therefore, the author
       is generally referred to as Scudéry, but for other works Georges
       and Madeleine are mentioned individually.
32. Huet, *Traité de l'origine des romans*, ed. Kok (Amsterdam, 1942),
    pp. 113-19.

PART I

Chapter I
1. Some of the Greek romances, notably Chariton's *Chaereas and
   Callirhoe*, Xenophon's *Ephesiaca*, and the *Apollonius of Tyre*,
   were not generally known until the eighteenth century when
   authoritative translations were published. Longus' *Daphnis and
   Chloe*, extremely popular in the sixteenth century thanks to
   Amyot's translation of 1559, does not resemble the other romances,
   being a static pastoral tale with none of the suspense characteristic
   of *Histoire ethiopique* and the other adventure-romances. It was
   eclipsed when *L'Astrée* appeared, offering a pastoral framework of
   much greater scope and without the explicit sexual references
   of Longus.
2. *L'Histoire aethiopique de Heliodorus*, trans. Amyot (Paris, 1547),
   fols. 53, 155-6, 157.
3. Ibid., fols. 127-37.
4. *Histoire aethiopique*, Le Proesme du translateur; Sorel, *La Bibliotheque françoise*, ed. cit., p. 182; Hotman de Latour, *Histoire
   celtique*, Advertissement.

5. Fumée, *Du vray et parfaict amour* (Paris, 1612). First edition 1599. This work was published as a translation of the second-century Greek philosopher, Athenagoras, but was later revealed as a forgery; see Huet, *Traité de l'origine des romans*, ed. cit., pp. 162-8.

6. Gerzan, *L'Histoire afriquaine de Cleomede et de Sophonisbe*, 3 vols. (Paris, 1627-8), I, 915.

7. Jean Baudoin (or Pierre de Boissat ?), *Histoire negrepontique, contenant la vie et les amours d'Alexandre Castriot* (Paris, 1631), pp. 223-4. My italics.

8. Ibid., pp. 234 et seq.

9. Boisrobert, *Histoire indienne d'Anaxandre et d'Orazie* (Paris, 1629), pp. 298 et seq., 152 et seq.

10. d'Urfé, *L'Astrée*, ed. Vaganay, 5 vols. (Lyon, 1925-8), I, 233.

11. Ibid., II, 239.

12. Ibid., I, 426-8; cf. I, 347.

13. cf. IV, 742-6.

14. Ibid., IV, 802.

15. See Pintard, 'Quelques aspects de l'héroïsme dans l'Astrée', *Héroïsme et création littéraire . . .* , pp. 233-42. Pintard confirms that the vocabulary of heroism in *L'Astrée* is infinitely less rich than that of love or *galanterie*.

16. On borrowings from *L'Astrée* by other novelists, see Magendie, *Le Roman français au XVIIe siècle de l'Astrée au Grand Cyrus* (Paris, 1932), pp. 100-7; cf. also R. Garapon, 'L'Influence de l'Astrée sur le théâtre français de la première moitié du XVIIe siècle', *Travaux de linguistique et de littérature* VI, 2 (1968), pp. 81-5. For examples of later pastorals, see Lansire, *La Diane desguisée* (Paris, 1647); *Le Grand Cyrus*, VI, Book II.

17. See R. Mandrou, *De la culture populaire aux XVIIe et XVIIIe siècles: la Bibliothèque bleue de Troyes* (Paris, 1964), pp. 131-41; N. Edelman, *Attitudes of Seventeenth-century France towards the Middle Ages* (New York, 1946), pp. 147-57.

18. *Les Prouvesses et vaillances du redouté Mabrian* (Troyes, 1625).

19. Quoted by G. Reynier, *Le Roman sentimental avant l'Astrée* (Paris, 1908), p. 177.

20. For full details of the Amadis cycle, see E. Baret, *De l'Amadis de Gaule et de son influence sur les mœurs et la littérature au XVIe et au XVIIe siècle*, 2nd edn. (Paris, 1873), pp. 224-30.

21. Du Verdier, *Le Romant des romans, où on verra la suitte & la conclusion de Don Belianis de Grece, du Chevalier du Soleil & des Amadis*, 7 vols. (Paris, 1627-9). Published by Courbé, du Bray, Sommaville, Loyson, Lacquehay, and Bessin. The original *privilège* refers to six volumes. Vol. IV appears to have been intercalated.

22. Logeas, *L'Histoire des trois freres, princes de Constantinople* (Paris, 1632), Au lecteur.

23. Logeas, *Le Romant heroïque, où sont contenus les memorables faits d'armes de Dom Rosidor, Prince de Constantinople* (Paris,

1632); *L'Histoire des trois freres; Les Travaux du prince incognu* (Paris, 1634). These three works reveal a development in the author's technique. *Le Romant heroïque* is a shapeless work, lacking any verisimilitude; *l'Histoire des trois freres* shows a somewhat greater concern for realism; *Les Travaux* is more polished, with fewer supernatural elements and a more central position accorded to women.

24. *Le Premier Livre de Amadis de Gaule*, trans. des Essarts (Paris, 1548), fols. 61–2.

25. Ibid., fol. 123.

26. *Le Romant des romans*, II, 773; III, 912–13.

27. Ibid., II, 34; II, 94; III, 869; V, 14, 15; V, 70; VI, 363; VI, 364.

28. Ibid., I, 540–1.

29. Fumée, *Du vray et parfaict amour*, ed. cit., fols. 288–9.

30. De Moreaux, *Peristandre ou l'illustre captif*, 2 vols. (Paris, 1642), II, 209–12.

31. fol. 334.

32. II, 310–11.

33. *Du vray et parfaict amour*, fol. 205.

34. *Peristandre*, II, 19.

35. *Le Polemire, ou l'Illustre Polonois* (Paris, 1646). Baldner lists the author as Père Calixte Auguste Deschaussée. Lever mentions no author's name. The *Epître* is signed V.F.

36. pp. 200–2.

37. Hotman de Latour, *Histoire celtique*, I, 9.

38. *Cleopatre*, X, 125; cf. *Ibrahim*, III, 287 and *Polexandre*, I, 705.

39. *Cleopatre*, II, 273.

40. Le Vayer de Boutigny, *Mitridate*, 4 vols. (Paris, 1648–51), I, 60.

41. Desmarets de Saint-Sorlin, *Rosane, histoire tirée de celle des Romains et des Perses* (Paris, 1639), p. 246.

42. *Axiane* (Paris, 1647), Au lecteur. Gomberville reveals himself to be nervous about exceeding the limits of credibility in *Polexandre* (IV, 623) where the hero is shown pacifying a kingdom in eight days. He explains for the benefit of those who do not know the provinces in question and who might think 'que je veux faire Polexandre pour un Amadis ou pour quelqu'autre Chevalier enchanté' that the area contained only three large villages and twenty to thirty hamlets.

43. *Polexandre*, II, 434–5; cf. ibid., I, 69, *Cassandre*, I, 35, 38, *Le Grand Cyrus*, VII, 105.

44. *Mitridate*, I, 100; cf. Chappuzeau, *Ladice ou les victoires du Grand Tamerlam* 2 vols. (Paris, 1650), I, 60–1.

45. P.A.D., *Alcide*, 2 vols. (Paris, 1647–8), I, 135–6. M. Lever has identified the author of this novel as le sieur d'Astorgues ('Romans en quête d'auteurs au XVIIe siècle', *RHLF* Jan.–Feb. 1973, pp. 7–21).

46. *Le Polemire*, p. 200 (rectified). A favourite source for details of youthful intellectual prowess was the *Cyropaedia* of Xenophon.

47. cf. Danjou (*Le Tableau de l'homme fort*, Nevers, 1645, pp. 5, 8): 'ce n'est pas assez qu'un homme courageux endure patiemment les peines & les travaux qui se presentent: il faut de plus qu'il agisse, & qu'il forme des desseins relevés, illustres & magnifiques ... L'action dit un principe & la passion une dependence: agir, c'est vaincre, pâtir, c'est estre vaincu: agir, c'est donner, pâtir, c'est recevoir: ... l'action est plus noble que la passion, puisque la premiere dit abondance & la seconde suppose disette & indigence.' See also Cériziers' attempts to establish the heroic basis of martyr-dom: *Le Philosophe françois*, 3 vols. (Paris, 1643), III, 365; *Les Trois Estats de l'innocence*, 3 vols. (Paris, 1640), III, 184 et seq.

48. *Ibrahim*, I, 740-1.

49. Du Cros, *Histoire de la vie de Henry, dernier duc de Montmorency* (Paris, 1643), pp. 7, 91-2.

50. Cériziers, *Le Heros françois ou l'idée du grand capitaine* (Paris, 1645), p. 3.

51. Guez de Balzac, *Œuvres*, 2 vols. (Paris, 1665), II, 491.

52. Du Bois-Hus, *Le Prince illustre* (Paris, 1645), pp. 34-5; cf. Saint-Évremond, *Eloge de Monsieur le Prince*, Arsenal MS 3135, fols. 61-9.

53. Le Moyne, *La Gallerie des femmes fortes* (Paris, 1647), p. 195.

54. Cériziers, *Le Tacite françois* (Paris, 1648), Part II, p. 245; cf. Richelieu, *Testament politique*, ed. André (Paris, 1947), p. 237.

55. e.g. Dubosc, *L'Honneste Femme*, 3rd edn., 2 vols. (Paris, 1635), II, 237.

56. Ibid., II, 240.

57. Dubosc, *Les Femmes heroïques comparées avec les heros*, 2 vols. (Paris, 1669), I, 218-19. First published as *La Femme heroïque, ou les heroïnes comparées avec les heros en toute sorte de vertus*, 2 vols. (Paris, 1645).

58. La Mothe le Vayer, *Œuvres*, 3rd edn., 2 vols. (Paris, 1662), II, 193, 197.

59. Vulson de la Colombière, *La Science heroïque* (Paris, 1644), pp. 1-2.

60. Vulson de la Colombière, *Le Vray Theatre d'honneur et de cheva-lerie, ou le miroir heroïque de la noblesse*, 2 vols. (Paris, 1648), I, Preface.

61. See Mayerne Turquet, *La Monarchie aristodemocratique* (Paris, 1611), p. 249; Chevreau, *L'Escole du sage, où il est traicté des vertus et des vices* (Paris, 1646), p. 148; Montagu de la Coste, *La Contention de l'espée avec la robbe sur les parties du prince* (Paris, 1610), pp. 147-8.

62. In *Cassandre*, *Le Grand Cyrus*, *Alcide*, and *Ladice* respectively.

63. III, 179.

64. III, 286.

65. V, 22.

66. XII, 212.

67. Juvenel, *Dom Pelage, ou l'entrée des Maures en Espagne*, 2 vols.

(Paris, 1645), I, 97.

68. I, 164.

69. I, 222.

70. Princess Godioze, beloved of Dom Pélage: 'cette injuste Princesse avoit tousjours plus d'égard à punir l'audace de mon amour qu'à reconnoistre la grandeur de mes services' (II, 208), but when she finds out his true identity, 'Godioze me fit paroistre ... une estime nonpareille' (II, 224).

71. I, 192.

72. Who naturally shares the open-minded attitude of the other characters: 'Non, non, Cratile, ... ne pensez pas que l'inégalité de vostre naissance à la mienne m'ayt faict condamner vostre passion. J'ay tousjours mieux aymé la vertu sans noblesse que la noblesse sans vertu' (I, 365).

73. cf. I, 107.

74. Desfontaines, *L'Illustre Amalazonthe* (Paris, 1645), p. 8. This novel is frequently attributed to Cériziers despite the fact that the title-page gives the author as le sieur Des Fontaines. There are three reasons, however, why the author is more likely to have been the actor and playwright, Desfontaines: (i) the novel includes an episode (see below, p. 88) out of which Desfontaines had already made a play, *Alcidiane ou les quatre rivaux* (1643); (ii) it reveals a leaning towards stoicism which was totally alien to Cériziers (see below, p. 66); (iii) Desfontaines liked to include the adjective 'illustre' in his titles, cf. *Eurimedon ou l'illustre pirate*, *L'Illustre Olympie*, *L'illustre Comédien*. He was associated with Molière's 'Illustre Théâtre'.

75. See J. Morel, 'L'Héroïsation des grands chefs de guerre en France au XVIIe siècle', *Revue des sciences humaines* (1966), pp. 5-11; cf. the distinction made by P.-H. Simon between the hero, the great man, and the superman (*Le Domaine héroïque des lettres françaises*, Paris, 1963, pp. 16 et seq.) and see also L. Braun, 'Polysémie du concept de héros', *Héroïsme et création littéraire* ..., pp. 19-28. It should be noted that the hero in the heroic novel is a direct descendant of the heroes of romance rather than of epic heroes in that he has no national or ethnic significance, generally lives in a vague, ill-defined world, and lacks a tragic dimension.

76. e.g. the tyrant Arcalaus who feeds his prisoners on salty bacon with no water, ambushes wandering knights, and abducts ladies, but who is basically cowardly and begs for mercy when his men have been defeated (*Le Tiers Livre de Amadis de Gaule*, Paris, 1547, fol. 30 et seq.).

77. *Le Premier Livre ...*, fol. 13.

78. *Le Quatriesme Livre d'Amadis de Gaule* (Paris, 1555), fol. 90.

79. Du Verdier, *Le Romant des romans*, vol. V.

80. Vol. VI.

81. Vol. VII.

82. *Ibrahim*, Preface.
83. *Mitridate*, II, 306.

Chapter II
1. Guez de Balzac, *Œuvres*, II, 173.
2. Richelieu, *Testament politique*, p. 234.
3. Silhon, *Le Ministre d'Estat* (Paris, 1665), p. 158.
4. Naudé, *Considerations politiques sur les coups d'Estat* (*s.l.*, 1679), p. 231.
5. Chevreau, *L'Escole du sage*, pp. 260-1, 267; cf. Sirmond, *Le Coup d'Estat de Louys XIII* (Paris, 1631), p. 42; Caussin, *La Cour sainte* (Paris, 1624), p. 327.
6. See Sutcliffe, *Le Réalisme de Charles Sorel* (Paris, 1965), pp. 16-25 for a wider analysis of these attitudes.
7. Danjou, *Le Tableau de l'homme fort*, p. 29.
8. Couraud, *Le Heros chretien* (Angers, 1655), p. 10.
9. Guérin de Bouscal, *Antiope*, 4 vols. (Paris, 1644), I, 109; III, 135.
10. Hobbes' views were known in France, where he lived from 1640 to 1651, but they were often identified with those of Machiavelli or the *libertins*. For that reason, Sorbière found it prudent to include in his translation of *De Cive*, published in Amsterdam in 1649 under the title of *Elemens philosophiques du citoyen*, a note claiming that he did not agree with the author and expressing the hope that some Frenchman would undertake the task of refuting his views, even though Sorbière in fact felt a good deal of sympathy for Hobbes' ideas (see *Sorberiana*, Paris, 1694, Art. 'Hobbes'). Sorel mentions that Hobbes' principles were not generally accepted and that Fortin de la Hoguette's *Elemens de la politique* (Paris, 1663), in which he attempted to show that society and mutual help are the state of nature and that men have always been interdependent, was 'plus approuvé' (*La Bibliotheque françoise*, p. 62).
11. *Antiope*, I, 104-5.
12. Ibid., I, 107-8.
13. Ibid., I, 283-5. A similar argument is used by the Prince d'Egine (IV, 137-8); cf. *Ariane*, p. 600.
14. Couraud, *Le Heros chretien*, pp. 9-10.
15. P. Bénichou, *Morales du Grand Siècle* (Paris, 1948), pp. 18-33; O. Nadal, *Le Sentiment de l'amour dans l'œuvre de Pierre Corneille* (Paris, 1948), pp. 283-323; Stegmann, op. cit., II, 417-98.
16. cf. Sutcliffe, *Guez de Balzac et son temps*, pp. 120-31.
17. Descartes' definition (*Les Passions de l'âme*, Art. 153) stops at this point: *générosité* is a determination to undertake 'toutes les choses qu'il jugera être les meilleures'.
18. Chevreau, *Scanderberg*, 2 vols. (Paris, 1644), I, 173. cf. Bonnet, *Berenger, comte de la Mark*, 4 vols. (Paris, 1645), III, 144.
19. Respectively *Ibrahim*, I, 42-3; *Le Polemire*, p. 270; *Axiane*, p. 141; *Scanderberg*, I, 496; *Ibrahim*, III, 290-1.
20. Respectively *Alcide*, I, 274; *Le Grand Cyrus*, IV, 237.

21. Respectively *Polexandre*, II, 151; *Ibrahim*, IV, 599.

22. Du Bail, *Le Prince ennemy du tyran*, 2 vols. (Paris, 1644), II, 95.

23. *Polexandre*, I, 586.

24. *Antiope*, I, 324-5, 367.

25. *Le Grand Cyrus*, I, 1080; cf. *Ibrahim*, I, 317-18.

26. cf. the definition given by Le Moyne (*La Gallerie des femmes fortes*, p. 209): 'La Generosité à la bien definir est une grandeur de Courage, ou une eslevation d'Esprit, par laquelle une Ame eslevée au dessus de l'Interest & de l'Utile se porte inviolablement & sans detour au Devoir qui est laborieux & à l'Honneste qui couste & qui paroist difficile.'

27. *Mitridate*, I, 272-4. *Courtoisie*, a term much used in the romances of chivalry, had all but disappeared from the heroic novel, *générosité* having replaced it. *Magnanimité* is closely allied to *générosité* and has equally strong moral overtones. For Gomberville, it is 'cette supreme & heroïque magnanimité qui acheve tousjours ce qu'elle commence, & fait faire les grandes actions par le seul motif de la vertu'; 'l'Oubly des injures receuës . . . est le supreme degré de la valeur, & le plus esclatant caractere de la vraye magnanimité' (*La Cytherée*, 2nd edn., 4 vols., Paris, 1642, II, 401, 135). La Serre puts it at a higher level than *générosité* because of the ease with which the latter can be counterfeited (*Le Portrait de la Reyne*, Paris, 1644, p. 116; cf. *Ibrahim*, II, 832; *Cleopatre*; I, 68; *Le Grand Cyrus*, III, 652), and indeed the term tended to be used by those who defined *générosité* in terms of physical courage to indicate that extra moral dimension which ensured that courage would never be used in a questionable cause.

28. Le Maire, *La Prazimene*, 4 vols. (Paris, 1638-43), II, 119-20.

29. Chevreau, *L'Escole du sage*, pp. 126, 128.

30. J. E. Fidao-Justiniani, *L'Esprit classique et la préciosité au XVIIe siècle* (Paris, 1914), p. 159.

31. *Polexandre*, II, 213-14.

32. Madeleine de Scudéry, 'Discours de la gloire', *Recueil de quelques pieces de prose et de vers faits* [sic] *pour les prix qui avoient esté proposez de la part de l'Academie Françoise en 1671* (Paris, 1671), p. 9. This point forms the basis of her definition of *gloire*: cf. 'La Gloire a besoin d'autruy; car un homme seul & absolument inconnu à tout le monde n'auroit point de gloire, quelque mérite qu'il pût avoir. Mais elle a aussi besoin de nous-mesmes; parce que si elle ne subsistoit qu'en autruy, il n'y auroit rien qui la rendist nostre, & qui l'attachast veritablement à nous' (p. 8). Madeleine de Scudéry's essay won the prize.

33. Dubosc, *L'Honneste Femme*, II, 206.

34. Camus, *La Caritée ou le pourtraict de la vraye charité* (Paris, 1641), p. 442.

35. Dubosc, op. cit., II, 224.

36. Camus, op. cit., pp. 329-30, 442.

37. Chevreau, op. cit., p. 136.

38. Dubosc, *Les Femmes heroïques*, II, 91-2; cf. La Mothe le Vayer, *Œuvres*, II, 412.

39. Cériziers, *Le Heros françois*, pp. 172-3.

40. *Le Grand Cyrus*, VI, 575; cf. ibid., II, 1149.

41. *Rosane*, pp. 406-7.

42. *La Cytherée*, II, 414.

43. *Cleopatre*, II, 18-19.

44. *Ibrahim*, IV, 498; cf. ibid., III, 298; *Ariane*, p. 667; *Le Grand Cyrus*, V, 1268-9. François de Sales stressed the duc de Mercœur's ability to carry out the 'office de cappitaine et soldat tout ensemble' in the latter's funeral oration (see J. Hennequin, 'Le Duc de Mercœur d'après son oraison funèbre par François de Sales', *Héroïsme et création littéraire . . .* , p. 188).

45. *Berenger*, II, 421; cf. ibid., III, 145-6.

46. *Cassandre*, IX, 536, 555 et seq.

47. *Scanderberg*, I, 315. Reservations in heroic novels about the dangers of allowing purely personal motives to dictate conduct in war evidently reflected similar reservations in real life. The episode in *Cassandre* mentioned above (IX, 555 et seq.) parallels an incident during the Lens campaign of 1647, when Marshals de Rantsau and de Gassion, 'competiteurs de gloire, . . . tousjours jaloux de la gloire l'un de l'autre et incompatibles, en sorte qu'ils se brouilloient souvent,' were leading separate columns. Both went forward alone to see whether the enemy was anywhere at hand and both came rushing back, having come across more than five hundred enemy soldiers on the top of a hill. Rantsau regained the head of his column, but Gassion was set upon. 'Mr le marechal de Rantsaw malicieux, arrivé à la teste de la colonne qui continuoit d'advancer, voioit avec plaisir l'embaras de son compagnon,' and was only persuaded to help his rival when the maréchal de Castelnau and Millet impressed upon him the dangers to which he was exposing not only Gassion but the whole body of troops under his command (*Mémoires de M. Millet*, Bibl. Méjanes MS 153, fols. 136-7). Similarly, Condé's exploits were interpreted in various lights, depending on the attitude of the author towards *gloire*. To La Serre, he is a magnificent individualist, always in the thick of the battle, every stroke a mortal one, always ready to follow *gloire* wherever it may lead him (*Les Sieges, les batailles, les victoires et les triomphes de Monseigneur le Prince de Condé*, Paris, 1651, *passim*), but Charrier is impressed by his ability to moderate his impetuousness when it is necessary for the cause he is serving (*Les Lauriers d'Enguien ou le parfait general d'armée*, Paris, 1645, *passim*). Du Bois-Hus admires his superb gestures of defiance and the way he makes his troops forget themselves in the service of his *gloire* (*Le Prince illustre, passim*) but Saint-Évremond notes approvingly Turenne's greater attachment to long-term advantages at the expense of his immediate reputation (*Comparaison de M. le Prince et M. de Turenne*, Bibl. de l'Arsenal MS 3135, fols. 69-71).

See M. R. Lida de Malkiel, *L'Idée de la gloire dans la tradition occidentale* (Paris, 1968) for an analysis of how opposing concepts of *gloire* manifested themselves in Roman and medieval literature.

48. Richelieu, *Testament politique*, p. 298.
49. Balzac, *Œuvres*, II, 420.
50. Chevreau, *L'Escole de sage*, pp. 22 et seq.; cf. Bardin, *Le Lycée*, 2 vols. (Paris, 1632-4), II, 411.
51. *Ariane*, pp. 233-4.
52. *Scanderberg*, I, 313; cf. Bardin, op. cit., II, 549, La Mothe le Vayer, op. cit., I, 877.
53. François de Sales, 'Traité de l'amour de Dieu', *Œuvres*, ed. Ravier and Davos (Paris, 1969), pp. 904-5. Stoic influences also affected the interpretation of *vertu*. Gomberville, for instance, often identified *vertu* with *gloire* in the sense of fidelity to an ideal of courage, humanity, and justice, but equally depicted *vertu* as an end in itself, its own reward (see S. Kévorkian, 'Le Héros dans l'œuvre romanesque de Gomberville: Polexandre et Araxez', *Héroïsme et création littéraire* . . . , pp. 243-9).
54. Dubosc, *Les Femmes heroïques*, II, 159.
55. Le Moyne, *La Gallerie des femmes fortes*, p. 311.
56. Cériziers, *Le Philosophe françois*, III, 317.
57. *La Cytherée*, II, 114.
58. *Ariane*, pp. 425, 426.
59. *Histoire celtique*, I, 198.
60. *Cleopatre*, VI, 29-30.
61. *Antiope*, I, 493.
62. *Cassandre*, III, 6.
63. *Antiope*, IV, 146.
64. *Le Grand Cyrus*, I, 68.
65. Segrais, *Berenice*, 4 vols. (Paris, 1648-9), II, 573.
66. Scudéry, *Clelie, histoire romaine*, 10 vols. (Paris, 1654-60), IX, 186.

Chapter III

1. Achilles Tatius, *Les Amours de Clytophon et de Leucippe*, trans. Baudoin (Paris, 1635), pp. 192-3.
2. Eustathius, *Ismene et Ismenie, histoire grecque*, trans. Colletet (Paris, 1625), p. 275.
3. cf. *Les Amours de Clytophon et de Leucippe*, pp. 13-14; *Histoire aethiopique*, fol. 33.
4. e.g. Gerzan, *Histoire afriquaine*, I, 30-1; Baudoin, *Histoire negrepontique*, p. 156.
5. Logeas, *Histoire des trois freres*, p. 231.
6. Fortin de la Hoguette, *Testament, ou conseils fideles d'un bon pere à ses enfans*, 9th edn. (Paris, 1658), p. 84; cf. Bardin, *Le Lycée*, II, 371-2; Chevreau, *Le Tableau de la fortune* (Paris, 1659), p. 10.
7. *Bérenger*, IV, 847.
8. *Ariane*, p. 489.
9. Camus, 'La Genereuse Vengeance', *L'Amphitheatre sanglant* (Paris,

1630), pp. 319-27.

10. *Le Grand Cyrus*, I, 617.

11. Guez de Balzac, *Œuvres*, II, 62-3.

12. *Testament politique*, p. 212. The morality of preventive detention was much debated during the ministries of Richelieu and Mazarin, particularly when the principle was put into effect, e.g. when Condé was imprisoned during the Fronde.

13. *Le Ministre d'Estat* (Paris, 1665), p. 219.

14. For a full account of the theory of political *prudence*, see E. Thuau, *Raison d'État et pensée politique à l'époque de Richelieu* (Paris, 1966), Chapter V, and F. E. Sutcliffe, *Guez de Balzac et son temps*, Chapter IV.

15. Mathieu de Morgues, *Diverses pieces pour la defense de la Reyne Mere du Roy Tres-chrestien Louys XIII* (Antwerp, 1637), p. 15.

16. Bibl. de l'Arsenal MS 5416, fols. 1921-34.

17. Du Refuge, *Traité de la cour, ou instruction des courtisans* (Paris, 1658), *passim.*

18. Faret, *L'Honneste Homme ou l'art de plaire à la court*, ed. M. Magendie (Paris, 1925), pp. 42-3.

19. Gerzan du Soucy, *La Conduite du courtisan* (Paris, 1646), pp. 41-2.

20. Jacques de Caillière, *La Fortune des gens de qualité et des gentils-hommes particuliers, enseignant l'art de vivre à la cour* (Paris, 1668), p. 308.

21. *L'Heros de Laurens Gracian*, trans. Gervaise (Paris, 1645), p. 6.

22. Ibid., p. 9.

23. Ibid., p. 57.

24. *Le Guerrier prudent et politique* (Paris, 1643), p. 3.

25. Ibid., pp. 263-4.

26. 'Jugement sur César et sur Alexandre', *Œuvres de Monsieur de Saint-Évremond*, 7 vols. (London, 1711), I, 165-80.

27. *Le Grand Cyrus*, I, 302-3; cf. ibid., I, 559; *Polexandre*, III, 562.

28. *Rosane*, p. 56; *Polexandre*, I, 106; *Ariane*, p. 658; cf. *Ibrahim*, III, 778-9.

29. *Cleopatre*, VIII, 290.

30. *Polexandre*, III, 15.

31. *Antiope*, I, 198.

32. *L'Illustre Amalazonthe*, p. 144; cf. ibid., p. 138, *Polexandre*, I, 781.

33. If a roundabout way of solving a problem has to be found, it is usually suggested to the hero by another character.

34. *Ibrahim*, III, 846.

35. Ibid., III, 877-8.

36. Retz, *La Conjuration de Fiesque*, ed. Watts (Oxford, 1967), pp. 44-5. See A. Coleman, 'A Source of *Ibrahim ou l'Illustre Bassa*', *Romanic Review* 29 (1938), pp. 129-40, for details of how Scudéry superimposed more heroic qualities onto Mascardi's original. In this respect, Retz was closer to Mascardi.

37. For a detailed analysis of the differences between the Scudéry

and the Retz versions, see C. Morlet, 'Jean-Louis de Fiesque, héros de roman', *XVIIe Siècle* 109 (1975), pp. 33-50; cf. also Pintard, 'La Conjuration de Fiesque ou l'héroïsation d'un factieux', *Héroïsme et création littéraire* . . . , pp. 225-30.

Chapter IV

1. Gomberville, Marin le Roy de, *La Doctrine des mœurs* (Paris, 1646), Tab. 71.

2. When Chevreau published a revised edition of *L'Escole du sage* (*L'Escole du sage ou le caractere des vertus et des vices*, Lyon, 1664), he added a second part in which the sympathies for stoicism discernible in the original edition are considerably diluted. *Le Tableau de la fortune* contains a thinly veiled admiration for the stoic attitude to death (Book II, chap. 7).

3. *Orasie*, 4 vols. (Paris, 1646), Preface. This novel was published by Mézeray who declares that the manuscript was given to him by a nobleman with the information that the author was a high-born lady. Mézeray expresses his surprise that a lady could write a work so accomplished. The lady has been taken to be Madame de Senecterre.

4. *Scanderberg*, I, 111; cf. Mégacle's rejection of the stoic admiration for Antony, Cato, and Brutus: 's'ils eussent marché la teste levée contre leur mauvais destin & se fussent presentez jusqu'à la fin à tout ce que le Ciel irrité leur pouvoit proposer, ils eussent laissé à la posterité une reputation plus entiere, & eussent passé pour fermes, pour intrepides & pour inesbranlables dans la bonne & dans la mauvaise fortune' (*Cleopatre*, VIII, 103). Cf. also *Ariane*, pp. 563-4.

5. Coeffeteau, *Tableau des passions humaines* (Paris, 1620), pp. 48 et seq.

6. Senault, *De l'usage des passions*, 8th edn. (Lyon, 1657), pp. 121 et seq. and *passim.*

7. Cériziers, *Le Philosophe françois*, III, 275.

8. Levi, *French Moralists*, Chapter 7.

9. Coeffeteau, op. cit., p. 26. Levi points out (op. cit., p. 145) that Coeffeteau's attribution of the primacy to the irascible over the concupiscible reverses the doctrine of Saint Thomas and describes it as 'the most considerable concession to the ethics of glory which we have so far met'.

10. Senault, op. cit., p. 6; cf. ibid., pp. 131, 143-4.

11. *Cleopatre*, I, 275.

12. *Rosane*, p. 527; cf. *Cleopatre*, VI, 158-9.

13. *Polexandre*, IV, 19.

14. Dubosc, *L'Honneste Femme*, II, 255.

15. *Ibrahim*, Preface.

16. *Le Grand Cyrus*, I, 345; cf. ibid., IV, 11; V, 323.

17. Ibid., V, 209.

18. *La Cytherée*, II, 329.

19. *Berenger*, I, 'A la noblesse françoise'.
20. *Polexandre*, V, 941-2.
21. Ibid., V, 944.
22. Ibid., V, 945-6.
23. Cf. above, pp. 44-5.
24. *Ariane*, pp. 635-6.
25. *La Cytherée*, II, 329; I, 182 et seq.; cf. *L'Illustre Amalazonthe*, pp. 418-26.
26. *Antiope*, IV, 150-1.
27. Caussin, *La Cour sainte*, pp. 97-8.
28. *L'Education heroïque. Recueillie d'un manuscrit et mise en lumiere par J. Ottonis, Chanoine de la cathedralle de Gand*, Bibl. Méjanes MS 411, fol. 1. I have not been able to find a printed copy of this work, though Chapelain's library contained a copy, published in Brussels in 1655 (see Searles, *Catalogue de tous les livres de feu M. Chapelain*, No. 2523).
29. *Scanderberg*, I, 189-90.
30. Consider Rouville's reply to the comtesse de Fiesque, who had remarked that she did not love Gramont, 'le plus grand fripon du monde': 'Voilà une plaisante raison, madame, que vous m'alléguez pour votre justification! Je sais que vous êtes encore plus friponne que lui, et je ne laisse pas de vous aimer.' (Bussy-Rabutin, *Histoire amoureuse des Gaules*, 2 vols., Paris, 1920, I, 40.)
31. See M. Magendie, *La Politesse mondaine et les théories de l'honnêteté en France au XVIIe siècle de 1600 à 1660*, 2 vols. (Paris, 1925), I, 195 et seq.; Coulet, *Le Roman jusqu'à la Révolution*, I, 150-2. For discussions in novels on the nature of love, see *Scanderberg*, I, 189 et seq., *Antiope*, II, 73 et seq., *Cassandre*, VI, 972 et seq.
32. *Ibrahim*, I, 155.
33. Ibid., IV, Book VI, 87-91; cf. ibid., II, 567-79.
34. e.g. Marcellin and Dicéarque in *Ariane*, Tisiphone and Syziphe in *Polexandre*. The virtuous pair, Histérie and Mélicerte, who both fall in love with Iphidamante, work their way from an irrational love of inclination to a rational love based on recognition (*Polexandre*, III, 891).
35. *L'Illustre Amalazonthe*, p. 493.
36. *Alcide*, II, 43. Pacore had evidently read *L'Astrée*.
37. *Axiane*, p. 278.
38. *Berenice*, II, 571.
39. See below, Chapters XI and XII.
40. *Polexandre*, IV, 459; cf. Araxez (*La Cytherée*, IV, 3-4): 'par la force du raisonnement, il surmonta la foiblesse de l'Amour & du desespoir'.
41. *Le Grand Cyrus*, VII, 753.
42. *Clelie*, II' 1045-6.
43. Ibid., II, 1052.
44. Ibid., II, 1053.

45. Ibid., II, 1054.
46. See below, Chapter XII.
47. *Clelie*, V, 332.
48. Ibid., V, 331.
49. Ibid., VI, 1354.
50. Ibid., IX, 351-2.
51. Cf. P. Zumthor, 'La Carte de Tendre et les précieux', *Trivium* VI (1948), pp. 263-73, and C. Dulong, *L'Amour au XVIIe siècle* (Paris, 1969), Chapter VI.
52. See below, Chapter XIII.

Chapter V
1. *Cassandre*, II, 86.
2. *Ibrahim*, II, 470, 489.
3. In *La Prazimène*, *Alcide*, *Axiane*, and *Le Prince ennemy du tyran* respectively.
4. *Cassandre*, III, 343.
5. Ibid., X, 1181-2; cf. ibid., III, 385-91.
6. *Rosane*, p. 289.
7. *Antiope*, I, 259. The cult of the Amazon in literature found its parallel in real life with the admiration accorded to those women who distinguished themselves in the predominantly male world of warfare, such as La Grande Mademoiselle and the redoubtable Madame de Saint-Balmont who reputedly killed or captured more than four hundred men (see Tallemant des Réaux, *Historiettes*, II, 596-7). The Académie française also took the subject seriously, if we are to judge by the *Discours des Amazones* (Bibl. de l'Arsenal MS 3259, fols. 61-72), seemingly delivered in 1655, which seeks to establish as many facts as possible about the Amazons; their historical existence is taken for granted. However, Noémi Hepp has pointed out pertinently that, despite the admiration accorded to women who displayed the virtues generally considered masculine, there was a feeling that, the nearer one came to real life, heroism in women was better expressed in terms of support for a man (through love or encouragement) or as a mediator ('La Notion d'héroïne', *Onze études sur l'image de la femme dans la littérature française du dix-septième siècle*, ed. W. Leiner, Tübingen and Paris, 1978, pp. 9-27). The heroic novel was set far apart from real life and willingly exploited the imaginative potential of every sort of heroic woman.
8. *Rosane*, pp. 197-8; cf. *Polexandre*, I, 241.
9. *Les Amours de Clytophon et de Leucippe*, pp. 592-4.
10. And Brantôme to declare, with a different emotion, 'je voudrois avoir autant de centaines d'escus comme il y a eu de filles, tant du monde que des relligieuses, qui se sont jeadis esmeues, pollues et depucellées par la lecture des *Amadis de Gaule*' (*Des dames galantes*, 3 vols. (Paris, 1933), III, 37).
11. *Le Tiers Livre de Amadis de Gaule*, fol. 22; cf. *Le Premier Livre*

..., fol. 9, and *Le Romant des romans*, I, 343.

12. *Le Romant heroïque*, pp. 373, 736.

13. *L'Astrée*, V, 424.

14. *Le Premier Livre de Amadis de Gaule*, fol. 124.

15. Cf. *Ismene et Ismenie*, pp. 166-74, 249; *L'Astrée*, I, 115-17, 169, II, 369; *Histoire afriquaine*, III, 1080; *Histoire indienne*, pp. 190-2; *Le Romant des romans*, III, 113.

16. *Cassandre*, II, 558-9.

17. *Polexandre*, V, 1320.

18. *Cassandre*, X, 1195-6; cf. *Polexandre*, IV, 491.

19. M. Magendie, *La Politesse mondaine*.

20. I. Maclean, *Woman Triumphant. Feminism in French Literature 1610-1652* (Oxford, 1977); C. C. Lougee, *Le Paradis des femmes. Women, Salons and Social Stratification in Seventeenth-century France* (Princeton, 1976).

21. Maclean, op. cit., pp. 266-7.

22. Cf. *Le Premier Livre de Amadis de Gaule*, fol. 4 and *Le Romant des romans*, II, 791-800; ibid., II, 249-91.

23. Marcassus, *L'Amadis de Gaule* (Paris, 1629), p. 10; pp. 14-15; pp. 171-4.

24. See Maclean, op. cit., Chapter III.

25. Gerzan, *Le Triomphe des dames* (Paris, 1646).

26. Dubosc, *La Femme heroïque ed. cit.*, I, 261-4.

27. Gilbert, *Panegyrique des dames* (Paris, 1650), p. 11.

28. Gerzan, op. cit., p. 57.

29. Le Moyne, *La Gallerie des femmes fortes*, pp. 273, 311. On chastity as moral independence, see Maclean, op. cit., pp. 84-7. The idea that chastity in women was the equivalent of courage in men was not new, but was given a new impetus in the 1640s.

30. See above, Chapter IV.

31. Cériziers, *Le Philosophe françois*, III, 289.

32. Gerzan, *Le Triomphe des dames*, p. 23.

33. Cf. *Orasie*, II, 270 et seq.

34. Saint-Gabriel, *Le Merite des dames*, 3rd edn. (Paris, 1660), pp. 251-2.

35. *Ibrahim*, III, 787.

36. *Cassandre*, I, 217-19; cf. *Polexandre*, I, 500-3.

37. *Alcide*, I, 499.

38. *Ladice*, II, 253.

39. *Le Grand Cyrus*, I, 136; cf. *Cleopatre*, XI, 253 et seq.

40. Even real-life heroes were apparently infected by this attitude, as a letter from the duc de Guise to Mazarin, written while he was on the Naples expedition of 1648, shows. Protesting at the way the Cardinal had removed Mademoiselle de Pons from the convent where she had been installed by the Duke before his departure, he writes: 'ny l'ambition ny le desir de m'immortaliser par des actions extraordinaires ne m'a embarqué dans un dessein sy perilleux que celuy où je me trouve mais la seulle pensée de mieux meriter

les bonnes graces de Mademoiselle de Pons en faisant quelque chose de glorieux' (Bibl. Mazarine MS 2117, fols. 242-3).

41. *Scanderberg*, II, 139–56, 461–74.
42. *Hermiogene*, 2 vols. (Paris, 1648), I, 161.
43. *Polexandre*, II, 863.
44. *Scanderberg*, I, 200, 202.
45. *Berenice*, IV, 173–6.
46. *L'Illustre Amalazonthe*, pp. 200–28. This episode was borrowed from Scudéry's translation of G.-B. Manzini, *Les Harangues ou discours academiques* (Paris, 1640). Euridème's devotion is abject. He tells his rivals: 'Je l'ayme seulement pour l'amour d'elle, & non pour l'amour de moy ... Vous l'aymez, orgueilleux, mais par la consideration de la recompence que vous esperez: Pour moy je l'ayme tousjours par l'estat present des choses, je ne crains pas qu'elle me soit rigoureuse, & je n'espere point qu'elle me soit favorable, je l'ayme seulement par ce que je l'ayme' (pp. 227–8).
47. *Le Grand Cyrus*, VI, 1221.
48. *Ladice*, II, 165; cf. ibid., II, 155–6.
49. *Axiane*, p. 695.
50. *Cleopatre*, II, 91.
51. *Ibrahim*, III, 393–4; cf. ibid., IV, Book X, 178–9.
52. *Le Grand Cyrus*, X, 577–80.
53. Ibid., IX, 1103–4; X, 1029.
54. Ibid., VII, 115.
55. Ibid., X, 647–50. All these points are remade in *Clelie*; cf. B. Treloar, 'Some Feminist Views in France in the Seventeenth Century', *AUMLA* X (1959), pp. 152–9.
56. *Le Grand Cyrus*, X, 587–8, 593; cf. Scarron, *Le Roman comique*, ed. Bénac, 2 vols. (Paris, 1951), II, 57.
57. See below, Chapter XII, and *Clelie*, VIII, 1250.
58. *Clelie*, IX, 363–4.
59. See Sister J. Sassus, *The Motif of Renunciation of Love in the Seventeenth-century French Novel* (Washington, 1963) for an alternative view that the strongly idealized love of this period derived from the post-Tridentine diffusion of Christian ideals.

Chapter VI
1. Martin, *Livre, pouvoirs et société ...*, pp. 522–4. Ariès explains the interest of the *robins* in history by the fact that it was in historical documents that they found the justification for their own prerogatives (*Le Temps de l'histoire*, Monaco, 1954, pp. 217–18).
2. See La Mothe le Vayer, *Œuvres*, I, 235. What might be described as a Renaissance theory of history was still being propounded in the 1650s by Bourdonné, *Le Courtisan des-abusé* (Paris, 1658), pp. 81–6, and others.
3. Quoted by Evans, *L'Historien Mézeray et la conception de l'histoire en France au XVIIe siècle* (Paris, 1930), pp. 84, 88.

4. Cf. Fortin de la Hoguette, *Testament*, p. 118.

5. The period since François Ier, however, being within living memory, was put into a different category and treated in the same way as contemporary events.

6. G. Snyders, *La Pédagogie en France aux XVIIe et XVIIIe siècles* (Paris, 1965), pp. 91-2.

7. Camus, *La Pieuse Jullie, histoire parisienne* (Paris, 1625), Dessert au lecteur, p. 573.

8. Dubosc, *L'Honneste Femme*, I, 29, 33.

9. Cf. Dubosc, *L'Honneste Femme*, I, 39-40; Vulson de la Colombière, *Le Vray Theatre d'honneur et de chevalerie*, I, Preface; Sorel, *De la connoissance des bons livres*, pp. 126-33.

10. Gerzan, *Histoire afriquaine*, Preface.

11. See Langlois, *Le Tombeau des romans*, p. 91. The second part of the anonymous *Roman de l'incogneu, ensemble quelques discours pour et contre les romans* (Paris, 1634) is a reprint of *Le Tombeau des romans* but in the wrong order, since the arguments 'pour' are an answer to points made 'contre'.

12. For a useful survey of the various approaches to the prose epic theory of the novel, see Ratner, *Theory and Criticism of the Novel in France from 'L'Astrée' to 1750* (*s.l.*, 1938), pp. 11-31; cf. also Dallas, *Le Roman français de 1660 à 1680* (Paris, 1932), Chapter I. A position intermediate between the prose epic theory and the arguments of those who decried history had been adopted by Amyot in the sixteenth century (*Histoire aethiopique*, Le Proesme du translateur) and was developed by Fortin de la Hoguette (*Testament*, p. 122).

13. *Histoire indienne*, Preface.

14. *Rosane*, Preface.

15. *Clorinde*, 2 vols. (Paris, 1654), Epistre à Lysis.

16. *Mitridate*, IV, Epistre.

17. Desmarets, *Rosane*, Preface; cf. *Axiane*, Preface.

18. *Antiope*, I, Preface.

19. *La Prazimene*, I, Au lecteur.

20. *Scanderberg*, I, Advertissement au lecteur.

21. *Axiane*, Preface.

22. *Ibrahim*, Preface. The relationship between history and fiction in the period from 1660 to 1700, after the period of the heroic novel's importance, has been studied by Marie-Thérèse Hipp in *Mythes et réalités*, pp. 132-94.

23. As Magendie tended to do (*Le Roman français*, pp. 222-34); cf. Coulet, *Le Roman jusqu'à la Révolution*, I, 136-7; Boorsch, 'About some Greek Romances', *Yale French Studies* 38 (1967), p. 81.

24. For examples of such works, see Du Verdier, *La Sibile de Perse* (Paris, 1632); Du Bail, *La Cefalie* (Paris, 1637); Du Verdier, *Fuite de Rozalinde* (Paris, 1643). In 'Romans et réalités, 1607-1628' (*XVIIe siècle* 104 (1974) pp. 29-43), E. Henein has shown how

such novels could combine the most grotesque fantasies with accurate observation of everyday life.

25. *Eloge de Monsieur le Prince*, Bibl. de l'Arsenal MS 3135, fols. 61-9. Authorship can be attributed to Saint-Évremond: see D. C. Potts, 'Saint Évremond and seventeenth-century "Libertinage"', (Oxford D. Phil. thesis, 1961), Appendix A, II, 1-5.

26. Segrais, *Les Nouvelles françoises, ou les divertissemens de la Princesse Aurélie*, 2 vols. (Paris, 1657), I, 26-7.

27. Sorel, *La Bibliotheque françoise*, pp. 183-5, 187; but cf. his views on the treatment of history in novels in *La Maison des jeux*, I, 390-1.

28. It is, however, notable that the earlier heroic novels, the authors of which are less obsessed with presenting models of *honnêteté*, display more imaginative power than the later ones, as Morillot (*Le Roman en France depuis 1610* . . . , p. 4) and Coulet (op. cit., I, 170-1) have pointed out.

29. Cf. the argument put forward by Chapelain in his *De la lecture des vieux romans*, ed. Feillet (Paris, 1870), pp. 21-2.

30. Sorel, *De la connoissance des bons livres*, pp. 106-8. Sorel implies that such anachronisms are due to the stupidity of the novelists and asserts that the meanest village sculptor or painter would know better. In the light of his comments, it is worth noting that separate conventions applied in the texts of novels and in the engravings which accompanied them. In volume VII of *Cleopatre*, there is an episode where Artaban is attacked by Tigrane and his men. Tigrane is wearing 'un petit chapeau ombragé de quelques plumes noires', but the rest of his body, we are told, is armed in the same way as his men. They appear to be wearing the medieval style of armour, since one of them is killed by a sword pushed 'par l'ouverture de la visiere'. The frontispiece to the volume, however, which depicts this scene, shows Artaban defending himself against seven men who are wearing tunics, breastplates and helmets of a style clearly belonging to the ancient world. The frontispiece to volume I of *Mitridate* shows the opening scene of the novel, where Ariarates attempts to escape from the besieged city of Ambracie, capital of Epirus. All the soldiers are wearing arms appropriate to the period and carrying small Grecian shields, though in the text there are references to visors and at one point, Pyrrhus being wounded, another man is dressed up in his armour so that his army, who see only the outward symbol, shall not be demoralized. The walls of the city and the background, on the other hand, are depicted in the frontispiece as medieval, with a portcullis and pavilion-tents. The same combination of classical costume and medieval architecture is found in the engravings accompanying the text of other novels, including the splendid plates in *Ariane*. Presumably, some of what was accepted as a convention in the text of a novel was sufficiently incongruous if shown pictorially to require modification. See D. Canivet, *L'Illustration de la poésie*

et du roman français au XVIIe siècle (Paris, 1957), pp. 52-9, for comments on the conventional nature of most plates in heroic novels, especially those by Chauveau.

31. See, for instance, G. Dulong, *L'Abbé de Saint-Réal Étude sur les rapports de l'histoire et du roman au XVIIe siècle*, 2 vols. (Paris, 1921), I, 71.

32. Du Plaisir, *Sentimens sur les lettres et sur l'histoire* (1683). Quoted in Coulet, op. cit., II, 89. Hipp has more accurately pointed out that what the readers were looking for after 1660 was veracity rather than mere credibility: 'aux inventions des écrivains, calculées selon une vérité moyenne, on préfère des aventures dont l'authenticité est garantie par le seul motif qu'elles sont arrivées' (*Mythes et réalités*, p. 45).

33. Scudéry reveals in the preface to *Almahide ou l'esclave reine*, 8 vols. (Paris, 1660-3), the beginnings of an awareness that the manners of one period cannot necessarily be transposed to another period: 'comme il est dangereux d'introduire l'usage de l'Antiquité dans nostre Temps, il ne l'est pas moins de faire remonter celuy de nostre Temps jusques à l'Antiquité'. This is a more rigorous view than that held by most novelists but it does not affect the ideals he is trying to represent and, in practice, *Almahide* shows no more historical sense than any other novel.

34. The 'Eloge de Mr le Prince' (Arsenal MS 3135) tells us that after Rocroi he was compared to his ancestor, the victor of Cérisolles, after Fribourg to Germanicus, after Nordlingen to Alexander the Great, and after Dunkirk to Julius Caesar. After Lens, 'les comparaisons cesserent et il n'y eust plus d'exemple pour luy que luy-mesme'.

35. See Mlle de Montpensier, *Mémoires*, Coll. Petitot, 2e série, vol. 40 (Paris, 1824), p. 450.

PART II

1. *La Prazimene*, IV, 393 (rectified).
2. Polexandre, III, 600-1; cf. IV, 128 et seq., IV, 260.
3. La Cytherée, Part II.
4. *Antiope*, Preface.
5. Ibid., II, 33-4; cf. the alternative explanation put forward in *Le Grand Cyrus*, V, 120-2.

Chapter VII
1. *Historiettes*, I, 400.
2. References are to the first quarto edition, *L'Ariane de Monsieur Des Marets, . . . De nouveau reveuë, et augmentée de plusieurs Histoires par l'Autheur, et enrichie de plusieurs figures* (Paris, 1639). The two-volume octavo edition of 1632 is rare and its text is largely the same as that of the 1639 edition. The copy of the

1632 edition in the Bibliothèque nationale contains the same text as the 1639 edition despite the claim that more stories have been added in the latter, though it is possible that augmented editions were published between 1632 and 1639 using the original engraved titles (see H. Gaston Hall, 'Jean Desmarets de Saint-Sorlin: his Background and Reception in the Seventeenth Century', unpublished Ph.D thesis, Yale, 1958, p. 387).

3. pp. 232-7; cf. *L'Astrée*, I, 286-91; II, 670.
4. *Le Parnasse reformé, nouvelle edition* (Paris, 1674), pp. 121-2.
5. e.g. the episode at Corinne's house in Book VI. H. Gaston Hall argues, however, that Desmarets used such episodes to show the disastrous effects of sensuality in contrast to the constant love of Mélinte for Ariane (op. cit., p. 44).
6. Book III.
7. pp. 202-3.
8. pp. 158-65.
9. pp. 339-42.
10. pp. 257-92.
11. p. 276.
12. pp. 5-6.
13. p. 6.
14. p. 358.
15. p. 481.
16. e.g. p. 359.
17. p. 95.
18. pp. 665-6.
19. p. 706.
20. p. 755. Desmarets had an eye for curiously gory details, e.g. Palamède chops off both the hands of a soldier who, having no means of staying on his horse, falls to the ground but finds his face saved from contact with the ground by 'les mains secourables' he had just lost (p. 143-4); cf. the dubious pun on p. 757.
21. p. 434.
22. p. 435 (my italics).
23. p. 263.
24. p. 662.
25. p. 218.
26. pp. 545-6.
27. pp. 130-1.
28. pp. 657-8. Ariane is herself capable of valour when pressed: see pp. 709, 713.
29. p. 756.
30. I, 5.
31. I, 19.
32. I, 203-4. The printing of all names in capitals is presumably an attempt to increase the heroic flavour of the work.
33. II, 547.
34. II, 502.

35. I, 100.
36. III, 901-2.
37. I, 200-1 (my italics).
38. I, 84.
39. I, 59-65; I, 125; II, 529-45.
40. I, 148-50.
41. I, 170-1.
42. I, 301-2.
43. e.g. I, 321-4.
44. 'Ils passerent quelques heures dans cet entretien, puis toute la compagnie se mit ensemble pour s'en aller à la pourmenade' (III, 899); cf. II, 663-4.
45. II, 571-2.
46. III, 778-80.
47. II, 382-3.
48. II, 733-4.
49. I, 90-1.
50. III, 960-1.
51. The most striking of such occasions is when Adalbert needs someone to subdue a rebel province: 'PALINGENE en ayant eu la commission l'emporta glorieusement' (II, 499).

Chapter VIII
1. The basic facts about these early versions are set out by Constans and van Roosbroeck, 'The Early Editions of Gomberville's *Polexandre*', *Modern Language Review* 18 (1923), pp. 302-8.
2. See Reynier, *Le Roman sentimental avant l'Astrée*, p. 302.
3. For a full account of the plot, see Wadsworth, *The Novels of Gomberville* (New Haven, 1942), pp. 10-11.
4. *L'Exil de Polexandre et d'Ericlée* (Paris, 1619), p. 637. The pagination is as follows: 1-610, 565-96, 579-638. References to pages within the overlapping sequences are indicated by (1), (2), or (3).
5. p. 508.
6. p. 529.
7. pp. 552-3, 571-2(1).
8. pp. 531-64; cf. *Ariane*, pp. 464-6.
9. It is interesting to note, in the light of Gomberville's Jansenist sympathies, that a hyperbolic style was considered a Jansenist characteristic: 'il n'y a rien de vertueux s'il n'est héroïque, rien de chrétien s'il n'est miraculeux, rien de tolérable s'il n'est inimitable ... la médiocrité à leur goût est un vice; ce qui n'est pas un succès est un manquement; ce qui n'est pas singulier est trop trivial. Ils ne trouvent grand que ce qui est immense. Ils n'estiment que ce qui ravit ou étonne ... Chacune de leurs paroles est une hyperbole; chaque maxime est un paradoxe, ... toutes leurs idées sont extrêmes, toutes leurs promesses immenses' (F. Bonal, 1655, quoted by Maillard, *Essai sur l'esprit du héros baroque (1580-1640)*, Paris, 1973, p. 16).

10. For an account of the plot, see Wadsworth, op. cit., pp. 14-16.
11. *L'Exil de Polexandre, premiere partie* (Paris, 1629), pp. 504-28.
12. *Mémoires de Nevers*, Preface, quoted by Wadsworth, op. cit., p. 13.
13. See pp. 119, 497-9; Book IV, *passim.*
14. *La Premiere (Seconde) Partie de Polexandre*, 2 vols. (Paris, 1632), II, 271-5. For an account of the plot, see Wadsworth, op. cit., pp. 21-6. Lever (*La Fiction narrative* . . .) lists only Parts III-V of the 1637 version of *Polexandre*, thus implying, erroneously, that the 1632 version constitutes the first two parts of the final version.
15. Cf. I, 22; 239-40; 519-20; 542-3.
16. *La Premiere (-Cinquiesme) Partie de Polexandre*, 5 vols., (Paris, 1637), V, 1329: 'La premiere fois que Polexandre vit le jour, il le vit par la puissance d'Eolinde & le perdit aussitost qu'elle eut cessé de luy prester sa lumiere. Neuf ans apres, il sortit des tenebres & eut l'obligation de ce nouveau jour à Zelmatide & à Izatide. Car il ne fut que le pretexte de mon travail. Les deux autres en furent la veritable cause.'
17. I, 346; II, 870-969; IV, 409-22.
18. II, 412.
19. IV, 719; V, 1024-7; cf. III, 261.
20. IV, 98.
21. III, 916.
22. II, 549.
23. III, 558.
24. I, 328.
25. III, 285; cf. II, 663, 742; III, 300, 564.
26. e.g. I, 134-5; II, 991-2.
27. II, 787.
28. I, 128-9; II, 735; III, 923; IV, 494-9.
29. III, 925 et seq.
30. Cf. I, 388-9; IV, 275-8, 322, 491.
31. For an analysis of the relationships between heroes and heroines in Gomberville, see Kévorkian, *Le Thème de l'amour dans l'œuvre romanesque de Gomberville*, especially Part II, Chapters II and IV.
32. *Polexandre*, I, 116-18; II, 593-4.
33. II, 389-91.
34. On the one occasion when specific features are described, her beauty is represented as almost supernatural: II, 689-90.
35. I, 136.
36. III, 320.
37. Gomberville was associated with Jansenism in his later years, and it is tempting to interpret the quasi-religious aspects of *Polexandre* in terms of Jansenism. In his chapter 'Un Monde tragique' (op. cit., pp. 217-25), Kévorkian paints a picture of Gomberville's world in which man is doomed to be the victim of his passions, his heredity, and malevolent 'gods'. However, he leaves out the all-pervading sense of providence which takes care of those areas in which man is most helpless and vulnerable and which leads him on, *provided he*

is trying to use his reason in the cause of good. Such a view was common to many people in Gomberville's day and need not necessarily be identified with Jansenism. Polexandre credits Alcidiane with the attributes of a loving, forgiving God: she is 'l'image vivante de cét Esprit Eternel qui tesmoigne tant d'amour à ses creatures. Comme luy, vous pardonnez infiniment & comme luy, vous troublez de faveurs ceux qui par leurs démerites ne devoient recevoir que des peines & des châtimens' (V, 1305). The most that can be said is that Gomberville wanted to represent heroic love as something approaching the purest possible form of love, that between God and man.

38. V, 1308-9.
39. Cf. II, 201.
40. IV, 596; V, 1070.
41. III, 6-7.
42. IV, 453.
43. IV, 387; cf. III, 743.
44. IV, 246-7.
45. V, 784-5.
46. V, 976.
47. III, 210; cf. V, 1260-1.
48. I, 569.
49. V, 1205.
50. V, 1301-2.
51. I, 767; II, 615; cf. II, 3 and an impatient attitude towards lovers on the part of other characters, II, 355-6, 686.
52. V, 1129.
53. V, 1320.
54. I, 903; see I, 845-959 for an analysis of Alcidiane's response to her emergent feelings of love.
55. I, 571-2.
56. V, 1155.
57. V, 1272.
58. V, 1320. It should be noted that, almost alone amongst the heroines of heroic novels, Alcidiane has no filial obligations.
59. Adam, *Histoire de la littérature française*, I, 414.
60. Kévorkian, 'Le Héros dans l'œuvre romanesque de Gomberville: Polexandre et Araxez', *Héroïsme et création littéraire . . .* , p. 247. See also Kévorkian, *Le Thème de l'amour . . .* , Part II, Chapter I.
61. Magendie and Coulet list *Polexandre* as a 'transitional' work (see above, p. 5); Adam (*L'Age classique*, pp. 145-6) classifies it as a *roman d'aventures* preceding the *roman héroïque* of La Calprenède and Scudéry. Cf. Kerviler (*Marin Le Roy, sieur de Gomberville*, Paris, 1876, p. 14) who acclaims Gomberville as the founder of the *roman chevaleresque*, later developed by La Calprenède and Scudéry.
62. III, 268; IV, 237; III, 924; II, 870 et seq.
63. II, 769-70. Technical terms are sometimes used to give an air of

verisimilitude, cf. II, 977.
64. V, 1327.

Chapter IX

1. *Ibrahim ou l'Illustre Bassa*, 4 vols. (Paris, 1641). See above, p. 203, note 31(d). References to volume IV indicate the Book in question because Book X is paginated separately.
2. Scudéry's claim to have taken so much care over realistic details left him all the more vulnerable to ridicule when he made one of his characters sail from the Black Sea into the Caspian (see Guéret, *Le Parnasse reformé*, pp. 128-9; Sorel, *De la connoissance des bons livres*, p. 105). Scudéry seems to have thought that the River Arax connected the two seas (*Ibrahim*, I, 902).
3. IV, Book VIII, 478-80.
4. III, 681.
5. Cf. I, 373, 666; II, 617; III, 586.
6. Preface.
7. The death of Ibrahim recounted by the historian Paul Jove was, it is claimed, a false report put out by the Sultan to cover Justinian's departure. The true story was contained in an account written by a 'Caloyer grec' who had heard it from Justinian and Isabelle themselves (IV, Book X, 176). It should be noted that *l'Histoire nègrepontique* was supposedly based on an account by 'un Caloyer grec'.
8. II, 210-11.
9. e.g. II, 640-3.
10. II, 517.
11. II, 521-2.
12. Vol. IV.
13. III, 851-2.
14. The *Bibliothèque universelle des romans* considered the Marquis français' story ('Le Feint Astrologue', II, 146-324) to be so different in tone from the rest of the novel that they printed it as a separate *nouvelle*, suggesting that Scudéry wrote it to prove that he could excel in more than one genre (Jan. 1777, II, 120).
15. I, 144.
16. I, 145-6.
17. I, 303; IV, Book X, 74-5.
18. I, 733.
19. I, 755.
20. III, 729-67; IV, Book IX, 636 et seq.
21. I, 104-5.
22. I, 538.
23. I, 431.
24. II, 471.
25. I, 179-82.
26. IV, Book X, 83; cf. II, 498, 507.
27. I, 368; cf. I, 213, but note IV, Book VIII, 411: 'je cesserois d'aimer

Ibrahim, s'il cessoit d'estre genereux'.

28. Lucien Braun ('Polysémie du concept de héros', *Héroïsme et création littéraire* . . . , p. 22) asserts that the heroic universe must exist outside the framework of ordinary life — 'il n'y a pas de passage du normal à l'héroïque. Le héros se pose en rupture' — and the great heroic traditions to which he refers support such a view. The institutional head, the king (and still less the minister) are not heroic simply by virtue of their functions and it is indicative of how radically Scudéry diverged from the heroic tradition that he could largely ignore the externals of heroism and concentrate almost exclusively on moral superiority.

29. II, 126–37.

30. Descartes, *Les Passions de l'âme*, Art. 50.

31. Bénichou, *Morales du Grand Siècle*, p. 21; see ibid., pp. 25–6.

32. I, 673; cf. I, 91–2.

33. e.g. Bajazet (II, 676–867), Dilament (III, 17–250).

34. I, 499–500; cf. III, 588.

35. I, 783.

36. III, 708–12.

37. IV, Book VIII, 395.

38. IV, Book IX, 526–606; I, 858–917.

39. III, 319–576.

40. IV, Book X, 144–5.

41. Descartes, *Les Passions de l'âme*, Arts. 155, 156.

42. IV, Book X, 15.

43. The distinction is borrowed from Doubrovsky (*Corneille et la dialectique du héros* (Paris, 1963), pp. 67–8) who contrasts the universality in Descartes with the singularity in Corneille.

44. They none the less manifest themselves at their best in France. The Marquis français is lionized by Genoese society because he teaches them the precepts of French *galanterie*.

Chapter X

1. References are to *Cassandre*, 10 vols. (Paris, 1642–5). For a detailed account of the plot, see T. J. Wilson, 'La Calprenède, romancier' (unpublished D.Phil. thesis, Oxford, 1927), I, 44–114.

2. VI, 835, 1033–5; VIII, 187, 189.

3. IV, 718; V, 535–6. La Calprenède creates his own clichés, such as the crossing of the hands on the stomach at moments of stress: cf. III, 192, 378; IV, 681; V, 205; VI, 926. (A special mention is made of this cliché by La Mothe le Vayer *fils*, *Le Parasite Mormon, histoire comique*, *s.l.*, 1650, p. 67). None the less, despite the clichés, the accounts of battles and sieges in *Cassandre* have a greater feeling of movement and action than those in any other heroic novel. The narrator's point of reference changes frequently from one part of the battlefield to another, giving the impression of surging armies: cf. II, 211–21; VI, 791–840; VIII, 154–208; IX, 271–301.

4. I, 206.
5. I, 232-3.
6. II, 185.
7. II, 207.
8. VIII, 36.
9. The secondary hero, Artaxerxe/Arsace, is however more aware of his filial responsibilities than Oroondate: see VII, 374-5.
10. X, 693-4.
11. X, 747.
12. III, 181.
13. VIII, 40-1.
14. Cf. III, 322-3; VIII, 403-4.
15. I, 425; cf. III, 230; X, 1060, 1064-5, 1094.
16. IX, 92.
17. IV, 683-4.
18. VIII, 285; cf. X, 667-8.
19. II, 362.
20. I, 143-4; V, 493; VIII, 429.
21. Cf. II, 162; IV, 642, 697; V, 14-17, 493; VI, 770-9, 1051-2.
22. II, 140-2; cf. IV, 699; IX, 379.
23. See Oroondate's behaviour in Vol. II, Part I, Book VI. All the major female characters except Talestris are in fact widows; see Tallemant des Réaux, *Historiettes*, II, 585 for a possible explanation of why this was so.
24. II, 330.
25. II, 437-8, 457-9. Statira's feelings for Alexander are ambivalent. He had been indirectly responsible for her father's death and she had not loved him when she married him, but after his death her memory of him is full of veneration and love. She decides to lock up all her love in his tomb and reject Oroondate, mainly from a feeling of guilt and duty towards Alexander (V, 73-4, 132, 162).
26. X, 912-25, cf. VI, 883 et seq.
27. III, 138.
28. III, 147.
29. III, 231.
30. After the death of Agis, she is persuaded by the other princesses to marry Démétrius who has attached himself devotedly to her (X, 1174).
31. II, 249.
32. IX, 323.
33. IX, 570-601.
34. VIII, 266-75.
35. X, 1159.
36. Seillière considers Démétrius to be a weakness in the novel because of his hypersensibility, 'un fâcheux exemple du romanesque outrancier qui nuit aux personnages masculins dans notre roman classique, héritier sur ce point d'une tradition trop despotique pour être parvenu à s'y soustraire' (*Le Romancier du Grand Condé*,

Paris, 1921, p. 109). Démétrius does not lack masculine qualities, however, and his emotional sensibility corresponds to a great *élan* on the battlefield.

37. The claims of some of the characters to royal descent are tenuous. Alexander's lieutenants have become kings as a result of the break-up of Alexander's empire; Darius had become King of Persia in a *coup d'état*. At one point, Oroondate insists on calling Statira Cassandre, the name she had borne before becoming a princess, because 'avec ce nom de la maison Royale, vous avez quitté tout ce que vous aviez de grand & de noble' (VI, 1052).

38. Cf. I, 60–3.

39. Cf. V, 56 and the huge numbers slaughtered in battle for purely personal quarrels (VI, 844; IX, 13-14).

40. Cf. V, 411-12.

41. II, 1–2.

42. Bénichou, *Morales du Grand Siècle*, p. 19.

43. Nadal, *Le Sentiment de l'amour . . .* , p. 312.

44. Cf. Morillot, op. cit., p. 70; Coulet, op. cit., I, 175. Certain episodes allow close parallels to be drawn, such as Oroondate's sparing of Perdicas' life so that it can be taken at the proper time and in the proper way (*Cassandre*, IV, 683–4) and Cornélie's *générosité* to-wards César (*La Mort de Pompée*, Act IV, sc. 4).

Chapter XI

1. References are to *Cleopatre*, 12 vols (Leiden, 1648–58). For a detailed account of the plot, see T. J. Wilson, *La Calprenède, romancier*, I, 120-57.

2. Mme de Sévigné, *Lettres*, 12 and 15 July 1671. The ability to deliver incredible blows is retained by the heroic characters through-out the novel: cf. I, 291; VII, 35, 361-72; IX, 310; XI, 207–8, 225.

3. e.g. I, 55, 245-50; II, 6, 78-9.

4. e.g. II, 97; V, 247-8; VIII, 317. Ménalippe is the only character with any Amazonian qualities.

5. V, 336.

6. *Cassandre*, VI, 1014.

7. See above, pp. 29.

8. Guéret, *Le Parnasse reformé*, p. 139.

9. 'Contre Mariane. A Mademoiselle de Guerchy', *Recueil de diverses poesies françoises 1648*, Bibl. Mazarine MS 3940.

10. Cf. 'Le Courrier burlesque de la guerre de Paris' (1650) (quoted by Magendie, *Le Roman français*, p. 405): 'On pensa chanter l'obit, de l'Ibrahim, de Polexandre, de Cleopatre, de Cassandre.'

11. e.g. 'Suitte de l'Histoire de Cesarion', X, 35-121.

12. Examples of ineptitude in the narrative are more frequent in *Cleopatre* than in *Cassandre*. The following passage gives an idea of the prolixity achieved by La Calprenède: 'Elise qui par le voisinage de l'Armenie aux Royaumes de son pere & de l'alliance qui avoit esté

dans leurs maisons, avoit appris avec toute l'Asie le naufrage
d'Ariobarzane & d'Arsinoé & les croyoit morts par l'opinion
generale, avançant la main & arrestant Olympie à ce commence-
ment de son discours: Quoy, luy dit-elle, ce bel Inconnu . . . est
Ariobarzane, Prince d'Armenie, qui par un naufrage connu à toute
l'Asie & qui luy fut commun avec la Princesse Arsinoé sa sœur
a passé pour mort jusqu'icy dans l'opinion de tout le monde!'
(VII, 13).
13. I, 72.
14. Mother of the heroine of the novel.
15. I, 172.
16. I, 215, III, 109.
17. IV, 18; cf. X, 46-7 and Oroondate's entirely masculine beauty
(*Cassandre*, I, 11).
18. Except Alcamène who is reminiscent of Oroondate; see below,
p. 160.
19. II, 64; cf. I, 193; II, 43, 183; IV, 315; V, 5, 95.
20. XI, 124.
21. I, 195-259; III, 35-169; X, 35-121.
22. VII, 11-218.
23. II, 10-153, 160-311; VIII, 23-81.
24. XI, 173 et seq.
25. IX, 142-5, 180-98.
26. IX, 197-8.
27. XI, 69.
28. VII, 227-34; XI, 11-18.
29. IX, 97; cf. IX, 95-101, 131; XI, 139 et seq.; 204 et seq.
30. VIII, 123.
31. This episode was used by Thomas Corneille as the basis for his very
successful play, *Timocrate*.
32. VIII, 205-18.
33. VIII, 305.
34. See above, pp. 145-9.
35. II, 70.
36. III, 275; cf. VI, 207.
37. VI, 65.
38. IV, 315.
39. V, 255-6; VI, 193; VII, 58; VIII, 301; IX, 45.
40. X, 57.
41. VI, 103.
42. X, 81; XI, 118.
43. VI, 121.
44. I, 39 et seq., I, 97.
45. VII, 280-1.
46. XI, 231; cf. VI, 287. Artémise develops a vehement passion for
Alexandre (IV, 131) but it is a rational passion based on obligation
as well as feeling (IV, 137-8, 149, 176).
47. XI, 235.

48. I, 143.
49. In the character of Julie, La Calprenède comes close to a genuine psychological realism. His accounts of the effects of jealousy have an emotional truth not found elsewhere in the work (II, 119-25, 193-205; V, 273 et seq.); cf. Junie in Segrais' *Berenice*.
50. 'Discours pour et contre l'amitié tendre': Sorel, *Œuvres diverses, ou discours meslez* (Paris, 1663), p. 134.
51. VII, 372.
52. X, 9.
53. XII, 332.
54. XII, 360.
55. Magendie, *Le Roman français*, pp. 257-8.
56. The reader is informed of the occasion when he had told an entire town that they were to be put to death and had replied to those going to execution who had asked for a proper burial 'que cette grace estoit en la disposition des corbeaux' (XII, 349).
57. XII, 348.
58. XII, 349; II, 51.
59. XII, 354. It is interesting to note that the *Bibliothèque universelle des romans* gives an entirely royalist interpretation to the episode in which Coriolan protects the Emperor, making him say: 'Ne frappez pas, ... cette tête est sacrée, ménageons-la' (April 1789, p. 187. cf. *Cleopatre*, XII, 301).
60. XII, 358.

Chapter XII
1. References are to *Artamene ou le Grand Cyrus*, 10 vols. (Paris, 1649-53). For a detailed account of the plot, see Madeleine de Scudéry, *Le Grand Cyrus; Clélie, hystoire romaine*, ed. Celoria (Turin, 1973), pp. 3-47.
2. I, 532.
3. I, 390.
4. I, 232, 473.
5. I, 325.
6. I, 343-6.
7. I, 593-4.
8. II, 25.
9. II, 271.
10. II, 717; cf. II, 209.
11. Crésus seriously suggests that the repeated abductions of Mandane are the method adopted by the gods to make Cyrus the conqueror of all Asia (VII, 27-28).
12. V, 821.
13. V, 27; VII, 601-2; VIII, 515; IX, 13.
14. 'Historie d'Artamene' (I, 167-704; II, 10-536), 'Histoire de Mandane' (II, 593-872), 'Histoire de la Princesse Araminte et de Spitridate' (III, 646-987), 'Histoire de la Princesse Palmis et de Cleandre' (IV, 60-367). Only two of the fifteen episodes in the second half

of the novel are of this sort: 'Histoire de Sesostris et de Timarete' (VI, 557-934), 'Histoire de Péranius et de la Princesse Cleonisbe' (VIII, 600-1050).

15. See V. Cousin, *La Société française au XVIIe siècle d'après le Grand Cyrus de Mlle de Scudéry*, 2 vols. (Paris, 1858), I, 370-413, 414-43. Cousin showed that the characters in *Le Grand Cyrus* are based on contemporaries of Madeleine de Scudéry and the portraits were no doubt recognizable in their day, but with many of the characters, the author's primary concern was to create psychological verisimilitude; cf. A. Le Breton, *Le Roman au XVIIe siècle*, 6th edn. (Paris, 1932), pp. 176-82.

16. VIII, 1085.

17. VIII, 1067.

18. VII, 610; cf. V, 193 et seq.

19. Cf. C. Aragonnès, *Madeleine de Scudéry, Reine du Tendre*, (Paris, 1934), pp. 149-50.

20. VI, 321; cf. III, 358-9: 'pourquoy ne m'aimez-vous point? c'est parce que je ne le puis, dit-elle; & c'est pour cette mesme raison, luy dis-je, que je ne sçaurois non plus cesser de vous aimer, que vous cesser de me haïr.'

21. VI, 1134.

22. X, 37, 48-9, 1084, 1385-9.

23. III, 345-6, 347.

24. VII, 710-903.

25. VII, 750-1.

26. VII, 756-7.

27. VII, 771-2.

28. VII, 901. The emotions of Myrinthe when he discovers that he is loved by Cléobuline are subjected to a similar close analysis (VII, 813-16, 843).

29. VII, 861.

30. VII, 870.

31. VII, 863-4.

32. VII, 886.

33. V, 869-1198.

34. I, 723-1079; IV, 442-746.

35. V, 1063-4.

36. V, 1173-4, 1187-8.

37. La Rochefoucauld, *Maximes*, ed. Truchet (Paris, 1967), Max. 10, p. 9. Comments in *Cyrus* such as that by Cléorante: 'ne nous y trompons pas, nostre interest particulier va tousjours devant l'interest general, & tous ces zelez pour la Patrie ne le sont bien souvent que pour leur propre bien' (IX, 1055) suggest that the ground was being prepared for La Rochefoucauld's *Maximes* even in the heroic novel.

38. VII, 713.

39. VII, 715-16.

40. X, 495.

41. X, 488.
42. III, 1279-80.
43. IV, 6; cf. IV, 1223; X, 1247-50.
44. VI, 525; cf. VI, 969-70; VII, 638.
45. *Cassandre*, X, 997.
46. This type of portrait does not appear in the earlier volumes.
47. VIII, 705-6.
48. IX, 553-4.
49. VII, 1243-4; cf. VIII, 696.
50. See Noromate's discourse on *gloire* in women: IX, 350-1.
51. VIII, 616-19, 823.
52. IX, 930.
53. III, 1111-2, X, 557-66. Sapho is, of course, Madeleine de Scudéry herself. Her brother (Charaxe) is treated with less sympathy. He has courage 'mais c'est de celuy qui rend les Taureaux plus vaillans que les Cerfs: & non pas de cette espece de courage que l'on confond quelquefois avec la generosité' (X, 566).
54. VI, 407.
55. V, 225, 227.
56. VII, 214-582. According to the key to *Cyrus*, Elise is Madeleine de Scudéry's close friend, Mlle Paulet.
57. VII, 575.
58. VII, 294.
59. VII, 247.
60. As when Asiadate offers to help her financially during a period of hardship (VII, 477-83).
61. VII, 589.
62. VII, 590.
63. VII, 592.
64. VII, 581-2.
65. See above, Chapter V.
66. *Antiope*, IV, 136 et seq.
67. *Rosane*, p. 409 et seq.
68. X, 888.
69. X, 891.
70. V, 57.
71. X, 892.
72. VII, 1127.
73. II, 897-8; cf. VI, 113 et seq.
74. VII, 1128-9.
75. X, 1161.
76. X, 1160.
77. Adam, *Histoire de la littérature française* ..., II, 132; cf. G. Mongrédien, *Madeleine de Scudéry et son salon* (Paris, 1946), p. 154: 'Si le *Grand Cyrus* trouvait son public dans l'entourage de Condé et dans la société fort choisie et, en définitive, assez restreinte de l'Hôtel de Rambouillet, la *Clelie* intéressait toute la bourgeoisie parisienne.'

PART III

Chapter XIII

1. On these two works, see J. W. Schweitzer, *Georges de Scudéry's Almahide: Authorship, Analysis, Sources and Structure* (Baltimore, 1939); S. Pitou, *La Calprenède's 'Faramond': a Study of the Sources, Structure and Reputation of the Novel* (Baltimore, 1938). Schweitzer makes a convincing case for Georges de Scudéry as the sole author of *Almahide*.
2. *Lettres de Jean Chapelain*, ed. Tamizey de Larroque, 2 vols. (Paris, 1880-3), II, 340. La Calprenède had died in October 1663.
3. Guéret, *La Promenade de Saint-Cloud*, ed. Monval (Paris, 1888), p. 99.
4. Quoted by Coulet, *Le Roman jusqu'à la Révolution*, II, 85.
5. Quoted by Coulet, op. cit., II, 88.
6. Lenglet du Fresnoy, *De l'usage des romans*, I, 319-20.
7. *Bibliothèque universelle des romans*, July 1775, I, 19-20.
8. The most recent re-statement is by E. Showalter, *The Evolution of the French Novel, 1641-1782* (Princeton, 1972), p. 27.
9. *Le Roman veritable, où sous des noms et des pays empruntez, dans un enchainement agreable, sont comprises les histoires et adventures amoureuses de plusieurs personnes de condition, tant dedans que dehors le Royaume*, 2 vols. (Paris, 1645).
10. Boisrobert, *Les Nouvelles heroïques et amoureuses* (Paris, 1657).
11. Sorel, *Polyandre, histoire comique*, 2 vols. (Paris, 1648); Scarron, *Le Romant comique*, ed. Bénac, 2 vols. (Paris, 1951).
12. *Ibrahim*, II, Book VII. The story is borrowed from Calderon.
13. *Berenger*, III, 106.
14. *Le Toledan*, 5 vols. (Paris, 1647-55). The *privilège* gives the author as M. D. L. C., but the novel is attributed variously to Segrais and Le Vert. It is virtually certain that the author was not La Calprenède, as the initials might suggest.
15. *Polyandre*, Advertissement aux lecteurs.
16. e.g. I, 51-61, 81-2.
17. Scarron, *Le Romant comique*, I, 122-3, 128, 235-6.
18. Cf. *Romanciers du XVIIe siècle*, ed. Adam (Paris, 1958), pp. 38-40; Coulet, op. cit., I, 205-7.
19. See the distinction made by H. Gaston Hall in 'Scarron and the travesty of Virgil', *Yale French Studies* 38 (1967), pp. 117-18.
20. Dassoucy, *Poesies et lettres, contenant diverses pieces heroïques, satiriques et burlesques* (Paris, 1653). The same is true of the *Poesies diverses* of both François Colletet (Paris, 1656) and Brébeuf (Paris, 1658). Brébeuf in particular shows himself to be capable of delicacy and *galanterie* in his burlesque verses, the only identifiable burlesque elements being the octosyllabic line and a certain lightness of touch.
21. *L'Arioste travesty en vers burlesques. Sur l'imprimé* (Paris, 1660).
22. *L'Odyssée d'Homere, ou les avantures d'Ulysse en vers burlesques*

(Paris, 1650), Epistre.

23. Guéret, *Le Parnasse reformé*, p. 27; cf. 'A un autheur, sur son Virgile travesty', *Recueil de diverses poesies des plus celebres autheurs de ce temps* (Paris, 1652), p. 56.

24. G. Colletet, *Le Parnasse françois, ou l'escole des muses* (Paris, 1664), p. 72.

25. *L'Heritier ridicule ou la dame interessée* (Paris, 1650), Epistre.

26. P. de Nouguier, *Œuvres burlesques* (Orange, 1650), pp. 59–60.

27. Sorel, *De la connoissance des bons livres*, p. 127.

28. See above, Chapter XII.

29. Only Part I was published.

30. The salon public would no doubt have approved, for instance, of the attitude adopted by the wicked pirate, Métraphane, who has Agiatis in his power but quails before her: 'Vous estes toûjours inhumaine, . . . belle Agiatis! & vous prenez plaisir à juger du pouvoir que vous avez sur moy par mon insensibilité aux offenses que vous me faites. Elles sont bien dures, ces rigoureuses épreuves que vous me faites souffrir, & à tout autre qu'à moy elles seroient insupportables,' etc. (I, 354).

31. See the naval battle, III, 622–3.

32. *Clelie*, VIII, 1136–7.

33. See A. Stegmann, 'L'Ambiguïté du concept héroïque dans la littérature morale en France sous Louis XIII', *Héroïsme et création littéraire* . . . , pp. 29–51.

34. Essential reading on this point is A. Levi's 'La Disparition de l'héroïsme: étapes et motifs', *Héroïsme et création littéraire* . . . , pp. 77–88.

35. See R. Godenne, 'Les Nouvelles de Mademoiselle de Scudéry', *Revue des sciences humaines* 37 (1972), pp. 503–14. See also N. Boursier, 'Du vaisseau à la barque: évolution d'un thème du 'Grand Roman' à la nouvelle classique', *XVIIe siècle* 110–11 (1976), pp. 45–56, for an interesting study of a link between novel and *nouvelle*.

Conclusion

1. Arland, 'Quelques étapes de l'évolution du roman au XVIIe siècle', *Le Préclassicisme français*, ed. Tortel (Paris, 1952), p. 200.

2. February 1780, p. 185.

3. Wadsworth, *The Novels of Gomberville*, p. 20. *Polexandre* certainly betrays a marked anti-Spanish feeling: see IV, 322, 356–7, 496.

4. loc. cit., p. 201.

5. Adam, *L'Age classique*, p. 148. On the relationship between heroism and society, see L. Braun, 'Polysémie du concept de héros', *Héroïsme et création litteraire* . . . , pp. 24–27.

6. See *Polexandre*, III, 791; V, 903.

7. Cf. J. Morel, 'Médiocrité et perfection dans la France du XVIIe siècle', *Revue d'histoire littéraire de la France* 69 (1969), pp. 441–50.

8. e.g. 'Il s'en faut bien que nous connaissions tout ce que nos passions nous font faire' (Max. 460), 'Si nous résistons à nos passions, c'est plus par leur faiblesse que par notre force' (Max. 122), 'Nos actions sont comme les bouts rimés, que chacun fait rapporter à ce qu'il lui plaît' (Max. 382).

BIBLIOGRAPHY

In addition to the standard bibliographical tools for seventeenth-century French literature (Arbour, Cioranescu, Goldsmith, etc.), the following are necessary for a study of the novel:

WILLIAMS, Ralph C. *Bibliography of the Seventeenth-century Novel in France.* New York, 1931.

BALDNER, Ralph W. *Bibliography of Seventeenth-century French Prose Fiction.* New York, 1967.

LEVER, Maurice. *La Fiction narrative en prose au XVIIe siècle.* Paris, 1976.

Each of these contains errors and omissions, but Lever's book is clearly superior to the two earlier works and has established itself as the standard work of reference in the area of prose fiction.

The bibliography that follows lists simply those manuscripts and printed works that have served as primary sources in the writing of this book and major secondary works.

Primary Sources

1. *Manuscripts*

Discours des Amazones (Arsenal 3259, fols. 61–72). An address delivered to the Académie française, probably in 1655.

L'Education heroïque. Recueillie d'un manuscrit et mis en lumiere par J. Ottonis, chanoine de la cathedralle de Gand (Bibl. Méjanes, Aix-en-Provence MS 411). Listed as No 115 in the *Catalogue général des manuscrits des bibliothèques publiques de France,* Paris, 1894.

Lettre de Monsieur de Guise au cardinal Mazarin (Mazarine 2117, fol. 242–3).

Manifeste du comte de Soissons (Arsenal 5416, fols. 1921–34).

Memoires de Monsieur Millet (Méjanes 153).

Recueil de diverses poesies françoises 1648 (Mazarine 3940).

SAINT-ÉVREMOND, sieur de. *Comparaison de M. le Prince et M. de Turenne* (Arsenal 3135, fols. 69–71).

—— *Eloge de Monsieur le Prince* (Arsenal 3135, fols. 61–9).

2. *Prose Fiction*

ACHILLES TATIUS. *Les quatre derniers livres des propos amoureux d'Achilles Tatius, contenant le discours des amours du seigneur Clitophant et damoiselle Leusippe,* trans. Jacques de Rochemaure. Lyon, 1556.

—— *Les Amours de Clitophon et de Leucippe*, trans. A. Rémy. Paris, 1625.

—— *Les Amours de Clytophon et de Leucippe*, trans. Baudoin. Paris, 1635.

Amadis de Gaule, Le Premier Livre de, trans. Des Essarts. Paris, 1548.

Amadis de Gaule, Le Second Livre de. Paris, 1550.

Amadis de Gaule, Le Tiers Livre de. Paris, 1547.

Amadis de Gaule, Le Quatriesme Livre d'. Paris, 1555.

ASTORGUES, le sieur d' (P.A.D.). *Alcide*, 2 vols. Paris, 1647–8.

Axiane. Paris, 1647.

BAUDOIN, Jean (or Pierre de BOISSAT?). *Histoire negrepontique, contenant la vie et les amours d'Alexandre Castriot*. Paris, 1631.

BOISROBERT, François le Métel de. *Histoire indienne d'Anaxandre et d'Orazie*. Paris, 1629.

—— *Les Nouvelles heroïques et amoureuses*. Paris, 1657.

BONNET, Pierre. *Berenger, comte de la Mark*, 4 vols. Paris, 1645.

BUSSY-RABUTIN, Roger de. *Histoire amoureuse des Gaules*, 2 vols. Paris, 1920.

C., M. D. L. *Le Toledan*, 5 vols. Paris, 1647–55.

CAMUS, Jean-Pierre. *La Pieuse Jullie, histoire parisienne*. Paris, 1625.

—— *L'Amphitheatre sanglant, où sont representées plusieurs actions tragiques de nostre temps*. Paris, 1630.

—— *Les Spectacles d'horreur, où se découvrent plusieurs tragiques effets de nostre siecle*. Paris, 1630.

CHAPPUZEAU, Samuel. *Ladice ou les victoires du Grand Tamerlam*, 2 vols. Paris, 1650.

CHEVREAU, Urbain. *Scanderberg*, 2 vols. Paris, 1644.

—— *Hermiogene*, 2 vols. Paris, 1648.

Clorinde, 2 vols. Paris, 1654.

D., P. A. see Astorgues.

DESCHAUSSÉE, Père Calixte Auguste (?). *Le Polemire, ou l'Illustre Polonois*. Paris, 1646.

DESFONTAINES, Nicolas-Marc. *L'Illustre Amalazonthe*. Paris, 1645.

DESMARETS DE SAINT-SORLIN, Jean. *Ariane*, 2 vols. Paris, 1632.

—— *L'Ariane de Monsieur Des Marets,* ... *De nouveau reveuë, et augmentée de plusieurs histoires par l'autheur, et enrichie de plusieurs figures*. Paris, 1639.

—— *Rosane, histoire tirée de celle des Romains et des Perses*. Paris, 1639.

DU BAIL, Louis Moreau, sieur. *La Cefalie*. Paris, 1637.

—— *Le Prince ennemy du tyran*, 2 vols. Paris, 1644.

DU VERDIER, Gilbert Saulnier, sieur. *Le Romant des romans, où on verra la suitte & la conclusion de Don Belianis de Grece, du Chevalier du Soleil & des Amadis*, 7 vols. Paris, 1627–9.

—— *Le Chevalier hypocondriaque*. Paris, 1632.

—— *La Sibile de Perse*. Paris, 1632.

—— *Fuite de Rozalinde*. Paris, 1643.

EUSTATHIUS. *Ismene et Ismenie, histoire grecque*, trans. G. Colletet. Paris, 1625.

FUMÉE, Martin. *Du vray et parfaict amour*. Paris, 1612.

GERZAN, François du Soucy, sieur de. *L'Histoire afriquaine de Cleomede et de Sophonisbe*, 3 vols. Paris, 1627-8.

GOMBERVILLE, Marin le Roy, sieur de. *L'Exil de Polexandre et d'Ericlée*. Paris, 1619.

—— *L'Exil de Polexandre, premiere partie*. Paris, 1629.

—— *La Premiere (Seconde) Partie de Polexandre*, 2 vols. Paris, 1632.

—— *La Premiere (-Cinquiesme) Partie de Polexandre*, 5 vols. Paris, 1637.

—— *La Cytherée*, 2nd edn., 4 vols. Paris, 1642.

GUERIN DE BOUSCAL, Guyon. *Antiope*, 4 vols. Paris, 1644.

HELIODORUS. *L'Histoire aethiopique de Heliodorus*, trans. Amyot. Paris, 1547.

—— *L'Histoire ethiopique d'Heliodore*. Paris, 1609.

—— *Les Amours de Theagene et Chariclée, histoire ethiopique d'Heliodore*, trans. Montlyard. Paris, 1622.

HOTMAN DE LATOUR, François. *Histoire celtique*, 3 vols. Paris, 1634.

JUVENEL, Félix de. *Dom Pelage, ou l'entrée des Maures en Espagne*, 2 vols. Paris, 1645.

LA CALPRENÈDE, Gautier de Coste, sieur de. *Cassandre*, 10 vols. Paris, 1642-5.

—— *Cleopatre*, 12 vols. Leiden, 1648-58.

—— *Faramond, ou l'histoire de France*, 7 vols. by La Calprenède. Paris, 1661-3.

LA MOTHE LE VAYER *fils*, François de. *Le Parasite Mormon, histoire comique*. *S.l.*, 1650.

LANSIRE. *La Diane desguisée*. Paris, 1647.

LE MAIRE. *La Prazimene*, 4 vols. Paris, 1638-43.

LE VAYER DE BOUTIGNY, Roland. *Mitridate*, 4 vols. Paris, 1648-51.

LOGEAS, Henry Maron, sieur de. *Le Romant heroïque, où sont contenus les memorables faits d'armes de Dom Rosidor, Prince de Constantinople*. Paris, 1632.

—— *L'Histoire des trois freres, princes de Constantinople*. Paris, 1632.

—— *Les Travaux du prince incognu*. Paris, 1634.

LONGUS. *Les Amours pastorales de Daphnis et de Chloé*, trans. Amyot. Paris, 1559.

MARCASSUS, Pierre. *L'Amadis de Gaule*. Paris, 1629.

MOREAUX, de. *Peristandre ou l'illustre captif*, 2 vols. Paris, 1642.

Les Prouvesses et vaillances du redouté Mabrian, lequel fut roy de Jerusalem. Troyes, 1625.

Roman de l'incogneu, ensemble quelques discours pour et contre les romans (by Antoine Humbert?). Paris, 1634.

Le Roman veritable, où sous des noms et des pays empruntez, dans

un enchainement agreable, sont comprises les histoires et adventures amoureuses de plusieurs personnes de condition, tant dedans que dehors le Royaume, 2 vols. Paris, 1645.
Romanciers du XVIIe *siècle*, ed. Adam. Paris, 1958.

SCARRON, Paul. *Le Romant comique*, ed. Bénac, 2 vols. Paris, 1951.
SCUDÉRY, Georges and/or Madeleine de. *Ibrahim ou l'illustre Bassa*, 4 vols. Paris, 1641.
—— *Artamene ou le Grand Cyrus*, 10 vols. Paris, 1649-53.
—— *Clelie, histoire romaine*, 10 vols. Paris, 1654-60.
—— *Almahide ou l'esclave reine*, 8 vols. Paris, 1660-3.
—— *Celinte, nouvelle premiere*. Paris, 1661.
—— *Le Grand Cyrus; Clélie, hystoire romaine*, ed. Celoria. Turin, 1973.
SEGRAIS, Jean Regnault de. *Berenice*, 4 vols. Paris, 1648-9.
—— *Les Nouvelles françoises, ou les divertissemens de la Princesse Aurelie*, 2 vols. Paris, 1657.
SENECTERRE, Madame de (?). *Orasie*, 4 vols. Paris, 1646.
SOREL, Charles. *Le Berger extravagant, où parmy des fantaisies amoureuses, on void les impertinences des romans et de la poesie*, 3 vols. Paris, 1627-8.
—— *Polyandre, histoire comique*, 2 vols. Paris, 1648.

URFÉ, Honoré d'. *L'Astrée*, ed. Vaganay, 5 vols. Lyon, 1925-8.

3. *Other Seventeenth-century Works*
L'Arioste travesty en vers burlesques. Sur l'imprimé. Paris, 1660.

BALZAC, Jean-Louis Guez de. *Œuvres*, 2 vols. Paris, 1665.
BARDIN, Pierre. *Le Lycée*, 2 vols. Paris, 1632-4.
BOILEAU-DESPREAUX, Nicolas. *Les Héros de roman*, ed. Crane. Boston, 1902.
BOURDONNÉ, de. *Le Courtisan des-abusé*. Paris, 1658.
BRANTÔME, Pierre de Bourdeille, sieur de. *Des dames galantes*, 3 vols. Paris, (1933).
BRÉBEUF, Georges de. *Poesies diverses*. Paris, 1658.

CAILLIÈRE, Jacques de. *La Fortune des gens de qualité et des gentilshommes particuliers, enseignant l'art de vivre à la cour*. Paris, 1668.
CAMUS, Jean-Pierre. *La Caritée ou le pourtraict de la vraye charité*. Paris, 1641.
Catalogue de tous les livres de feu M. Chapelain, ed. Searles. Stanford, 1912.
CAUSSIN, Nicolas. *La Cour sainte, ou l'institution chrestienne des grands*. Paris, 1624.
CÉRIZIERS, René. *Les Trois Estats de l'innocence*, 3 vols. Paris, 1640.
—— *Le Philosophe françois*, 3 vols. Paris, 1643.
—— *Le Heros françois ou l'idée du grand capitaine*. Paris, 1645.
—— *Le Tacite françois*. Paris, 1648.
CHAPELAIN, Jean. *De la lecture des vieux romans*, ed. Feillet. Paris, 1870.

—— *Lettres de Jean Chapelain*, ed. Tamizey de Larroque, 2 vols. Paris, 1880-3.

—— 'Dialogue de la gloire' *in* J. E. Fidao-Justiniani, *L'Esprit classique et la préciosité au XVIIe siècle.* Paris, 1914.

CHARRIER. *Les Lauriers d'Enguien ou le parfait general d'armée.* Paris, 1645.

CHEVREAU, Urbain. *L'Escole du sage, où il est traicté des vertus et des vices.* Paris, 1646.

—— *Le Tableau de la fortune.* Paris, 1659.

—— *L'Escole du sage ou le caractere des vertus et des vices.* Lyon, 1664.

COEFFETEAU, Nicolas. *Tableau des passions humaines, de leurs causes et de leurs effets.* Paris, 1620.

COLLETET, François. *Poesies diverses.* Paris, 1656.

COLLETET, Guillaume. *Le Parnasse françois, ou l'escole des muses.* Paris, 1664.

COURAUD, Élie. *Le Heros chretien.* Angers, 1655.

DANJOU, Jean. *Le Tableau de l'homme fort.* Nevers, 1645.

DASSOUCY, Charles Coypeau. *Poesies et lettres, contenant diverses pieces heroïques, satiriques et burlesques.* Paris, 1653.

—— *L'Ovide en belle humeur, augmenté du ravissement de Proserpine et du jugement de Paris.* Paris, 1659.

DESCARTES, René. *Œuvres et lettres,* ed. Bridoux. Paris, 1952.

DESMARETS DE SAINT-SORLIN, Jean. *Les Morales d'Epictete, de Socrate, de Plutarque et de Seneque.* Paris, 1653.

DU BOIS-HUS, Michel Yvon. *Le Prince illustre.* Paris, 1645.

DUBOSC, Jacques. *L'Honneste Femme,* 3rd edn., 2 vols. Paris, 1635.

—— *Le Femme heroïque, ou les heroïnes comparées avec les heros en toute sorte de vertus,* 2 vols. Paris, 1645.

—— *Les Femmes heroïques comparées avec les heros,* 2 vols. Paris, 1669.

DU CROS, Simon. *Histoire de la vie de Henry, dernier duc de Montmorency.* Paris, 1643.

DU PLAISIR. *Sentimens sur les lettres et sur l'histoire, avec des scrupules sur le stile.* Paris, 1683.

DU REFUGE, Eustache. *Traité de la cour, ou instruction des courtisans. Derniere edtion.* Paris, 1658.

FARET, Nicolas. *L'Honneste Homme ou l'art de plaire à la court,* ed. Magendie. Paris, 1925.

FORTIN DE LA HOGUETTE, Philippe. *Testament, ou conseils fideles d'un bon pere à ses enfans,* 9th edn. Paris, 1658.

—— *Elemens de la politique.* Paris, 1663.

GERZAN, François du Soucy, sieur de. *La Conduite du courtisan.* Paris, 1646.

—— *Le Triomphe des dames.* Paris, 1646.

GILBERT, Gabriel. *Panegyrique des dames.* Paris, 1650.

GOMBERVILLE, Marin le Roy, sieur de. *Discours des vertus et des vices de l'histoire.* Paris, 1620.

— *La Doctrine des mœurs.* Paris, 1646.

GRACIAN, Baltasar. *L'Heros de Laurens Gracian,* trans. Gervaise. Paris, 1645.

GUERET, Gabriel. *Le Parnasse reformé, nouvelle edtion.* Paris, 1674.

— *La Promenade de Saint-Cloud,* ed. Monval. Paris, 1888.

Le Guerrier prudent et politique. Paris, 1643.

HOBBES, Thomas. *Elemens philosophiques du citoyen. Traicté politique où les fondemens de la societé civile sont découverts, par Thomas Hobbes,* trans. Sorbière. Amsterdam, 1649.

HUET, Pierre-Daniel. *Traité de l'origine des romans,* ed. Kok. Amsterdam, 1942.

LA MOTHE LE VAYER, François de. *Œuvres,* 3rd edn., 2 vols. Paris, 1662.

LANGLOIS, François, sieur de Fancan. *Le Tombeau des romans où il est discouru I Contre les romans II Pour les romans.* Paris, 1626.

LA ROCHEFOUCAULD, François de. *Maximes,* ed. Truchet. Paris, 1967.

LA SERRE, Jean Puget de. *Le Portrait de la Reyne.* Paris, 1644.

— *Les Sieges, les batailles, les victoires et les triomphes de Monseigneur le Prince de Condé.* Paris, 1651.

LE MOYNE, Pierre. *La Gallerie des femmes fortes.* Paris, 1647.

MANZINI, Gianbattista. *Les Harangues ou discours academiques,* trans. G. de Scudéry. Paris, 1640.

MAYERNE TURQUET, Louis de. *La Monarchie aristodemocratique.* Paris, 1611.

MONTAGU DE LA COSTE, Henry de. *La Contention de l'espée avec la robbe sur les parties du prince.* Paris, 1610.

MONTPENSIER, Anne-Marie-Louise-Henriette d'Orléans, duchesse de. *Mémoires,* Coll. Petitot, 2e série, Vol. 40–43. Paris, 1824.

MORGUES, Mathieu de. *Diverses pieces pour la defense de la Reyne Mere du Roy Tres-chrestien Louys XIII.* Antwerp, 1637.

NAUDÉ, Gabriel. *Considerations politiques sur les coups d'Estat. S.l.,* 1679.

NOUGUIER, Pierre de. *Œuvres burlesques.* Orange, 1650.

PICOU, Hugues de. *L'Odyssée d'Homere, ou les avantures d'Ulysse en vers burlesques.* Paris, 1650.

Recueil de diverses poesies des plus celebres autheurs de ce temps. Paris, 1652.

RETZ, Jean-François-Paul de Gondi, cardinal de. *La Conjuration de Fiesque,* ed. Watts. Oxford, 1967.

RICHELIEU, Armand-Jean Du Plessis, cardinal duc de. *Testament politique,* ed. André. Paris, 1947.

SAINT-ÉVREMOND, Charles de Marguetel de Saint-Denis, sieur de. *Œuvres de Monsieur de Saint-Évremond, publiées sur les manuscrits de l'auteur,* 7 vols. London, 1711.

SAINT-GABRIEL. *Le Merite des dames*, 3rd edn. Paris, 1660.

SALES, François de. *Œuvres*, ed. Ravier and Davos. Paris, 1969.

Les Satires françaises du XVIIᵉ siècle, ed. Fleuret and Perceau, 2 vols. Paris, 1923.

SCARRON, Paul. *L'Heritier ridicule ou la dame interessée*. Paris, 1650.

SCUDÉRY, Madeleine de. 'Discours de la gloire' *in Recueil de quelques pieces de prose et de vers faits pour les prix qui avoient esté proposez de la part de l'Academie Françoise en 1671*. Paris, 1671.

SENAULT, Jean-François. *De l'usage des passions*, 8th edn. Lyon, 1657.

SÉVIGNÉ, Marie de Rabutin-Chantal, marquise de. *Lettres*, ed. Grouvelle, 12 vols. Paris, 1811.

SILHON, Jean de. *Le Ministre d'Estat*. Paris, 1665.

SIRMOND, Jean. *Le Coup d'Estat de Louys XIII*. Paris, 1631.

Sorberiana. Paris, 1694.

SOREL, Charles. *La Maison des jeux*, 2 vols. Paris, 1657.

—— *Œuvres diverses, ou discours meslez*. Paris, 1663.

—— *La Bibliotheque françoise*, 2nd edn. Paris, 1667.

—— *De la connoissance des bons livres, ou examen de plusieurs autheurs*. Paris, 1671.

TALLEMANT DES RÉAUX, Gédéon. *Historiettes*, ed. Adam, 2 vols. Paris, 1960.

TROUSSET, Alexis. *Alphabet de l'imperfection et malice des femmes*. Paris, 1617.

VULSON DE LA COLOMBIÈRE, Marc. *La Science heroïque*. Paris, 1644.

—— *Le Vray Theatre d'honneur et de chevalerie, ou le miroir heroïque de la noblesse*, 2 vols. Paris, 1648.

Secondary Sources

1. *Unpublished Theses*

HALL, H. Gaston. 'Jean Desmarets de Saint-Sorlin: his background and reception in the seventeenth century'. Yale Ph.D., 1958 (microfilm).

POTTS, D. C. 'Saint Évremond and seventeenth-century "Libertinage".' Oxford D.Phil., 1961.

TRELOAR, Bronnie. 'Preciosity: a social and literary study'. Oxford D.Phil., 1949.

WILSON, T. J. 'La Calprenède, romancier.' Oxford D.Phil., 1927.

2. *Printed Works*

ADAM, Antoine. *Histoire de la littérature française au XVIIᵉ siècle*, 5 vols. Paris, 1948-56.

—— *L'Age classique 1624-1660*. Paris, 1968.

ARAGONNÈS, Claude. *Madeleine de Scudéry, Reine du Tendre*. Paris, 1934.

ARIÈS, Philippe. *Le Temps de l'histoire*. Monaco, 1954.

ARLAND, Marcel. 'Quelques étapes de l'évolution du roman au XVIIe siècle' in *Le Préclassicisme français*, ed. Tortel. Paris, 1952. pp. 196-207.

BARET, Eugène. *De l'Amadis de Gaule et de son influence sur les mœurs et la littérature au XVIe et au XVIIe siècle*, 2nd edn. Paris, 1873.

BAUDOUIN, Charles. *Le Triomphe du héros*. Paris, 1952.

BÉNICHOU, Paul. *Morales du Grand Siècle*. Paris, 1948.

BERTAUD, Madeleine. *La Jalousie dans la littérature au temps de Louis XIII*. Geneva, 1981.

BEUGNOT, Bernard. 'L'Héroïsation des vertus solitaires', *Héroïsme et création littéraire sous les règnes d'Henri IV et de Louis XIII*, ed. Hepp and Livet. Paris, 1974. pp. 173-82.

Bibliothèque universelle des romans, ouvrage périodique dans lequel on donne l'analyse raisonnée des romans anciens et modernes, françois, ou traduits dans notre langue, 224 vols. Paris, 1775-89.

BOLLÈME, G. *La Bibliothèque bleue: littérature populaire en France du XVIIe au XIXe siècle*. Paris, 1971.

BOORSCH, Jean. 'About some Greek romances', *Yale French Studies* 38 (1967), pp. 72-88.

BOURSIER, Nicole. 'Du vaisseau à la barque: évolution d'un thème du "Grand Roman" à la nouvelle classique', *XVIIe siècle* 110-11 (1976), pp. 45-56.

BRAUN, Lucien. 'Polysémie du concept de héros' in *Héroïsme et création littéraire sous les règnes d'Henri IV et de Louis XIII*, ed. Hepp and Livet. Paris, 1974. pp. 19-28.

CALI, Andrea *et al*. *Il Romanzo al tempo di Luigi XIII*. Bari and Paris, 1976.

CAMPBELL, Joseph. *The Hero with a Thousand Faces*, 2nd edn. Princeton, 1971.

CANIVET, Diane. *L'Illustration de la poésie et du roman français au XVIIe siècle*. Paris, 1957.

COLEMAN, Algernon. 'A Source of *Ibrahim ou l'Illustre Bassa*', *Romanic Review* 29 (1938), pp. 129-40.

CONSTANS, Antony and G. L. van ROOSBROECK. 'The early editions of Gomberville's *Polexandre*', *Modern Language Review* 18 (1923), pp. 302-8.

COULET, Henri. *Le Roman jusqu'à la Révolution*, 2 vols. Paris, 1967.

—— 'Un siècle, un genre?', *Revue d'histoire littéraire de la France* 77 (1977), pp. 359-72.

COUSIN, Victor. *La Société française au XVIIe siècle d'après le Grand Cyrus de Mlle de Scudéry*, 2 vols. Paris, 1858.

DALLAS, Dorothy. *Le Roman français de 1660 à 1680*. Paris, 1932.

DELOFFRE, Frédéric. *La Nouvelle en France à l'âge classique*. Paris, 1967.

DOUBROVSKY, Serge. *Corneille et la dialectique du héros*. Paris, 1963.

DULONG, Claude. *L'Amour au XVIIe siècle*. Paris, 1969.

DULONG, Gustave. *L'Abbé de Saint-Réal. Étude sur les rapports de l'histoire et du roman au XVIIe siècle*, 2 vols. Paris, 1921.

DUMONCEAUX, Pierre. *Langue et sensibilité au XVIIe siècle. L'évolution du vocabulaire affectif.* Geneva, 1975.

EDELMAN, Nathan. *Attitudes of seventeenth-century France towards the Middle Ages.* New York, 1946.

EVANS, W. H. *L'Historien Mézeray et la conception de l'histoire en France au XVIIe siècle.* Paris, 1930.

FRANCILLON, R. *L'Œuvre romanesque de Madame de La Fayette.* Paris, 1973.

GARAPON, Robert. 'L'Influence de l'Astrée sur le théâtre français de la première moitié du XVIIe siècle', *Travaux de linguistique et de littérature* VI, 2 (1968), pp. 81–5.

GODENNE, René. *Histoire de la nouvelle française aux XVIIe et XVIIIe siècles.* Geneva, 1970.

—— 'Les Nouvelles de Mademoiselle de Scudéry', *Revue des sciences humaines* 37 (1972), pp. 503–14.

GREEN, Frederick C. 'The Critic of the Seventeenth Century and his Attitude toward the French Novel', *Modern Philology* 24 (1926–27), pp. 285–95.

—— *French Novelists, Manners and Ideas from the Renaissance to the Revolution.* London and Toronto, 1928.

HALL, H. Gaston. 'Scarron and the travesty of Virgil', *Yale French Studies* 38 (1967), pp. 115–27.

HENEIN, Eglal. 'Romans et réalités, 1607–1628', *XVIIe siècle* 104 (1974), pp. 29–43.

HENNEQUIN, Jacques. 'Le duc de Mercœur d'après son oraison funèbre par François de Sales' in *Héroïsme et création littéraire sous les règnes d'Henri IV et de Louis XIII*, ed. Hepp and Livet. Paris, 1974. pp. 183–94.

—— *Henri IV dans ses oraisons funèbres ou la naissance d'une légende.* Paris, 1977.

HEPP, Noémi. 'La Notion d'héroïne' in *Onze études sur l'image de la femme dans la littérature française du dix-septième siècle*, ed. Leiner. Tübingen and Paris, 1978.

Héroïsme et création littéraire sous les règnes d'Henri IV et de Louis XIII, ed. Hepp and Livet. Paris, 1974.

HIPP, Marie-Thérèse. *Mythes et réalités. Enquête sur le roman et les mémoires (1660–1700).* Paris, 1976.

KERVILER, René. *Marin le Roy, sieur de Gomberville, l'un des quarante fondateurs de l'Académie Française (1600–1674).* Paris, 1876.

KÉVORKIAN, Séro. *Le Thème de l'amour dans l'œuvre romanesque de Gomberville.* Paris, 1972.

—— 'Le Héros dans l'œuvre romanesque de Gomberville: Polexandre et Araxez' in *Héroïsme et création littéraire sous les règnes d'Henri IV et de Louis XIII*, ed. Hepp and Livet. Paris, 1974. pp. 243–9.

KÖRTING, Heinrich. *Geschichte des französischen Romans im XVII Jahrhundert*, 3 parts in one vol. Leipzig, 1885.

KRAILSHEIMER, A. J. *Studies in Self-Interest from Descartes to La Bruyère*. Oxford, 1962.

LANCASTER, Henry C. *A History of French Dramatic Literature in the Seventeenth Century*, 9 vols. Baltimore, 1929-42.

LE BRETON, André. *Le Roman au XVIIe siècle*, 6th edn. Paris, 1932.

LENGLET DU FRESNOY, abbé Nicolas. *De l'usage des romans où l'on fait voir leur utilité et leurs differens caractères*, 2 vols. Amsterdam, 1734.

LEVER, Maurice. 'Romans en quête d'auteurs au XVIIe siècle', *Revue d'histoire littéraire de la France* 73 (1973), pp. 7-21.

—— 'Etat présent des études sur le roman français au XVIIe siècle (1973-1977)', *XVIIe siècle* 30, 4 (1978), pp. 309-14.

LEVI, Anthony. *French Moralists. The Theory of the Passions, 1585 to 1649*. Oxford, 1964.

—— 'La Disparition de l'héroïsme: étapes et motifs' in *Héroïsme et création littéraire sous les règnes d'Henri IV et de Louis XIII*, ed. Hepp and Livet. Paris, 1974. pp. 77-88.

LIDA DE MALKIEL, M. R. *L'Idée de la gloire dans la tradition occidentale*. Paris, 1968.

LOUGEE, Carolyn C. *Le Paradis des femmes. Women, Salons and Social Stratification in Seventeenth-century France*. Princeton, 1976.

MACLEAN, Ian W. F. *Woman Triumphant. Feminism in French Literature, 1610-1652*. Oxford, 1977.

MAGENDIE, Maurice. *La Politesse mondaine et les théories de l'honnêteté en France au XVIIe siècle de 1600 à 1660*, 2 vols. Paris, 1925.

—— *Le Roman français au XVIIe siècle de l'Astrée au Grand Cyrus*. Paris, 1932.

MAILLARD, Jean-François. *Essai sur l'esprit du héros baroque (1580-1640): le même et l'autre*. Paris, 1973.

MANDROU, Robert. *De la culture populaire aux XVIIe et XVIIIe siècles: la Bibliothèque bleue de Troyes*. Paris, 1964.

MARTIN, Henri-Jean. *Livre, pouvoirs et société à Paris au XVIIe siècle (1598-1701)*, 2 vols. Geneva, 1969.

MOLINIÉ, Georges. *Du roman grec au roman baroque: un art majeur du genre narratif en France sous Louis XIII*. Toulouse, 1982.

MONGRÉDIEN, Georges. *Madeleine de Scudéry et son salon*. Paris, 1946.

MOREL, Jacques. 'L'Héroïsation des grands chefs de guerre en France au XVIIe siècle', *Revue des sciences humaines* (1966), pp. 5-11.

—— 'Médiocrité et perfection dans la France du XVIIe siècle', *Revue d'histoire littéraire de la France* 69 (1969), pp. 441-50.

MORILLOT, Paul. *Le Roman en France depuis 1610 jusqu'à nos jours*. Paris, s.d.

MORLET, Chantal. 'Jean-Louis de Fiesque, héros de roman', *XVIIe

siècle 109 (1975), pp. 33–50.

—— 'Mort d'un personnage', *Revue d'histoire littéraire de la France* 77 (1977), pp. 459–69.

NADAL, Octave. *Le Sentiment de l'amour dans l'œuvre de Pierre Corneille*. Paris, 1948.

NIDERST, Alain. *Madeleine de Scudéry, Paul Pellisson et leur monde*. Paris, 1976.

Nouvelle bibliotheque de campagne, ou choix d'episodes intéressans et curieux, tiré des meilleurs romans, tant anciens que nouveaux, 3 vols. Amsterdam and Paris, 1769.

PICARD, Raymond. 'Remises en question', *Revue d'histoire littéraire de la France* 77 (1977), pp. 355–8.

PINTARD, René. 'La Conjuration de Fiesque ou l'héroïsation d'un factieux' in *Héroïsme et création littéraire sous les règnes d'Henri IV et de Louis XIII*, ed. Hepp and Livet. Paris, 1974. pp. 225–30.

—— 'Quelques aspects de l'héroïsme dans l'Astrée', in *Héroïsme et création littéraire sous les règnes d'Henri IV et de Louis XIII*, ed. Hepp and Livet. Paris, 1974. pp. 233–42.

PITOU, Spire. *La Calprenède's 'Faramond': a Study of the Sources, Structure and Reputation of the Novel*. Baltimore, 1938.

RANUM, Orest. *Artisans of Glory. Writers and Historical Thought in Seventeenth-century France*. Chapel Hill, 1980.

RATNER, Moses. *Theory and Criticism of the Novel in France from 'L'Astrée' to 1750*. S.L., 1938.

REYNIER, Gustave. *Le Roman sentimental avant l'Astrée*. Paris, 1908.

'Le Roman au XVIIe siècle', *Revue d'histoire littéraire de la France* 77 (1977), Nos. 3–4.

RONZEAUD, P. 'La Femme au pouvoir ou le monde à l'envers', *XVIIe siècle* 108 (1975), pp. 9–33.

SAINTSBURY, George. *A History of the French Novel to the Close of the Nineteenth Century*, 2 vols. London, 1917.

SASSUS, Jeannine. *The Motif of Renunciation of Love in the Seventeenth-century French Novel*. Washington, 1963.

SCHWEITZER, Jerome W. *Georges de Scudéry's Almahide: Authorship, Analysis, Sources and Structure*. Baltimore, 1939.

SEILLIÈRE, Ernest. *Le Romancier du Grand Condé: Gautier de Coste, sieur de la Calprenède*. Paris, 1921.

SELLIER, Philippe. *Le Mythe du héros*. Paris, 1973.

SHOWALTER, English. *The Evolution of the French Novel, 1641–1782*. Princeton, 1972.

SIMON, Pierre-Henri. *Le Domaine héroïque des lettres françaises*. Paris, 1963.

SNYDERS, Georges. *La Pédagogie en France aux XVIIe et XVIIIe siècles*. Paris, 1965.

STEGMANN, André. *L'Héroïsme cornélien. Genèse et signification*, 2 vols. Paris, 1968.

—— 'L'Ambiguïté du concept héroïque dans la littérature morale en France sous Louis XIII' in *Héroïsme et création littéraire sous les règnes d'Henri IV et de Louis XIII*, ed. Hepp and Livet. Paris, 1974. pp. 29-51.

STEINER, A. 'Les Idées esthétiques de Mademoiselle de Scudéry', *Romanic Review* 16 (1925), pp. 174-84.

SUTCLIFFE, F. E. *Guez de Balzac et son temps: littérature et politique*. Paris, 1959.

—— *Le Réalisme de Charles Sorel.* Paris, 1965.

TAVENEAUX, René. 'Port-Royal ou l'héroïsme de la sainteté' in *Héroïsme et création littéraire sous les règnes d'Henri IV et de Louis XIII*, ed. Hepp and Livet. Paris, 1974. pp. 99-109.

THUAU, Étienne. *Raison d'Etat et pensée politique à l'époque de Richelieu*. Paris, 1966.

TRELOAR, Bronnie. 'Some feminist views in France in the seventeenth century', *AUMLA* 10 (1959), pp. 152-9.

TURK, Edward B. *Baroque Fiction-making: a study of Gomberville's 'Polexandre'*. Chapel Hill, 1978.

WADSWORTH, Philip A. *The Novels of Gomberville. A Critical Study of 'Polexandre' and 'Cytherée'*. New Haven, 1942.

WENTZLAFF-EGGEBERT, Harald. *Der französische Roman um 1625*. Munich, 1973.

ZUMTHOR, Paul. 'La Carte de Tendre et les précieux', *Trivium* 6 (1948), pp. 263-73.

INDEX

References to the notes are included only when a substantial item of information is involved. Authors of secondary works are listed only if they are mentioned in the text.